Arthur Sherburne Hardy

Francesca of Rimini

A Poem

Arthur Sherburne Hardy

Francesca of Rimini
A Poem

ISBN/EAN: 9783744705479

Printed in Europe, USA, Canada, Australia, Japan

Cover: Foto ©Thomas Meinert / pixelio.de

More available books at **www.hansebooks.com**

Thomas Carew
from the Picture by Vandyke at Windsor Castle
photographée by permission of Her Majesty the Queen

THE POEMS AND MASQUE

OF

HOMAS CAREW.

GENTLEMAN OF THE PRIVY-CHAMBER TO
KING CHARLES I., AND CUP-BEARER
TO HIS MAJESTY.

With an Introductory Memoir, an Appendix of
Unauthenticated Poems from MSS., Notes,
and a Table of First Lines.

EDITED BY

JOSEPH WOODFALL EBSWORTH,

M.A., F.S.A., ETC.

LONDON:
EEVES AND TURNER, 196 STRAND.
1893.

Dedicatory Prelude

THE POEMS OF THOMAS CAREW.

AD PSYCHEM.

MAIDEN FAIR, we bring to thee
Choicest Lyric Pöesy,
Such as our world rarely hears,
After five times fifty years :
No crude jests of mocking tongue ;
Sweeter songs were never sung,
When both Time and Love were young.

Hearken strains from One who knew
How to praise, and how to sue :
Celia's lover, TOM CAREW.
He had bask'd in Beauty's smile,
Learn'd to prize her daintiest wile,
Yet could chide her, when he found
She would crush him to the ground ;
Gave her worship, gave her fame—
Though we may not guess her name ;
Saw her fickle, coy and cold,
Sometimes radiant, with the gold
Nimbus of her hair (like thine,
Where my fingers love to twine) :
Now, a sun, begirt with rays ;
Then, chill, with a moon-lit haze
Of impenetrable sadness,
Driving men to gloom or madness,
Till she won them back to gladness.

Live in verse the varied charms
That allured him to her arms ;
Live in verse, no less complete,
Pride, that trod him 'neath her feet ;
Till her petty scorn set free
Outraged Love from tyranny :
Then to others would he turn,
Hoping some new flame might burn
With unwavering warmer light—
Seeking peace, in her despite.
Still misled by fen-fire gleams,
These too were illusive dreams,
 While his memory retain'd
 Thoughts of her, whose love was feign'd,
 Who had yet unequall'd reign'd.

Blame not, thou, his wasted hours,
Flitting round those fading flowers ;
Nor account his labour vain
Whilst he Celia *sought to gain—*
Fairest face that Vandyck drew,
Of Whitehall's bewildering crew ;
Nymphs, who laughing partners play'd
p. 129.] *In his Shrove-tide masquerade :*
Love its own pursuit can bless,
Though it never meet success.
Happy he, whom Celia *foil'd,*
Since to grace his Queen he toil'd ;
Faithful to the Martyr-King,
Of whose worth he lov'd to sing ;
Happy, with unshaken trust
That his reign was wise and just.
Unforeseen were all the woes
Following swiftly his life's close ;
When the Revels ebb'd away,
Soon would dawn the Evil Day.
1638.] *Happier he, thus laid to rest,*
Ere Rebellion rear'd its crest ;
 Folly's thraldom from him cast,
 Contrite for all errors past :
 Peace and Wisdom found at last.

Heed not, thou, the envious scribes
Who assail with heartless gibes
Those who true and loyal stand,
As he stood, in our dear Land.
Wanton triflers could not dare
Rise to breathe such purer air;
Pedant Puritans, with spite,   [p. 252.
Strove to darken his clear light.
Let him reap what he had sown,
Let his merit now be known.
Few the lines we wish unwrit,
Of his courtly mirth and wit;
Few, though lawless passion pain'd,
Warmth of youth left soil'd or stain'd.
A Knightly Gentleman was he,
Who bent in loyal faith the knee,
And would with sword and pen have striven,
Had life prolong'd to him been given.
        Time then had nobler gifts reveal'd;
        False could he never be—or yield:
        He would have died on Naseby-field.

J. WOODFALL EBSWORTH.

MOLASH PRIORY, KENT, 1892.

The Portrait of Thomas Carew.

(A Note.

The pretended 'Medallion portrait of Thomas Carew, †
Poet, Gentleman of the Privy Chamber to King Charles
which was advertised for publication in 1811–1814 by Jo
Fry of Bristol—after the profile medal by Jean Varin, al
Warin, is not here re-engraved and reproduced: for
'excellent reason' that it proves to be a portrait of the ot
poet, 'Thomas Cary' (pp. 105, 239), attested as such by
inscription; which was falsified in 1870: it is, distinct
'THO. CARY. R. CAROL. CVBICVLAR. ÆTATIS. SVÆ. 35. 163
Signed, below, 'VARIN.' In high relief: no reverse. It
singularly beautiful, with chastened and noble features; h
flowing, with a love-lock. Jean Varin was born at Sed
in 1599, and died at Paris in 1672. There is one genu
portrait of the true poet, THOMAS CAREW, painted by Anto
Vandyck, and preserved in Her Majesty's Collection
Windsor. It is of this portrait, a little more than pro
(sketched as Frontispiece) that 'Barry Cornwall,' himself
poet, the father of Adelaide Anne Procter, wrote in 1824:

'What a graceful picture is this, carrying about it all t
fine air and fantastic gentility of Vandyke! CAREW w
a man of family, a courtier, and a poet, and was mu
beloved by the wits of his time. Some of his smaller piec
are exceedingly graceful, and indeed, beautiful. He was
much of an amorist as Sir Philip Sidney, and his verses ha
more ease, though scarcely the same depth of sentiment,
those by that Prince of Chivalry. Although Carew h
been classed by Pope with the 'mob of gentlemen,' the
are few of them who may be compared with him. B
little poem, beginning,

p. 69.]   "Ask me no more where Jove bestows," etc.,

is the most elegant little thing that ever was built up
conceits; and his Masque of Cœlum Britannicum, thoug
of course, infinitely below Milton's Comus, reminds us
parts of that delightful poem.'—Effigies Poeticæ, No. 30.

But Cœlum Britannicum preceded Comus in publicatio
Comus, first acted privately by the two Egertons (p. 16;
and others, on 29th September, 1634, at Ludlow Castle, w
not printed until 1637. Carew could not borrow from it.

Introductory Memoir.

' Again she said—"I woo thee not with gifts :
Sequel of guerdon could not alter me
To fairer. Judge thou me by what I am,
So shalt thou find me fairest." '—*Œnone.*

§ I.

THOMAS CAREW died more than two
hundred and fifty years ago. There are
many of our ' Early Poets ' who are best
represented by brief specimens of their
shorter works, to win attention from the present
race of languid or impatient readers, and some
fragment of praise or blame from the unsatisfactory
critics, who affect to be their supreme tasters and
advisers. Of the longer narratives in verse, the
dramas, epics, and allegories, the monodies and
epithalamia, a few mutilated extracts are held
sufficient to preserve the brilliant lines, the ' gems
of thought,' torn ruthlessly and destructively out
of their original setting, although it were of gold,
leaving the battered shell of context to be flung
aside on the dust-heap as ' alms for oblivion.'

But Thomas Carew deserves better treatment
than this. The total bulk of his poetry is not

large, its quality is almost always good, and in many of his charming love-songs to Celia he had reached excellence. His every word has value, worthy of being received with thanks. His verbal 'concetti,' yielded to suit the dainty fashion of his time, are singularly few, in comparison with those of Donne, Suckling, and others at the same date. If occasionally, but not often, there is found in him an excess of amatory warmth and directness of speech, such as Court ladies encouraged of old, he stands comparatively stainless, where others had given the reins to their licentious fancy, and been led into sensual imagery or into voluptuous impurity. We object entirely to literature being emasculated; if regulated solely by the supposed requirements and approval of the conventional 'young person.' But purity and sweetness are inestimable. Neither Spenser's '*Epithalamion*' nor 'A Rapture' was written for vicious minds. No one need feel injury or disgust, when reading the present text of Carew.

Since he wrote many of the most tender and faultless love-songs, any 'English Anthology' would be grievously incomplete without them. His *Cœlum Britannicum*, far superior to the ordinary Court masques of the reign, has passages of grandeur and true feeling, never wearisome. Although the flattery of King Charles I. and of his Queen, Henrietta Maria, may be deemed too laudatory by the modern code, which begrudges flattery to monarchs, and restricts it to the dispensers of patronage, place, and power, we have every reason to believe that from Carew it was loyally sincere,

ind rendered in affectionate gratitude to those who
iad invariably treated him with kindness. The
jrodigal outlay, lavished in the production of such
i Masque as this, its adornment regardless of cost
ind labour, the scenery, machinery, dresses, and
nusic by Henry Lawes, suggest to remembrance
.he speedy approach of evil days. The continual
lrain of money, required for such costly pleasures,
;ompelled the King to strain to the utmost his
jrivileges and prerogative, while stinted grudgingly
)f supplies for all expenditure by the Commons ;
;o that the Masques at Whitehall, leading towards
.he exactions of Ship-money and Poundage, followed
jefore long by the open rebellion of the King's
:nemies, and their cold-blooded murder of his
:hief adherents, Strafford and Laud, were events
:hat held a logical sequence.

Thomas Carew was perfectly sincere in his
'Commendatory Verses' (pp. 117 to 128), his praise
)f the living patrons, the King, or the Villiers family;
ind of the dead, in his funeral verses or 'Obsequies'
:pp. 17, 51 to 55, 106 to 118). This, his wedding
:ongratulations (pp. 63, 81 to 84), his descriptive
:hanks for hospitality at Saxham and Wrest (pp.
:4, 125), no less than all his friendly greetings to
Aurelian Townsend, George Sandys, Ben Jonson,
Walter Montague, William Davenant, and even the
Monody on Donne of St. Paul's (pp. 59, 111, 114,
:15, 120, 124), their unaffected heartiness and
:implicity of language surely prove. They raise
lis character high in esteem. He was devoid of
:ealousy or malice, and must have despised the
mseemly railing of faction, as he despised all

that was disloyal to his lord or lady. He bear
well every searching ordeal, and the more we have
studied him the better we have learned to love him
as an honourable man who reverenced the truth
in others, and who was no less faithful in religion
than he was in obedience to his sovereign.

Piecemeal biographers have disparaged him
according to their use and wont ; using him as a
target whereat to shoot their moral pellets and
cheap thunderbolts against the Court of the Stuarts
(since, according to one of them, Charles I. was 'a
king who the less he knew the more he meddled ')
accepting without examination, and as if already
proved, whatsoever convenient slanderous gossip
may have floated down the ages from the Puritans
It is supposed by them to be sufficient, that a loyal
Cavalier would necessarily be grossly immoral
and opposed to national liberty.   Such mockery of
liberty as these advocates admire, the demagogues
and parliament-men of old were before long trying
to bring in : 'The Dominion of the Sword,' when
'Law lies a-bleeding,' or the greatest anarchy of
the biggest number.   This could be seen within
four years—nay, little more than two years—after
Carew's death.   Truly, it was time for him to go.

An attempt has been made, by the present editor
and publishers, to atone for the neglect into which
Carew had fallen ; also for the sins and absurdities
of those who had hitherto done little to restore to
him his true position in the affectionate remembrance
of all who have faculties to prize genuine merit.
The reader has here as pure and perfect a text as
can be recovered, unburdened by footnotes on the

ige, to distract attention from the poetry, and
) outward sign shown too obtrusively of the
igrudging labour expended in reproduction. The
ithentic reading has in every case been searched
r, amid contrasted manuscripts and printed
ersions, thus to reach, if possible, the *ipsissima
rba* of the poet.   From every known source
mething has been drawn of gain, and a full
:knowledgment of such help is made in the
·oup of 'Poems from Manuscripts,' and in the
her 'Appendix of Notes' (pp. 171 to 208, and
(1 to 248).   The indisputable authority for the
:xt of the *Cœlum Britannicum*, 163¾, was the
·st edition, in quarto, dated 1634; printed four
:ars before Carew's death, and probably with his
vn revision.*   Little is won from reproductions
' later date, 1640, etc., including Robert Southey's,
331; he, with other editors, was grossly remiss in
itention to the text (*e.g.*, misprinting '*right* hand'
·r '*rigid* hand' of p. 150; spoiling the passage

---

* Thomas Warton (*History of English Poetry*, ii. 538,
homas Tegg's edit., 1871), has a footnote telling of
arew's Masque, 'written by the King's command, and
ayed by his majesty, with many of the nobility and their
ms who were boys. The machinery by Inigo Jones, and
e music by H. Lawes. It has been given to Davenant,
it improperly.' Warton says it was the masque with
hich the King returned the compliment paid by 'a little
ece called *The Inns of Court Anagrammatist*, or, *The
'asquers Masqued in Anagrams*, written by Francis Lenton,
e Queen's poet, London, 1634,' 4to. 'In this piece the names
id respective houses of each masquer are specified, and in
mmendation of each there is an epigram.' (Reeves and
urner's ed., 1871, iii. 318. *Cf.* Strafford's letters, 360.)

concerning the double changes of Jupiter's favourite
by misreading 'transformed ;' one, in 1870, actuall
accentuating 'transformèd,' to eke out the damage
line, which ought to read thus, 'And in despite h
re-transform'd to stars :' (p. 133).

In old printing the capital letters were in exces
but the reprints in our modern times injuriousl
restrict or banish them, quite as capriciously.   W
have exercised our own discretion in retaining them
where important, and also the italic type, thereb
to distinguish proper names in the original text
How execrably that text had been treated, elsewhere
needs no laboriously specific demonstration.

§ II.—Birth, Parentage, and Education.

In attempting to write a memoir of any earl
poets and dramatists one is perpetually met by th
obstacle of their having been seldom mentioned b
their contemporaries with the fulness and fervou
that might have been expected, and that had bee
their due.   A few dates can be found, when the
chanced to take part in some public ceremony, c
became involved in any questionable transactior
Often, as in the case of Thomas Carew, we hav
no certain evidence regarding the place and dat
of his birth or of his death ; though we hav
good reason to believe that he was born in 1598
at Wickham in Kent ; and that he died, probabl
at Sunninghill in Windsor Forest, or possibly i
King Street, Westminster, in the month of Marc
or in the first week of April, 1638.

He was youngest of three children (Martha, Matthew,
and Thomas), who, out of a large family, survived their
father, Sir Matthew Carew of Middle-Littleton, Worcester-
shire (a Master in Chancery, and son of Sir Wymond
Carew, K.B., of East Anthony, near Plymouth, also of
Kingsland, Hackney, Middlesex, and Martha, his wife,
daughter of Sir Edmund Denny, of Cheshunt, Herts.);
he was knighted in 1603, and buried at St. Dunstan's-
in-the-West, August 2, 1618, where his monument was
raised. His wife, Alice, Lady Carew, mother of Thomas,
was a daughter of Sir John Rivers, Lord Mayor of London
in 1573, and grand-daughter of Richard Rivers of Penhurst
Stow: *Survey of London*, 1720, Bk. v. p. 135). It was her
second marriage, her first was with one Ingpenny.

Martha, only surviving daughter, wife of James Cromer,
Kent, became Lady Cromer; and afterwards married
Sir Edward Hales. Since her daughter Elizabeth was
baptized out of Dr. Carew's house,' at St. Dunstans-in-
the-West, Nov. 11, 1599 (Nichols, *Collectanea Topographica
et Genealogica*, 1838, v. 368), Martha must have been much
elder than her two brothers; the elder one, Matthew (made
knight banneret in 1609), having been born April 3, 1590, at
Wickham in Kent. Their father had lost his fortune four
years before his death (some £8000 or £10,000 lost by one
borrower, who never repaid: see Lansdowne MS. 163, fol.
87, quoted by Cecil Monro, *Acta Cancellariæ*, 1847, p. 3).
He must have resided occasionally, in vacation time, at
Middle-Littleton, for his daughter Christian was buried
here, March 1, 159⅝ (Nash's *Worcestershire*, ii. 105), but
her age is not mentioned on the brass tablet. It is possible
that Thomas was born at Middle-Littleton two years later,
and not in Kent at Wickham.

Thomas is supposed to have studied early, like his father,
or his elder brother Matthew, at Westminster School, and
thence went to Corpus Christi, at Oxford, but left without
taking a degree. Anthony à Wood says that Carew 'had
his academical education in Corp. Ch. Coll., as those that
knew him have informed me; yet he occurs not matriculated
as a member of that house, or that he took a scholastical
degree' (*Athenæ Oxonienses*, ed. Philip Bliss, ii. 657, 1815).

§ III.—Early Troubles.

In the absence of dates to this account of Carew's Oxford experience, we suppose him to have left College early, 1615, his studies being interrupted by Sir Matthew's losses. Thomas may have indulged beyond his means in such expensive habits as his open friendliness and the knowledge of belonging to a good family, connected with many of the nobility by blood or marriage, must inevitably have encouraged. His father's impoverishment came from profusely lending money without security or ultimate repayment. His son inherited his generous disposition, but had no fixed professional income; while ' drawing of affidavits' remained a profitable employment for Sir Matthew until his death, 1618. At that time Thomas was only twenty years old, and had already been repulsed in his attempts to gain or retain employment on foreign affairs. To speak of Carew having ' surrendered himself to idle habits,' and also of his having ' developed an unfortunate propensity at an early age for neglecting the work of preparation for making his way in the world ' (*Roxb. Library: Carew*, p. xxii. 1870), is to press unduly against him a charge which might as justly be brought to disparage every other poet: in whom the imaginative temperament, the love of meditation, art, song, and even the pursuit of science and philosophy, instead of commerce and diplomacy, have frequently proved obstacles to an early success in making money : Pope mentions

' A Clerk foredoom'd his father's soul to cross,
Who pens a stanza, when he should engross.'

t is open to demonstration that Carew can never
ave been an idler. He had not only great abilities
aturally, but he must have been laborious and
onscientious in his determined improvement of
is faculties ; the artistic finish of all that he had
ought and wrote. Such friends as he won, and
eld securely, were not men of slight or frivolous
haracter. By them he was loved and respected.
nce for all, we must reject alike the slanders of
ie precisian John Hales, and the distasteful in-
nuations of the conceited voluptuary and trifler,
ir John Suckling (p. 244).

So early as February 25, 1613 (161$\frac{3}{4}$, our 1614),
hen Thomas was not older than sixteen, Sir
Iatthew, in a letter to Dudley Carleton, mentions
that one of his sons is roving after hounds and
awks ; the other studying in the temple, but doing
ttle at law.' It has been assumed, rashly, that it
as Thomas who was wasting time with hawks (he
ertainly uses a term of falconry, ' to *imp* the wings,'
p. 15, 216, but it was a proverbial common-place,
iown on pp. 217, 253) ; this probably means the
.der son, Matthew, who adopted a military life ;
id leaves Thomas to a novitiate of law-study, in
adiness to help his father as secretary.

Three years later, on September 2, 1616, Sir
'udley Carleton being at the Hague, English
Ambassador to the united Provinces of the Low
ountrys,' and a connection of the Carew family
y marriage, a letter was written to him by Thomas   [p. 256.
State Papers, Domestic, of James I., 1616, July
› October, vol. 88, No. 67), telling of his new
ideavour to take service with a kinsman, George,

b

Lord Carew, at Woodstock, where fair promise but no real help had been given to him. Nin days later he had better hopes from the Earl o Arundel, to whom he was recommended by Lor Carew (*Ibid.*, *Domest.*, James I., vol. 88, Nos. 77 87); but it came to nothing, owing to some grudg on the part of Dudley Carleton: with whom Si Matthew nevertheless kept correspondence, telling on October 4, 1617, that his son has nothing t do, and is leading a loose and debauched life Later, March 24, 1618, less than four month before his own death, he writes to Lady Carleton Thomas Carew's position had improved, he agai living with his father, and expressing sorrow for hi previous irregularities. (Sir Dudley became Viscoun Dorchester in 1628, and died in Feb. 163½.)

That Carew had been previously employed ii foreign correspondence and familiar intercours with the Carletons before this date is ascertained they had both been absent from England sinc November 1610 at Venice, Turin, and elsewhere until Sir Dudley succeeded Winwood at the Hagu in March 1616, remaining there five years. Som heedlessness of talk or writing on the part of Carev concerning them, when he had left them suddenl abroad, in his youth, had been taken bitterly an revengefully to heart by the lady. She managed t sway her uxorious husband, for her own unknowi reasons, against the handsome youth; who failed perhaps, to treat her with sufficient deference She was Anne, daughter of Sir Henry Saville, th editor of Chrysostom, and had been married at th Temple Church in 1607. Such a woman neve

forgives a slight or a repulse. Before indulging
in blame of Carew, on such a quarrel, we should
remember the probability of her being the sole
aggressor : arrogant and indignant that her waning
beauty, *in the 'thirties,'* met less adoration. If
' he comes too near, who comes to be denied,' there
are others, like Carew, who incur hatred because of
not coming near enough to please.

Service of some sort, as tutor or secretary, was
secured, by 1619, soon after the death of his father,
and foreign travel with all its advantages was thus
regained. The Oxford residence had been earlier,
circâ 1615. Our best authority is again Anthony
Wood, whose richly-annotated Diary is now being
published by the Oxford Historical Society. He says,

' Afterwards [*i.e.*, after leaving Christ Church, Oxford],
improving his parts by travelling and conversation with
ingenious men in the metropolis, he became reckon'd among
the chiefest of his time for delicacy of wit and poetic fancy.
About which time, being taken into the Royal Court for his
most admirable ingenuity, he was made Gentleman of the
Privy-chamber, and Sewer in ordinary to King Charles I.,
who always esteemed him to the last one of the most cele-
brated wits in his court. . . . Carew was much valued by the
King, and was a great favourite among his poetical and other
acquaintances, among whom must not be omitted Walt.
Montague, afterwards Lord Abbot of Pontois ; Aurelian
Townsend, of the same family with those of Raynham
in Norfolk ; Tho. May, afterwards the long parliament's
historian ; George Sandys, the traveller and poet ; Will.
Davenant.'—*Wood's Athenæ*, ii. 658. (*The Life and Times of
Anthony Wood, Antiquary of Oxford*, 1632-1695 ; *described
by Himself;* is edited most satisfactorily, a thorough,
elaborate, and convincing work of immense value, by the
Rev. Andrew Clark, M.A., Fellow of Lincoln College, and
Vicar of S. Michael's, Oxford. 1891, 1892. *In progress.*)

Many more names might have been added, especially Edward Hyde, the Chancellor; Lord Clarendon; John Donne, Dean of St. Paul's; James Howell, of the *Epistolae Ho-ellianæ;* James Shirley, dramatist; Sir John Crofts, of Saxham, Cup-bearer to the King; the Neville family—Gilbert, Catherine, and Mary (pp. 101, 125, 186); Henry Carey, second Earl of Monmouth (pp. 118, 246); John Selden, Sir Kenelm Digby, John Vaughan, Charles Cotton, Lord Herbert of Cherbury (with whom in 1619 he went to the French Court). Also two, who were more dangerous in their brilliant immorality and looseness of principle than all his other acquaintances, the Circean Lucy, Countess of Carlisle (pp. 29, 99, 218, 237 to 239), and the lively Sir John Suckling (pp. 219, 244), who gave to the world his matchless 'Ballad on a Wedding,' "I tell thee, Dick, where I have been."

It may have been during the unsettled time, while his prospects were dark and uncertain, that he wrote the beautiful lines on the 'Parting of Two Lovers' (p. 175). They were evidently sincere and of personal experience.

§ IV.—Known and Loved.

Probably before the accession of Charles I., in March 1625, and while he was still Prince of Wales (created Nov. 4, 1616), Lord Beauchamp was attended by Carew as Squire. He soon rose in favour with the King; was appointed by him Sewer in Ordinary, involving duties as arranger of the banquet-table, and Cup-bearer to his Majesty, and

Gentleman of the Privy-chamber. (Not 'of the Bed-chamber,' *Cubicularis*, as was Thomas Carey : see p. viii.)

Carew won more solid bounty, King Charles bestowing on him the royal domain of Sunninghill, part of the Windsor great forest. Whether he died there, or at one of his friends' houses, Wrest in Suffolk, or Saxham, near Bedford (pp. 24, 27, 218), or was able after sickness to return to his town-house in King Street, Westminster (pp. 242, 256), is not ascertained ; for no monument or church register of burial has been discovered. It seems probable that when he sent requesting John Hales to visit him, from Eton (p. 252), Carew had been dwelling at Sunninghill, in the near neighbourhood. The chief aid to an estimate of the time of Carew's death, lies in his relation to Ben Jonson, who died August 6, 1637, and the poets of the day speedily contributed their tributary verses in his memory : the collection is entitled *Jonsonus Virbius.* From this Thomas Carew's memorial lines are absent. But he had loved the man, and could properly value his genius (see Carew's address to him, on the publication in 1631 of Ben's Ode, angrily denouncing those who had rejected his comedy of *The New Inn*, 16$\frac{29}{30}$, pp. 61, 225, 226). It is deemed almost certain, that sickness and death must have caused Carew's silence. Anthony à Wood says, 'He was much respected, if not ador'd, by the poets of his time, especially by Ben Jonson.' A trustworthy anecdote of both Carew and Jonson is preserved in a letter from James Howell to Sir Thomas Hawke, April 5, 1636. It deserves to be reproduced here :—

'I was invited yesternight to a solemn supper by *B[en]*
J[onson], where you were deeply remembered; there was
good Company, excellent Cheer, choice Wines, and jovial
welcome : One thing intervened, which almost spoiled the
relish of the rest, that *B.* began to engross all the Discourse,
to vapour extremely of himself, and by vilifying others to
magnify his own Muse. *T. Ca.* buzzed me in the ear, that
though *Ben* had barrelled up a great deal of knowledge,
yet it seems he ad not read the *Ethics,* which, among other
Precepts of Morality, forbid Self-commendation.'

Carew's estimate was justified. Ben Jonson had previously
found a spiteful chronicler in Wm. Drummond, of Hawthorn-
den, a libellous diarist and traducer of his guest. See his
'*Conversations,*' of January 16$\frac{18}{20}$:—'*He is a great lover and
praiser of himself: a contemner and scorner of others;* given
rather to lose a friend than a jest; *jealous of every word and
action of those about him (especially after drink, which is one
of the elements in which he liveth);*' etc., with much bitterness.

§ V.—His Death.

In the *Jonsonus Virbius* poem, written by Lucius
Carey, Lord Falkland, 'On the Death of Ben
Jonson,' *Carew's name occurs, as if he were alive.*

> ' Let *Digby, Carew, Killigrew,* and *Maine,*
> *Godolphin, Waller,* that inspired train—
> Or whose rare pen beside deserves the grace
> Or of an equal, or a neighbouring place—
> Answer thy wish, for none so fit appears
> To raise his Tomb, as who are left his heirs.'
>
> —*An Eclogue on the Death of Ben Jonson.*
> (*Miscellanies of Fuller Worthies Lib.,* iii. 1871.)

Carew must have been still alive, *or not known
to be dead,* until the earliest days of spring, 1638.
He probably died suddenly, during March, or the
first week of April, at latest; but after more than

one forewarning from severe illness, 'in the country.'
His friend Will. Davenant had addressed to him a
poem, playfully anticipating the effect of his death,
whensoever it might take place, in releasing from
rivalry the crowd of hitherto eclipsed amatory poets,
who would straightway throng King Street, West-
minster, where Carew had dwelt, even as though
Parliament were again sitting in the neighbour-
hood. This poem, having been written recently,
is at the end of the volume; which was licensed
on 26th of February, 163⅞, and published early in
March. Moreover, Clement Barksdale sent a copy
of it to Carew, under care of his friend John Crofts
of Saxham, Suffolk, and wrote in it his own lines
beginning, 'Teque meum,' etc., that were afterwards
printed in his *Nympha Libethris; or, The Cotswold
Muse*, 1651. (See pp. 245, 254, for both these
poems. They form documentary evidence of date,
in regard to Carew's death.) Had Davenant known
that Carew no longer lived, he would not have
permitted the lines to go forth, for he loved him.
It was different with the less affectionate and more
flippant Sir John Suckling, who felt no scruple
against circulating in manuscript his own three
jests at Carew's expense; they remained unprinted
until 1646, and Suckling died *circâ* 1642.

Carew had died *before the* 17*th* of April 1638, for
in the *Domestic Series of State Papers*, Charles I.,
of that date, vol. 387, No. 31, viz., the humble
petition of John Robinson, Vicar of Sunninghill
in the county of Berks., it mentions that 'your
Majesty was graciously pleased to part with the
Park of Sunninghill in the Forest of Windsor to

Mr. Tho. Carew,' and he personally requests an inquiry to be made, by summoning '*the executors of the said Mr. Carew,*' etc. Parsondom and money!

§ VI.—Conclusion.

Thus bald and scanty is the record that is called biography of Thomas Carew. Had he chosen to have kept a Diary or Itinerary in his youthful days of travel, noting what he saw for himself at the Hague, in Venice, Turin, Paris, and Florence, cities which he visited diplomatically or for pleasure, and with such descriptions of men, manners, and scenery as he has proved himself to have at will, we should have possessed a more charming book than Lord Herbert of Cherbury could give, or grave John Evelyn, men whose talents were respectable and habits decorous, but who certainly gave way to sententious dulness and sanctimonious pretences.

It seems idle to burden this necessarily brief Introduction with the eulogies on Carew, seldom enthusiastic, from fifth-rate critics. Phillips of *Theatrum Poetarum* need not be summoned again as a witness. Headley, Hallam, and a score more, who wrote their commendation respectfully, cannot equal the interest of Clarendon's affectionate words (p. 246). Robert Baron's frigid compliments (p. 253) in 'Truth and Tears,' of *Pocula Castalia*, 1650, or George Daniel of Beswick's mere mention of Carew's name, cannot advance his reputation greatly, so neither can he be injured by the carping insolence of George Wither, or whosoever it may have been that wrote the libellous satire entitled

The Great Assizes Holden in Parnassus by Apollo and his Assessors, 1645. We are led away too much in modern days by the opinions of people who ill deserve to possess any authority. We read criticisms, comments, and ' elucidations' which darken counsel with much speaking, when we ought to devote attention to the author himself; not the scene-shifter, or the roguish link-boy who too often dashes the flame in our face, and robs us unblushingly, as link-bearers used to do of old. When reading Thomas Carew, what need have we of more than Carew himself? If ponderous tomes are written about a man, how little it avails, unless he himself interests us, and is worthy of our regard? There are in Carew sufficient attractions, beyond the fact of his long-continued faithfulness in love, towards the one woman, whom he protects from gossip by disguising her name, as '*Celia.*' Throughout the Notes and incidental comments, we have spoken all that we needed to say, except—availing ourself of an old custom—what we have tried to sing, in the *Prelude* and the *Epilogue,* avowing our love and admiration for the man himself, the writer, no less than for the *Poems of Thomas Carew.*

J. W. Ebsworth.

Molash Priory, Kent, 1892.

In Memoriam: Thomas Carew.

(Natus circâ, 1598 ; Obiit, 1638.)

— ◦◦◦ —

WE know not where thy dust is laid,
    Perchance in some forgotten glade,
Under the Yew-trees' hallow'd shade ;

Since, haply, thy last breath was drawn
In a lone distant Grange, when dawn
Show'd glittering dew-drops on the lawn ;

Or, home return'd, to be more near
The Court of CHARLES, *who held thee dear :*
Death found thee, sad, yet without fear.

And friends, who oft had shared thy quest,
Bore thee in silence to thy rest :
That long sweet sleep we count the best.

They knew thy worth.   The crowd press'd on
To civil-war, with shout or moan :
For thee rose no memorial-stone.

Yet all whose hearts were sound could prize
Thy songs, thy tender melodies,
That still win tears from loving eyes.

Early recall'd :—the better doom!
We mourn thee not, as lost in gloom :
But lay this White Rose on thy tomb.

MOLASH PRIORY : KENT.   J. W. E.

xxvi

CONTENTS.

he original title-page of the MASQUE, 1634, *is on p.* 129;
title of editio princeps, 1640, *reproduced here.*]

POEMS

By

THOMAS CAREVV,

Esquire.

One of the Gentlemen of the
Privie-Chamber, and Sewer in
Ordinary to His Majesty.

———————— —— — —— — -

————————————

LONDON,

Printed by *I. D.* for *Thomas Walkley,*
and are to be Sold at the Signe of the
Flying Horfe, between Brittain's
Burfe and York-Houfe.

1640

Imprimatur,

MATTHEW CLAY.

Aprill, 29.   1640.

THE POEMS

OF

THOMAS CAREW.

The Spring.

NOW that the Winter's gone, the Earth hath
     lost
    Her snow-white robes ; and now no more
     the frost
    Candies the grass, or casts an icy cream
Upon the silver lake or crystal stream :
But the warm sun thaws the benumbed earth,
And makes it tender ; gives a second birth
To the dead Swallow ; wakes in hollow tree
The drowsy Cuckoo and the Humble-Bee.
Now do a choir of chirping minstrels sing,
In triumph to the world, the youthful Spring :
    The valleys, hills, and woods in rich array
    Welcome the coming of the long'd-for *May*.

    Now all things smile : only my Love doth lour,
Nor hath the scalding noon-day sun the power
To melt that marble ice, which still doth hold
Her heart congeal'd, and makes her pity cold.
The ox, which lately did for shelter flie
Into the stall, doth now securely lie

In open field ; and love no more is made
By the fire-side, but in the cooler shade.
Amyntas now doth by his *Cloris* sleep
Under a Sycamore, and all things keep
  Time with the season : only she doth carry
  June in her eyes, in her heart *January*.

His Counsel to his Mistress, *A. L.* Persuasions to Love.

THINK not, 'cause men flatt'ring say
 You're fresh as *April*, sweet as *May*,
Bright as is the morning star,
That you are so ; or, though you are,
Yet be not therefore proud, and deem
All men unworthy your esteem :
For, being so, you lose the pleasure
Of being fair, since that rich treasure
Of rare beauty and sweet feature
Was bestow'd on you by nature
To be enjoy'd ; and 'twere a sin
There to be scarce, where she hath been
So prodigal of her best graces :
Thus common beauties and mean faces
  Shall have more pastime, and enjoy
  The sport you lose by being coy.

 Did the thing for which I sue
Only concern myself, not you ;
Were men so framed as they alone
Reap'd all the pleasure, women none ;
Then had you reason to be scant :
But here 'tis madness not to grant
That which affords—if you consent—
To you, the giver, more content
Than me, the beggar. Oh, then be
Kind to yourself, if not to me.

Starve not yourself, because you may
Thereby make me to pine away ;
Néither let brittle beauty make
You your wiser thoughts forsake ;
For that same lovely face will fail :
Beauty is sweet, Beauty is frail.
'Tis sooner past, 'tis sooner done,
Than Summer's rain, than Winter's sun ;
 Most fleeting, when it is most dear :
 'Tis gone, while we but say 'tis here.

These curious locks, so aptly twin'd,
Whose every hair a soul doth bind,
Will change their auburn hue, and grow
White and cold as Winter's snow.
That eye, which now is *Cupid's* nest,
Will prove his grave, and all the rest
Will follow him ; on cheek, chin, nose,
Will be no lily found, nor rose.
And what will then become of all
Those whom now you Servants call ?
 Like swallows, when the Summer's done,
 They'll fly, and seek some warmer sun.

Then wisely choose one for your Friend
Whose love may, when your beauties end,
Remain still firm : be provident,
And think, before your Summer's spent,
Of following-Winter ; like the ant,
In plenty hoard for time of scant.
Cull out, amongst the multitude
Of lovers, who seek to intrude
Into your favour, one that may
Love for an age, not for a day ;
One that will cool your youthful fires,
And speed in age your hot desires.
For when the storms of time have moved
Waves on that cheek which was beloved ;

When a fair Lady's face is pined,
And yellow spread where red once shined ;
When beauty, youth, and all sweets leave her,
Love may return, but Lovers never :
    And old folks say, there are no pains
    Like itch of love in aged veins.

O love me, then, and now begin it,
Let us not lose this precious minute ;
For time and age will work that wrack
Which time and age can ne'er call back.
The Snake each year fresh skin resumes,
And Eagles change their aged plumes ;
The faded Rose each Spring receives
A fresh red tincture on her leaves ;
    But if your beauties once decay,
    You ne'er shall know a second *May*.

O then, be wise, and whilst your season
Affords you days for sport, do reason ;
Spend not in vain your life's short hour,
But crop in time your beauty's flower,
    Which will away, and doth together
    Both bud and fade, both blow and wither.

A Strife between *Celia's* Lips and Eyes.

IN *Celia's* face a question did arise,
    Which were more beautiful, her Lips or Eyes ?
"We," said the Eyes, "send forth those pointed darts
Which pierce the hardest adamantine hearts."
"From us," replied the Lips, "proceed those blisses
Which lovers reap by kind words and sweet kisses."
Then wept the Eyes, and from their springs did pour
Of liquid Oriental pearls a shower ;
Whereat the Lips, moved with delight and pleasure,
Through a sweet smile unlock'd *their* pearly treasure
    And bade Love judge, whether did add more grace
    Weeping or smiling Pearls to *Celia's* face.

A Divine Mistress.

I N Nature's pieces still I see
   Some error that might mended be ;
Something my wish could still remove,
Alter or add ; but my fair Love
Was framed by hands far more divine,
For she hath every beauteous line :
    Yet I had been far happier
    Had Nature, that made me, made her.

   Then likeness might (that Love creates)
Have made her love, what now she hates ;
Yet, I confess, I cannot spare
From her just shape the smallest hair ;
Nor need I beg from all the store
Of heaven for her one beauty more.
    She hath too much Divinity for me :
    You Gods, teach her some more humanity.

On his Beautiful Mistress.

SONG.

I F when the Sun at noon displays
         His brighter rays,
   Thou but appear,
He then, all pale with shame and fear,
        Quencheth his light,
Hides his dark brow, flies from thy sight,
   And grows more dim,
Compared to thee, than stars to him.

If thou but show thy face again,
When darkness doth at midnight reign,

The darkness flies, and light is hurl'd
Round about the silent world :
 So as alike thou drivest away
 Both light and darkness, night and day.

A CRUEL MISTRESS.

WE read of Gods and Kings that kindly took
 A pitcher full of water from the brook ;
But I have daily tender'd without thanks
Rivers of tears that overflow their banks.
 A slaughter'd bull appeased angry *Jove*,
A horse the Sun, a lamb the God of Love ;
But she disdains the spotless sacrifice
Of a pure heart, that on her altar lies.
 Vesta is not displeased, if her chaste urn
Doth with repaired fuel ever burn ;
But my Saint frowns, though to her honour'd name
I consecrate a never-dying flame.
 Th' *Assyrian* King did none i' th' furnace throw
But such as would not to his Image bow ;
With bended knees I daily worship her,
Yet she consumes her own Idolater.
  Of such a Goddess no times have record,
  Who burns the temple where she was adored.

MURDERING BEAUTY.

I'LL gaze no more on her bewitching face,
 Since ruin harbours there in every place ;
For my enchanted Soul alike she drowns
With calms and tempests, of her smiles and frowns.
 I'll love no more those cruel eyes of hers,
Which, pleased or anger'd, still are murderers :
For if she dart, like lightning, through the air
Her beams of wrath, she kills me with despair :
  If she behold me with a pleasing eye,
  I surfeit with excess of joy, and die.

My Mistress Commanding me to Return her Letters.

SO grieves th' advent'rous Merchant, when he throws
   All the long toil'd-for treasure his ship stows
Into the angry main, to save from wrack
Himself and men, as I grieve to send back
These letters : yet so powerful is your sway
That, if you bid me die, I must obey.
   Go then, blest papers, you shall kiss those hands
That gave you freedom, but hold me in bands ;
Which with a touch did give you life, but I,
Because I may not touch those hands, must die.
   Methinks, as if they knew they should be sent
Home to their native soil from banishment,
I see them smile, like dying Saints, that know
They are to leave earth, and tow'rd heaven go.
   When you return, pray tell your sovereign
And mine, I gave you courteous entertaine ;
Each line received a tear, and then a kiss ;
First bathed in that, it 'scaped unscorch'd from this :
I kiss'd it 'cause her hand had once been there ;
But, 'cause it is not now, I shed a tear.
   Tell her, no length of time, no change of air,
No cruelty, disdain, absence, despair ;
No, nor her steadfast constancy, can deter
My vassal heart from ever honouring her.
Though these be powerful arguments to prove
I love in vain, yet I must ever love.
   Say, if she frown, when you that word rehearse,
Service in prose is oft called love in verse :
Then pray her, since I send back on my part
Her papers, she will send me back my heart.
     If she refuse, warn her to come before
     The God of Love, whom I will thus implore :
" Trav'lling thy countries o'er, great God, I spied
By chance this lady, and walk'd by her side,

From place to place, fearing no violence ;
For I was well-arm'd, and had made defence
In former fights 'gainst fiercer foes than she
Did at the first encounter seem to be.
But, going farther, every step reveal'd
Some hidden weapon, till that time conceal'd.

"Seeing these outward arms, I did begin
To fear some greater strength was lodged within.
Looking into her mind, I might survey
An host of beauties, that in ambush lay,
And won the day, before they fought the field :
For I, unable to resist, did yield.

"But the insulting tyrant foe destroys
My conquer'd mind, my ease, my peace, my joys,
Breaks my sweet sleep, invades my harmless rest,
Robs me of all the treasures of my breast,
Spares not my heart, nor yet a greater wrong,
For, having stol'n my heart, she binds my tongue.
But at the last her melting eyes unseal'd
My lips, enlarged my tongue : then I reveal'd
To her own ears the story of my harms,
Wrought by her virtues and her beauty's charms.

"Now hear, just Judge, an act of savageness ;
When I complain, in hope to find redress,
She bends her angry brow, and from her eye
Shoots thousand darts.   Then I well hoped to die ;
But in such sovereign balm Love dips his shot,
That, though they wound a heart, they kill it not.
She saw the blood gush forth from many a wound,
Yet fled, and left me bleeding on the ground,
Nor sought my cure, nor saw me since : 'tis true,
Absence and Time, two cunning Leaches, drew
The flesh together ; yet, sure, though the skin
Be closed without, the wound festers within.

"Thus hath this cruel Lady used a true
Servant and subject to herself and you ;
Nor know I, great Love, if my life be lent
To show thy mercy or my punishment :

Since by the only magic of thy Art
A lover still may live that wants his heart.
  " If this indictment 'fright her, so that she
Seem willing to return my heart to me,
But cannot find it (for perhaps it may,
'Mongst other trifling hearts, be out o' th' way);
    If she repent, and would make me amends,
    Bid her but send me her's, and we are friends."

SECRECY PROTESTED.

FEAR not, dear Love, that I'll reveal
    Those hours of pleasure we two steal ;
No eye shall see, nor yet the Sun
Descry, what thou and I have done.

No ear shall hear our love, but we
As silent as the night will be ;
The God of Love himself (whose dart
Did first wound mine, and then thy heart),

Shall never know that we can tell
What sweets in stol'n embraces dwell.
This only means may find it out :
If, when I die, physicians doubt

What caused my death, and there to view
Of all their judgments which was true,—
Rip up my heart, oh ! then, I fear,
The world will see thy picture there.

A PRAYER TO THE WIND.
SONG: A SIGH.

GO, thou gentle whispering wind,
    Bear this Sigh ! and if thou find
Where my cruel fair doth rest,
Cast it in her snowy breast,

So, inflamed by my desire,
It may set her heart on fire.
  Those sweet kisses thou shalt gain,
Will reward thee for thy pain ;
Boldly light upon her lip,
There suck odours, and thence skip
To her bosom : lastly fall
Down, and wander over all.
  Range about those ivory hills,
From whose every part distils
Amber dew ; there spices grow,
There pure streams of nectar flow :
There perfume thyself, and bring
All those sweets upon thy wing.
  As thou return'st, change by thy power
Every weed into a flower ;
Turn every thistle to a Vine,
Make the bramble Eglantine :
For so rich a booty made,
Do but this, and I am paid.
  Thou can'st with thy powerful blast
Heat apace, and cool as fast ;
Thou can'st kindle hidden flame,
And again destroy the same :
Then, for pity, either stir
Up the Fire of Love in her,
    That alike both flames may shine,
    Or else quite extinguish mine.

MEDIOCRITY IN LOVE REJECTED.

SONG.

G IVE me more Love, or more Disdain ;
   The torrid or the frozen zone
Bring equal ease unto my pain,
  The temperate affords me none :
Either extreme, of love or hate,
Is sweeter than a calm estate.

Give me a storm : if it be Love,
　Like *Danæ* in that golden shower,
I swim in pleasure ; if it prove
　Disdain, that torrent will devour
My vulture-hopes ; and he's possessed
Of Heaven, that's but from Hell released.
　　　Then crown my joys, or cure my pain :
　　　Give me more Love, or more Disdain.

GOOD COUNSEL TO A YOUNG MAID.

SONG.

G AZE not on thy beauties' pride,
　　Tender Maid, in the false tide
That from Lovers' eyes doth slide.

Let thy faithful Crystal show
How thy colours come and go :
Beauty takes a foil from woe.

Love, that in those smooth streams lies
Under Pity's fair disguise,
Will thy melting heart surprise.

Nets of Passion's finest thread,
Snaring poems, will be spread,
All to catch thy maidenhead.

Then beware ! for those that cure
Love's disease, themselves endure
For reward a Calenture.　　　　　　[= a hot
　　　　　　　　　　　　　　　　　　 fever.

Rather let the Lover pine,
Than his pale cheek should assign
A perpetual blush to thine.

To my Mistress, sitting by a River's side.

AN EDDY.

MARK, how yon Eddy steals away
    From the rude stream into the Bay ;
There, lock'd up safe, she doth divorce
Her waters from the channel's course,
And scorns the torrent that did bring
Her headlong from her native spring.
      Now doth she with her new Love play,
      Whilst he runs murmuring away.

Mark, how she courts the banks, whilst they
As amorously their arms display,
T' embrace, and clip her silver waves :
See how she strokes their sides, and craves
An entrance there, which they deny ;
Whereat she frowns, threat'ning to fly
Home to her stream, and 'gins to swim
Backward, but from the channel's brim
      Smiling returns into the creek,
      With thousand dimples on her cheek.

Be thou this Eddy, and I'll make
My breast thy shore, where thou shalt take
Secure repose, and never dream
Of the quite forsaken stream ;
Let him to the wide Ocean haste,
There lose his colour, name, and taste :
      Thou shalt save all, and, safe from him,
      Within these arms for ever swim.

Conquest by Flight : A Song.

LADIES, fly from Love's soft tale !
    Oaths steep'd in tears do oft prevail ;
Grief is infectious, and the air
Enflamed with sighs will blast the Fair.

Then stop your ears, when Lovers cry,
Lest yourselves weep, when no soft eye
    Shall with a sorrowing tear repay
    That pity which you cast away.

  Young men, fly ! when Beauty darts
Amorous glances at your hearts :
The fix'd mark gives the shooter aim ;
And Ladies' looks have power to maim ;
Now 'twixt their lips, now in their eyes,
Wrapt in a smile or kiss, Love lies :
    Then fly betimes, for only they
    Conquer Love that run away.

To my Inconstant Mistress.

SONG.

WHEN thou, poor Excommunicate
    From all the joys of Love, shalt see
The full reward and glorious fate
    Which my strong faith shall purchase me,
    Then curse thine own Inconstancy.

A fairer hand than thine shall cure
    That heart, which thy false oaths did wound ;
And to my soul a soul more pure
    Than thine shall by Love's hand be bound,
    And both with equal glory crown'd.

Then shalt thou weep, entreat, complain
    To Love, as I did once to thee ;
When all thy tears shall be as vain
    As mine were then : for thou shalt be
    Damn'd for thy false Apostacy.

Persuasions to Joy: A Song.

I F the quick spirits in your eye
  Now languish, and anon must die ;
If every sweet, and every grace
Must fly from that forsaken face :
    Then, *Celia*, let us reap our joys
    Ere time such goodly fruit destroys.

Or, if that golden fleece must grow
For ever, free from aged snow ;
If those bright suns must know no shade,
Nor your fresh beauties ever fade,
Then fear not, *Celia*, to bestow
What, still being gather'd, still must grow.
    Thus, either Time his sickle brings
    In vain, or else in vain his wings.

A Deposition from Love.

I WAS foretold, your Rebel sex
  Nor Love nor Pity knew ;
And with what scorn you use to vex
  Poor hearts that humbly sue.
Yet I believed, to crown our pain,
  Could we the fortress win,
The happy Lover sure should gain
  A Paradise within :
I thought Love's plagues, like dragons, sate
Only to fright us at the gate.

But I did enter, and enjoy
  What happier Lovers prove ;
For I could kiss, and sport, and toy,
  And taste those sweets of Love,
Which, had they but a lasting state,
  Or if in *Celia's* breast

The force of love might not abate,
   Jove were too mean a guest :
But now her breach of faith far more
Afflicts, than did her scorn before.

Hard fate ! to have been once possess'd
   As Victor of a heart,
Achieved with labour and unrest,
   And then forced to depart.
If the stout Foe will not resign,
   When I besiege a Town,
I lose but what was never mine ;
   But he that is cast down
From enjoy'd Beauty, feels a woe
Only deposed kings can know.

INGRATEFUL BEAUTY THREATENED.

KNOW, *Celia*, since thou art so proud,
   'Twas I that gave thee thy renown.
Thou had'st in the forgotten crowd
   Of common Beauties lived unknown,
Had not my verse extoll'd thy name,
And with it ympt the wings of Fame.   [*Note.*

That killing power is none of thine :
   I gave it to thy voice and eyes ;
Thy sweets, thy graces, all are mine ;
   Thou art my Star, shin'st in my skies :
Then dart not from thy borrow'd sphere
Lightning on him that fix'd thee there.

Tempt me with such affrights no more,
   Lest what I made I uncreate ;
Let fools thy mystic forms adore,
   I know thee in thy Mortal state.
Wise poets that wrapt Truth in tales,
Knew her themselves through all her veils.

DISDAIN RETURNED.

H E that loves a rosy cheek,
　　Or a coral lip admires,
Or, from star-like eyes, doth seek
　　Fuel to maintain his fires ;
As old Time makes these decay,
So his flames must waste away.

But a smooth and steadfast mind,
　　Gentle thoughts and calm desires,
Hearts with equal love combined,
　　Kindle never-dying fires.
Where these are not, I despise
Lovely cheeks, or lips, or eyes.

No tears, *Celia*, now shall win
　　My resolved heart to return ;
I have search'd thy soul within,
　　And find nought but pride and scorn.
I have learn'd thy arts, and now
Can disdain as much as thou.
　　Some Power in my revenge convey
　　That Love to her I cast away.

A LOOKING-GLASS.

T HAT flatt'ring Glass, whose smooth face wear
　　Your shadow, which a Sun appears,
Was once a river of my tears.

About your cold heart they did make
A circle, where the briny lake
Congealed into a Crystal cake.

Gaze no more on that killing eye,
For fear the native cruelty
Doom you, as it doth all, to die :

For fear lest the fair object move
Your froward heart to fall in love :
Then you yourself your Rival prove.

Look rather on my pale cheeks pined,
There view your beauties, there you'll find
A fair face, but a cruel mind.

Be not for ever frozen, coy !
One beam of Love will soon destroy
And melt that ice to floods of joy.

An Elegy on the Lady *Pennington* :
Sent to my Mistress out of *France*.

LET him, who from his tyrant Mistress did
This day receive his cruel doom, forbid
His eyes to weep that loss, and let him here
Open those flood-gates to bedew this Bier ;
So shall those drops, which else would be but brine,
Be turned to Manna, falling on her shrine.
Let him who, banish'd far from her dear sight,
Whom his soul loves, doth in that absence write,
Or lines of passion, or some powerful charms,
To vent his own grief, or unlock her arms ;
Take off his pen, and in sad verse bemoan
This general sorrow, and forget his own.
So may those Verses live, which else must die ;
For though the Muses give eternity
When they embalm with verse, yet she could give
Life unto that Muse by which others live.

Oh, pardon me, fair Soul ! that boldly have
Dropp'd, though but one tear, on thy silent grave,
And writ on that earth, which such honour had,
To clothe that flesh wherein thy self was clad.

B

And pardon me, sweet Saint ! whom I adore,
That I this tribute pay out of the store
Of lines and tears that were due unto thee :
Oh, do not think it new Idolatry,
Though you are only-sovereign of this Land,
Yet universal losses may command
A subsidy from every private eye,
And press each pen to write : so to supply
And feed the common grief.   If this excuse
Prevail not, take these tears to your own use,
As shed for you : for when I saw her die,
I then did think on your mortality.
   For since nor virtue, will, nor beauty, could
Preserve from Death's hand this their heavenly mould
Where they were framed all, and where they dwelt,
I then knew you must die too, and did melt
Into these tears ; but, thinking on that day,
And when the gods resolved to take away
A Saint from us, I that did know what dearth
There was of such good souls upon the earth,
Began to fear lest Death, their officer,
Might have mistook, and taken thee for her :
So had'st thou robb'd us of that happiness
Which she in heaven, and I in thee possess.
   But what can heaven to her glory add ?
The praises she hath, dead, living she had.
To say she's now an Angel, is no more
Praise than she had, for she was one before.
Which of the Saints can show more votaries
Than she had here ?   Even those that did despise
The Angels, and may her, now she is one,
Did whil'st she lived with pure devotion
Adore and worship her : Her virtues had
All honour here, for this world was too bad
To hate or envy her ; these cannot rise
So high as to repine at Deities :
     But now she's 'mongst her fellow-Saints, they ma,
     Be good enough to envy her, this way.

There's loss i' th' change 'twixt heaven and earth, if she
Should leave her servants here below to be
Hated of her competitors above ;
But sure her matchless goodness needs must move
Those blest souls to admire her excellence ;
By this means only can her journey hence
To heaven prove gain, if, as she was but here
Worshipp'd by Men, she be by Angels there.

But I must weep no more over this Urn,
My tears to their own channel must return ;
And having ended these sad obsequies,
My Muse must back to her old exercise,
To tell the story of my martyrdom.
But oh, thou Idol of my soul ! become
Once pitiful, that she may change her style,
Dry up her blubber'd eyes, and learn to smile.
Rest then, blest Soul ! for, as ghosts fly away
When the shrill cock proclaims the infant-day,
So must I hence, for lo ! I see from far
The minions of the Muses coming are :
  Each of them bringing to thy sacred Hearse
  In either eye a tear, each hand a verse.

To his Mistress in Absence.

THOUGH I must live here, and by force
  Of your command suffer divorce ;
Though I am parted, yet my mind
(That's more my self) still stays behind.
I breathe in you, you keep my heart,
'Twas but a carcass that did part.
Then though our bodies are disjoin'd,
As things that are to place confined,
Yet let our boundless spirits meet,
And in Love's sphere each other greet ;
There let us work a mystic wreath,
Unknown unto the world beneath :

There let our clasp'd loves sweetly 'twine,
There let our secret thoughts unseen
Like nets be weaved and inter-twined,
Wherewith we'll catch each other's mind.
    There, whilst our souls do sit and kiss,
Tasting a sweet and subtle bliss,
(Such as gross lovers cannot know,
Whose hands and lips meet here below),
Let us look down, and mark what pain
Our absent bodies here sustain ;
And smile to see how far away
The one doth from the other stray,
Yet burn and languish with desire
To join, and quench their mutual fire ;
Where let us joy to see from far
Our emulous flames at loving war :
Whilst both with equal lustre shine,
Mine bright as yours, yours bright as mine.
There, seated in those heavenly bowers
We'll cheat the lag and ling'ring hours,
        Making our bitter absence sweet,
        Till souls and bodies both may meet.

To Her in Absence.

A SHIP.

TOST in a troubled sea of griefs, I float
    Far from the shore, in a storm-beaten boat ;
Where my sad thoughts do, like the Compass, show
The several points from which cross-winds do blow.
My heart doth, like the needle, touch'd with love,
Still fix'd on you, point which way I would move ;
You 're the bright Pole-star, which, in the dark
Of this long absence, guides my wand'ring bark ;
Love is the Pilot : but, o'er-come with fear
Of your displeasure, dares not homewards steer.
My fearful hope hangs on my trembling sail,
Nothing is wanting but a gentle gale ;

Which pleasant breath must blow from your sweet lip :
Bid it but move, and quick as thought this Ship
    Into your arms, which are my port, will fly,
    Where it for ever shall at Anchor lie.

ETERNITY OF LOVE PROTESTED.

SONG.

HOW ill doth he deserve a Lover's name
      Whose pale weak flame
      Cannot retain
His heat, in spite of absence or disdain ;
But doth at once, like paper set on fire,
      Burn and expire !
True love can never change his seat ;
Nor did he ever love that can retreat.

That noble flame, which my breast keeps alive,
      Shall still survive
      When my soul's fled ;
Nor shall my love die, when my body's dead ;
That shall wait on me to the lower shade,
      And never fade :
My very ashes in their urn
Shall, like a hallowed lamp, for ever burn.

UPON SOME ALTERATIONS IN MY MISTRESS,

AFTER MY DEPARTURE INTO *FRANCE.*

OH, gentle Love, do not forsake the guide
    Of my frail Bark, on which the swelling tide
      Of ruthless Pride
Doth beat, and threaten wrack from every side.
Gulfs of Disdain do gape to overwhelm
This boat, nigh sunk with grief ; whilst at the helm
      Despair commands ;
And, round about, the shifting sands

Of faithless love and false inconstancy,
               With rocks of Cruelty,
Stop up my passage to the neighbour Lands.

My sighs have raised those winds, whose fury bears
My sails o'erboard, and in their place spreads fears ;
               And from my tears
This Sea is sprung, where nought but death appears.
A mystic cloud of anger hides the light
Of my fair Star ; and everywhere black night
               Usurps the place
Of those bright rays, which once did grace
My forth-bound Ship : but when it could no more
               Behold the vanish'd shore,
In the deep flood she drown'd her beamy face.

GOOD COUNSEL TO A YOUNG MAID.

p. 11.]

WHEN you the sun-burn'd Pilgrim see
               Fainting with thirst, haste to the springs ;
Mark how at first with bended knee
               He courts the crystal Nymph, and flings
His body to the earth, where he
Prostrate adores the flowing Deitie.

But when his heated face is drench'd
               In her cool waves, when from her sweet
Bosom his burning thirst is quench'd,
               Then mark, how with disdainful feet
He kicks her banks, and from the place
That thus refresh'd him, moves with sullen pace.

So shalt thou be despised, fair Maid,
               When by the sated Lover tasted ;
What first he did with tears invade
               Shall afterward with scorn be wasted :
When all thy Virgin-springs grow-dry,
Then no stream shall be left but in thine eye.

CELIA BLEEDING.

TO THE SURGEON.

FOND man, that can'st believe her blood
   Will from those purple channels flow ;
Or that the pure untainted flood
   Can any foul distemper know ;
Or that thy weak steel can incize
The crystal case wherein it lies :—

Know, her quick blood, proud of his seat,
   Runs dancing through her azure veins ;
Whose harmony nor cold nor heat
   Disturbs, whose hue no tincture stains :
And the hard rock, wherein it dwells,
The keenest darts of Love repels.

But thou reply's 'Behold, she bleeds !'
   Fool ! thou'rt deceived, and do'st not know
The mystic knot whence this proceeds,
   How Lovers in each other grow :
Thou struck'st her arm, but 'twas my heart
Shed all the blood, felt all the smart.

To *T. H.*, A LADY RESEMBLING MY MISTRESS.

FAIR copy of my *Celia's* face,
   Twin of my Love, thy perfect grace
May claim with her an equal place.

Disdain not a divided heart ;
Though all be hers, you shall have part :
Love is not tied to rules of art.

For as my soul first to her flew,
Yet stay'd with me, so now 'tis true
It dwells with her, though fled to you.

Then entertain this wand'ring guest,
And if not love, allow it rest :
It left not, but mistook, the nest.

Nor think my Love, or your fair eyes,
Cheaper, 'cause from the sympathies
You hold with her these flames arise.

To lead or brass, or some such bad
Metal, a Prince's stamp may add
That value which it never had :

But to the pure refined Ore
The stamp of kings imparts no more
Worth, than the metal held before.

Only the image gives the rate,
To subjects of a foreign state :
'Tis prized as much for its own weight.

So though all other hearts resign
To your pure worth, yet you are mine
Only because you are her coin.

ON HIS ENTERTAINMENT AT *SAXHAM*, 1634.

THOUGH frost and snow lock'd from mine eyes
    That beauty which without-door lies,
Thy gardens, orchards, walks, that so
I might not all thy pleasures know,
Yet, *Saxham*, thou within thy gate
Art of thy self so delicate,
So full of native sweets, that bless
Thy roof with inward happiness,
As neither from, nor to, thy store
Winter takes aught, or Spring adds more.

The cold and frozen air had starved
Much Poor, if not by thee preserved,
Whose prayers have made thy table blest
With plenty, far above the rest.
The season hardly did afford
Coarse cates unto thy neighbours' board,
Yet thou had'st dainties : as the sky
Had only been thy Votary ;
Or else the birds, fearing the snow
Might to another Deluge grow,
The pheasant, partridge, and the lark
Flew to thy house, as to the Ark.
The willing ox of himself came
Home to the slaughter, with the lamb ;
And every beast did thither bring
Himself, to be an offering.
The scaly herd more pleasure took,
Bathed in thy dish, than in the brook ;
Water, earth, air, did all conspire
To pay their tribute to thy fire,
Whose cherishing flames themselves divide
Through every room, where they deride
The night and cold abroad : whilst they,
Like suns, within, keep endless day.
 Those cheerful beams send forth their light
To all that wander in the night,
And seem to beckon from aloof
The weary Pilgrim to thy roof ;
Where, when refresh'd, if he'll away,
He's fairly welcome ; but, if he stay,
Far more ; which he shall hearty find
Both from the master and the hind :
The Stranger's Welcome each man there
Stamp'd on his cheerful brow doth wear.
Nor doth his welcome or his cheer
Grow less, 'cause he stays longer there.
There's none observes, much less repines,
How often this man sups or dines.

Thou hast no Porter at thy door
To examine or keep back the Poor ;
Nor locks nor bolts : thy gates have been
Made only to let strangers in.
Untaught to shut, they do not fear
To stand wide open all the year,
Careless who enters, for they know
Thou never did'st deserve a foe :
    And as for thieves, thy bounty's such,
    They cannot steal, thou givest so much.

Upon a Ribbon, tied about his Arm by a Lady.

THIS silken wreath, that circles-in my arm,
    Is but an emblem of that mystic charm
Wherewith the magic of your Beauty binds
My captive soul, and round about it winds
Fetters of lasting love. This hath entwined
My flesh alone ; that hath empaled my mind.
Time may wear out these soft weak bands, but those
Strong chains of brass Fate shall not discompose.
    This holy relic may preserve my wrist,
But my whole frame doth by that power subsist :
To that my prayers and sacrifice, to this
I only pay a superstitious kiss.
This but an idol, that's the Deity :
Religion there is due ; here, ceremony.
That I received by faith, this but in trust ;
Here I may tender duty : there, I must.
This order as a layman I may bear,
But I become Love's Priest when *that* I wear.
This moves like air, that as the centre stands ;
That knot your virtues tied : this, but your hands.
    That, Nature framed ; but this was made by Art :
    This, makes my arm your prisoner ; that, my heart.

To the King, at his Entrance into *Saxham.*

SPOKEN BY MASTER JOHN CROFTS.

SIR, ere you pass this threshold, stay,
 And give your creature leave to pay
Those pious rites, which unto you,
As to our household gods, are due.
In stead of sacrifice, each breast
Is like a flaming altar drest
  With zealous fires, which from pure hearts
  Love mixed with loyalty imparts.

 Incense nor gold have we, yet bring
As rich and sweet an offering ;
And such as doth both these express,
Which is our humble thankfulness ;
By which is paid the all we owe
To gods above, or men below.
The slaughter'd beast, whose flesh should feed
The hungry flames, we for pure need
Dress for your supper ; and the gore
Which should be dash'd on every door,
We change into the lusty blood
Of youthful Vines, of which a flood
  Shall sprightly run through all our veins,
  First to your health, then your fair Train's.

 We shall want nothing but good fare,
To show your welcome and our care ;
Such rarities, that come from far,
From poor men's houses banish'd are :
Yet we'll express in homely cheer
How glad we are to see you here.
We'll have what-soe' the season yields,
Out of the neighbouring woods and fields ;
For all the dainties of your board
Will only be what those afford,
  And, having supp'd, we may perchance
  Present you with a Country dance.

Thus much your servants, that bear sway
Here in your absence, bade me say ;
And beg, besides, you'ld hither bring
Only the mercy of a King,
And not the greatness : since they have
A thousand faults must pardon crave,
But nothing that is fit to wait
Upon the glory of your State.
Yet your gracious favour will,
They hope, as heretofore, shine still
    On their endeavours, for they swore
    Should *Jove* descend, they could no more.

Upon the Sickness of *E. S.*

M UST she then languish, and we sorrow thus,
    And no kind god help her, or pity us ?
Is justice fled from heaven ? can that permit
A foul deformed ravisher to sit
Upon her virgin cheek, and pull from thence
The rose-buds in their maiden excellence ?
To spread cold paleness on her lips, and chase
The frighted rubies from their native place ?
To lick up with his searching flames a flood
Of dissolved coral, flowing in her blood ;
    And with the damps of his infectious breath
    Print on her brow moist characters of death ?

Must the clear light, 'gainst course of nature, ce:
In her fair eyes, and yet the flames increase ?
Must fevers shake this goodly tree, and all
That ripen'd fruit from the fair branches fall,
Which princes have desired to taste ?   Must she,
Who hath preserved her spotless chastity
From all solicitation, now at last
By agues and diseases be embraced ?

Forbid it, holy *Dian !* else who shall
Pay vows, or let one grain of incense fall
On thy neglected altars, if thou bless
No better this thy zealous votaress ?
Haste then, O maiden Goddess ! to her aid ;
Let on thy quiver her pale cheek be laid,
And rock her fainting body in thine arms ;
Then let the God of Music with still charms
Her restless eyes in peaceful slumbers close,
And with soft strains sweeten her calm repose.
   Cupid, descend ! and whilst *Apollo* sings,
Fanning the cool air with thy panting wings
Ever supply her with refreshing wind ;
Let thy fair mother with her tresses bind
Her labouring temples, with whose balmy sweat
She shall perfume her hairy Coronet,
Whose precious drops shall upon every fold
Hang like rich pearls about a wreath of gold ;
Her looser locks, as they unbraided lie,
Shall spread themselves into a canopy ;
Under whose shadow let her rest secure
From chilling cold or burning Calenture :   [p. 11.
Unless she freeze with ice of chaste desires,
Or holy *Hymen* kindle nuptial fires :
   And when at last Death comes to pierce her heart,
   Convey into his hand thy golden dart.

A NEW-YEAR'S SACRIFICE.
TO LUCINDA, 1632.

THOSE that can give, open their hands this day ;
   Those that cannot, yet hold them up to pray,
That health may crown the seasons of this year,
And mirth dance round the circle ; that no tear,
Unless of joy, may with its briny dew
Discolour on your cheek the rosy hue ;
That no access of years presume t' abate
Your Beauty's ever-flourishing estate.

Such cheap and vulgar wishes I could lay
As trivial offerings at your feet this day ;
But that it were apostacy in me
To send a prayer to any Deity
But your divine self, who have power to give
Those blessings unto others : such as live,
Like me, by the sole influence of your eyes,
Whose fair aspects govern our destinies.

    Such incense, vows, and holy rites as were
To the Involved Serpent of the Year
Paid by *Egyptian* priests, lay I before
Lucinda's sacred shrine, whilst I adore
Her beauteous eyes, and her pure altars dress
With gums and spice of humble thankfulness.
So may my Goddess from her heaven inspire
My frozen bosom with a *Delphic* fire ;
      And then the world shall, by that glorious flam
      Behold the blaze of thy immortal name.

SONG : TO ONE WHO, WHEN I PRAISED MY MISTRESS
        BEAUTY, SAID I WAS BLIND.

WONDER not, though I am blind,
        For you must be
Dark in your eyes or in your mind,
        If, when you see
Her face, you prove not blind like me.
    If the powerful beams that fly
        From her eye,
And those amorous sweets that lie
Scatter'd in each neighbouring part,
Find a passage to your heart ;
Then you'll confess your mortal sight
Too weak for such a glorious light :
For if her graces you discover,
You grow, like me, a dazzled lover :
      But if those beauties you not spy,
      Then are you blinder far than I.

To my Mistress, I burning in Love.

SONG.

I BURN ! and cruel you, in vain
   Hope to quench me with disdain ;
If from your eyes those sparkles came
That have kindled all this flame,
What boots it me, though now you shroud
Those fierce comets in a cloud ?
Since all the flames that I have felt
Could your snow yet never melt :
Nor can your snow, though you should take
Alps into your bosom, slake
The heat of my enamour'd heart ;
But, with wonder, learn Love's art :
No seas of ice can cool desire,
Equal flames must quench Love's fire.
    Then, think not that my heat can die,
    Till you burn as well as I.

To her again, she Burning in a Fever.

SONG.

NOW she burns, as well as I,
   Yet my heat can never die ;
She burns, that never knew desire,
She that was ice, she now is fire.
She whose cold heart chaste thoughts did arm
So as Love's flames could never warm
The frozen bosom where it dwelt,
She burns, and all her beauties melt.
She burns, and cries, ' Love's fires are mild :
Fevers are Gods, and he is a Child.'
Love, let her know the difference
'Twixt the heat of soul and sense :
    Touch her with thy flames divine,
    So shalt thou quench her fire, and mine.

Upon the King's Sickness.

SICKNESS, the minister of Death, doth lay
   So strong a siege against our brittle clay,
As, whilst it doth our weak forts singly win,
It hopes at length to take all mankind in.
First, it begins upon the womb to wait,
And doth the unborn Child there uncreate ;
Then rocks the cradle where the Infant lies,
Where, ere it fully be alive, it dies.
It never leaves fond Youth, until it have
Found or an early or a later grave.
By thousand subtle sleights from heedless Man
It cuts the short allowance of a span ;
And where both sober life and art combine
To keep it out, Age makes them both resign.
    Thus, by degrees, it only gain'd of late
    The weak, the aged, or intemperate.

But now the Tyrant hath found out a way
By which the sober, strong, and young decay ;
Ent'ring his Royal limbs that is our head :
Through us (his mystic limbs) the pain is spread.
That man who doth not feel his [share] hath none
In any part of his dominion ;
    If he hold land, that earth is forfeited,
    And he unfit on any ground to tread.

This grief is felt at Court, where it doth move
Through every joint, like the true soul of love.
All those fair stars, that do attend on Him
Whence they derived their light, wax pale and dim.
That ruddy morning beam of Majesty,
Which should the sun's eclipsed light supply,
Is overcast with mists, and in the lieu
Of cheerful rays sends us down drops of dew.

That curious form, made of an earth refined,
At whose blest birth the gentle Planets shined
With fair aspects, and sent a glorious flame
To animate so beautiful a frame,
That Darling of the gods and men doth wear
A cloud on 's brow, and in his eye a tear.
And all the rest, save when his dread command
Doth bid them move, like lifeless statues stand.
    So full a grief, so generally worn,
    Shows a good King is sick, and good men mourn.

SONG.

To a Lady, not yet enjoyed by her Husband.

COME, *Celia*, fix thine eyes on mine,
    And through those crystals our souls flitting
Shall a pure wreath of eye-beams twine,
    Our loving hearts together knitting.
Let Eaglets the bright Sun survey,
Though the blind Mole discern not day.

When clear *Aurora* leaves her mate,
    The light of her grey eyes despising,
Yet all the world doth celebrate
    With sacrifice her fair up-rising.
Let Eaglets the bright Sun survey,
Though the blind Mole discern not day.

A Dragon kept the golden fruit,
    Yet he those dainties never tasted;
As others pined in the pursuit,
    So he himself with plenty wasted.
Let Eaglets the bright Sun survey,
Though the blind Mole discern not day.

c

The Willing Prisoner to his Mistress.

SONG.

LET fools great *Cupid's* yoke disdain,
　　Loving their own wild freedom better;
Whilst, proud of my triumphant chain,
　　I sit, and court my beauteous fetter.

Her murd'ring glances, snaring hairs,
　　And her bewitching smiles so please me;
As he brings ruin, who repairs
　　The sweet afflictions that disease me.

Hide not those panting balls of snow
　　With envious veils from my beholding;
Unlock those lips, their pearly row
　　In a sweet smile of love unfolding.

And let those eyes, whose motion wheels
　　The restless Fate of every lover,
Survey the pains my sick heart feels,
　　And wounds, themselves have made discover.

A Fly that flew into his *Celia's* eye.

WHILE this Fly lived, she used to play
　　In the bright sunshine all the day;
Till, coming near my *Celia's* sight,
She found a new and unknown light,
　　　So full of glory that it made
　　　The noon-day Sun a gloomy shade.

At last this Amorous Fly became
My rival, and did court my flame.
She did from hand to bosom skip,
And from her breath, her cheek, and lip,
　　　Suck'd all the incense and the spice;
　　　So grew a Bird of Paradise.

At last into her eye she flew,
There, scorch'd in heat and drown'd in dew,
Like *Phaëton* from the sun's sphere
She fell ; and with her dropp'd a tear :
Of which a pearl was straight composed,
Wherein her ashes lie enclosed.
    Thus she received from *Celia's* eye
    Funeral, flame, tomb, obsequy.

SONG.

On *Celia* singing to her Lute, in Arundel Garden.

HARK, how my *Celia*, with the choice
    Music of her hand and voice,
Stills the loud wind, and makes the wild
Enraged boar and panther mild.
Mark how those statues like men move,
While men with wonder statues prove.
    The stiff rock bends to worship her :
    The Idol turns idolater.

Now, see how all the new inspired
Images with love are fired !
Hark how the tender marble groans,
And all the late transformed stones
Court the fair Nymph, with many a tear,
Which she—more stony than they were—
Beholds with unrelenting mind ;
When they, amazed to see combined
    Such matchless beauty with disdain,
    Are all turn'd into stone again.

CELIA SINGING.

SONG.

YOU that think Love can convey
            No other way
But through the eyes into the heart
            His fatal dart,
Close up those casements, and but hear
            This Syren sing ;
            And on the wing
Of her sweet voice it shall appear
That Love can enter at the ear :

Then unveil your eyes : behold
            The curious mould
Where that voice dwells : and, as we know
            When the cocks crow,
We freely may gaze on the day ;
So may you, when the Music's done,
Awake, and see the rising Sun.

SONG.

To ONE THAT DESIRED TO KNOW MY MISTRESS.

SEEK not to know my Love, for she
      Hath vow'd her constant faith to me ;
HER mild aspects are mine, and thou
Shalt only find a stormy brow :
        For if her beauty stir desire
        In me, her kisses quench the fire.

Or I can to Love's fountain go,
Or dwell upon her hills of snow ;
But when thou burn'st, she will not spare
One gentle breath to cool the air :
        Thou shalt not climb those Alps, nor spy
        Where the sweet springs of *Venus* lie.

Search hidden Nature, and there find
A treasure to enrich thy mind ;
Discover arts not yet reveal'd,
But let my Mistress live conceal'd :
    Though men by knowledge wiser grow,
    Yet Her 'tis wisdom not to know.

SONG.

IN THE PERSON OF A LADY TO HER INCONSTANT SERVANT.

WHEN on the altar of my hand,
    Bedew'd with many a kiss and tear,
Thy now-revolted heart did stand
    An humble martyr, thou did'st swear
    Thus (and the God of Love did hear) :
' By those bright glances of thine eye,
Unless thou pity me, I die.'

When first those perjured lips of thine,
    Be-paled with blasting sighs, did seal
Their violated faith on mine,
    From the soft bosom that did heal
    Thee, thou my melting heart did'st steal :
My soul, enflamed with thy false breath,
Poison'd with kisses, suck'd in death.

Yet I nor hand nor lip will move,
    Revenge or mercy to procure
From the offended God of Love :
    My curse is fatal, and my pure
    Love shall beyond thy scorn endure.
If I implore the Gods, they'll find
Thee too ungrateful, me too kind.

Truce in Love Intreated.

NO more, Blind God! for see, my heart
    Is made thy quiver, where remains
No void place for another dart;
    And, alas! that conquest gains
Small praise, that only brings away
A tame and unresisting prey.

Behold! a nobler foe, all arm'd,
    Defies thy weak artillery;
That hath thy bow and quiver charm'd
    A rebel Beauty, conquering Thee:
If thou darest equal combat try,
Wound her, for 'tis for her I die.

SONG.

To My Rival.

HENCE, vaine Intruder, haste away!
    Wash not with thy unhallow'd brine
The footsteps of my *Celia's* shrine;
Nor on her purer altars lay
Thy empty words, accents that may
    Some looser Dame to love incline:
    She must have offerings more divine.

Such pearly drops, as youthful *May*
Scatters before the rising day;
Such smooth soft language, as each line
    Might stroke an angry God, or stay
Jove's thunder, make the hearers pine
    With envy: do this, thou shalt be
    Servant to her, Rival to me.

BOLDNESS IN LOVE.

(*THE MARIGOLD.*)

MARK how the bashful morn, in vain,
 Courts the amorous Marigold,
With sighing blasts and weeping rain ;
 Yet she refuses to unfold.
But when the Planet of the Day
Approacheth, with his powerful ray,
  Then she spreads, then she receives
  His warmer beams into her virgin leaves.

So shalt thou thrive in love, fond Boy !
 If thy tears and sighs discover
Thy grief, thou never shalt enjoy
 The just reward of a bold Lover.
But when with moving accents thou
Shalt constant faith and service vow,
  Thy *Celia* shall receive those charms
  With open ears, and with unfolded arms.

A PASTORAL DIALOGUE :

BETWEEN CELIA AND CLEON.

AS *Celia* rested in the shade
 With *Cleon* by her side,
The Swain thus courted the young Maid,
 And thus the Nymph replied.

Cleon.—'Sweet ! let thy Captive fetters wear,
  Made of thine arms and hands ;
 Till such as thraldom scorn, or fear,
  Envy those happy bands.'

Celia.—'Then thus my willing arms I wind
  About thee, and am so
 Thy prisoner : for my self I bind,
  Until I let thee go.'

Cleon.—' Happy that slave whom the fair foe
          Ties in so soft a chain.'
Celia.—' Far happier I, but that I know
          Thou wilt break loose again.'

Cleon.—' By thy immortal beauties, never !'
   Celia.—' Frail as thy love 's thine oath.'
Cleon.—' Though beauty fade, my love lasts ever.'
   Celia.—' Time will destroy them both.'

Cleon.—' I dote not on that snow-white skin.'
   Celia.—' What then ?'   *Cl.*—' Thy purer mind.'
Celia.—' It loved too soon.'   *Cl.*—' Thou had'st not been
          So fair, if not so kind.'

Celia.—' Oh strange vain fancy !'   *Cl.*—' But yet true.'
   Celia.—' Prove it !'   *Cleon.*—' Then make a braid
          Of those loose flames that circle you,
          My sun's, and yet your shade.'

Celia.—' 'Tis done.'   *Cleon.*—' Now give it me.'
   Celia.—   ' Thus thou
          Shalt thine own error find ;
          If these were beauties, I am now
          Less fair, because more kind.'

Cleon.—' You shall confess you err : that hair,
          Shall it not change the hue,
          Or leave the golden mountain bare ?'
   Celia.—' Ay me ! it is too true.'

Cleon.—' But this small wreath shall ever stay
          In its first native prime ;
          And smiling, when the rest decay,
          The triumph sing of Time.'

Celia.—' Then let me cut from thy fair grove   .
          One branch, and let that be
          An emblem of eternal Love :
          For such is mine to thee.

Both.—'Thus are we both redeem'd from Time.'
 Cleon.—'I by thy grace.' *Celia.*—'And I
  Shall live in thy Immortal rhyme,
   Until the Muses die.'

Cleon.—'By heaven !' *Celia.*—'Swear not ! if I must
    weep,
   Jove shall not smile at me.
  This kiss, my heart, and thy faith keep !'
 Cleon.—'This breathes my soul to thee.'

  Then forth the thicket *Thyrsis* rush'd,
   Where he saw all their play ;
  The Swain stood still, and smiled, and blush'd :
   The Nymph fled fast away.

GRIEF ENGROSSED.

WHEREFORE do thy sad numbers flow,
   So full of woe ?
Why dost thou melt in such soft strains,
   Whilst she disdains ?
  If she must still deny,
  Weep not, but die !
  And in thy Funeral fire
  Shall all her fame expire :
Thus both shall perish, and as thou, upon thy Hearse
Shall want her tears, so she shall want thy Verse.

  Repine not then at thy blest state :
  Thou art above thy fate.
  But my fair *Celia* will not give
  Love enough to make me live ;
  Nor yet dart from her eye
  Scorn enough to make me die.
Then let me weep alone, till her kind breath
Or blow my tears away, or speak my death.

A Pastoral Dialogue.

SHEPHERD, NYMPH, AND CHORUS.

Shepherd.

'THIS mossy bank they press'd.'
    Nymph.—'That aged Oak
Did canopy the happy pair
All night from the dank air.'

Chorus.—' Here let us sit, and sing the words they spoke,
    Till, the day breaking, their embraces broke.'

Shepherd.—'See, Love, the blushes of the Morn appear,
    And now she hangs her pearly store
    (Robb'd from the Eastern shore),
    I' th' cowslip's bell, and roses rare :
    Sweet, I must stay no longer here.'

Nymph.—'Those streaks of doubtful light usher not Day,
    But show my sun must set : no Morn
    Shall shine till thou return :
    The yellow Planets, and the grey
    Dawn, shall attend thee on thy way.'

Shepherd.—'If thine eyes gild my path, they may
    forbear
    Their useless shine.' *Nymph.*—' My tears
    will quite
    Extinguish their faint light.'

Shepherd.—'Those drops will make their beams more
    clear,
    Love's flames will shine in every tear.'

Chorus.

' They kiss'd ; and wept, and from their lips and eyes,
    In a mixed dew of briny sweet,
    Their joys and sorrows meet.
But she cries out.' *Nymph.*—' Shepherd, arise !
The sun betrays us else to spies.'

Shepherd.—'The winged hours fly fast,—whilst we
  embrace ;
   But when we want their help to meet,
   They move with leaden feet.'
Nymph.—'Then let us pinion Time, and chase
   The day for ever from this place.'

Shepherd.—'Hark !' *Nymph.*—'Ay me, stay !' *Shep-*
  herd.—'For ever ?' *Nymph.*—'No, arise !
  We must be gone.' *Shepherd.*—'My nest of
  spice !'
Nymph.—'My soul !' *Shepherd.*—'My Paradise !'

Chorus.

Neither could say farewell, but through their eyes :
Grief interrupted speech, each tear supplies.

RED AND WHITE ROSES.

READ in these Roses the sad story
 Of my hard fate and your own glory ;
In the White you may discover
The paleness of a fainting lover ;
In the Red, the flames still feeding
On my heart, with fresh wounds bleeding.
 The White will tell you how I languish,
And the Red express my anguish ;
The White my innocence displaying,
The Red my martyrdom betraying.
The frowns, that on your brow resided,
Have these Roses thus divided.
  Oh ! let your smiles but clear the weather,
  And then they both shall grow together.

To my Cousin, *C. R.*, marrying my Lady *A*[LTHAM]

HAPPY Youth ! that shalt possess
    Such a spring-tide of delight,
  As the sated appetite
Shall, enjoying such excess,
Wish the flood of Pleasure less ;
  When the *Hymeneal* rite
  Is perform'd, invoke the night,
That it may in shadows dress
Thy too real happiness :
  Else (as *Semele*) the bright
  Deitie, in her full might,
May thy feeble soul oppress.
  Strong perfumes and glaring light
  Oft destroy both smell and sight.

A Lover consults with Reason :
Upon an Accident necessitating his Departure.

Lover.

WEEP not, nor backward turn your beams,
    Fond eyes ! Sad sighs, lock in your breath,
Lest on this wind, or in those streams,
  My grieved Soul fly or sail to death.
Fortune destroys me if I stay,
Love kills me if I go away :
  Since Love and Fortune both are blind,
  Come, Reason, and resolve my doubtful mind.

Reason.

Fly ! and blind Fortune be thy guide,
  And 'gainst the blinder God rebel.
Thy love-sick heart shall not reside
  Where scorn and self-will'd error dwell ;
Where entrance unto Truth is barr'd,
Where Love and Faith find no reward :
  For my just hand may sometimes move
  The wheel of Fortune, not the sphere of Love.

at,
' etc.]

Parting, *Celia* Weeps.

WEEP not, my Dear, for I must go
 Laden enough with mine own woe ;
Add not thy heaviness to mine,
Since fate our pleasures must disjoin :
Why should our sorrows meet ? If I
Must go, and lose thy company,
I wish not theirs : It shall relieve
My grief, to think thou dost not grieve.
 Yet grieve, and weep, that I may bear
Every sigh and every tear
Away with me ; so shall thy breast
And eyes, discharged, enjoy their rest :
  And it will glad my heart to see
  Thou art thus loath to part with me.

A Rapture.

I WILL enjoy thee now, my *Celia*, come,
 And fly with me to Love's *Elysium.*
The Giant, Honour, that keeps cowards out,
Is but a masquer, and the servile rout
Of baser subjects only bend in vain
To the vast Idol ; whilst the nobler train
Of valiant Lovers daily sail between
The huge Colossus' legs, and pass unseen
Unto the blissful shore. Be bold and wise,
And we shall enter : the grim *Swiss* denies [= Warder.
  Only to fools a passage, that not know
  He is but form, and only frights in show.

Let duller eyes that look from far, draw near,
And they shall scorn what they were wont to fear.
We shall see how the stalking Pageant goes
With borrow'd legs, a heavy load to those
That made and bear him : not, as we once thought,
The seed of Gods, but a weak model, wrought

By greedy men, that seek t' enclose the common,
And within private arms impale free Woman.

Come, then, and mounted on the wings of Love
We'll cut the fleeting air, and soar above
The Monster's head, and in the noblest seat
Of those blest shades quench and renew our heat.
There shall the Queens of Love and Innocence,
Beauty and Nature, banish all offence
From our close Ivy-twines : there I'll behold
Thy bared snow and thy unbraided gold ;
There my enfranchised hand on every side
Shall o'er thy naked polish'd ivory slide.
No curtain there, though of transparent lawn,
Shall be before thy virgin-treasure drawn ;
But the rich Mine, to the enquiring eye
Exposed, shall ready still for mintage lie :
And we will coin young *Cupids.* There a bed
Of roses and fresh myrtles shall be spread,
Under the cooler shade of Cypress groves ;
Our pillows, of the down of *Venus'* doves ;
Whereon our panting limbs we'll gently lay,
In the faint respites of our amorous play :
That so our slumbers may in dreams have leisure
To tell the nimble fancy our past pleasure,
    And so our souls—that cannot be embraced—
    Shall the embraces of our bodies taste.

Meanwhile the babbling stream shall court the shor
Th' enamour'd chirping Wood-choir shall adore
In varied tunes the Deity of Love ;
The gentle blasts of Western wind shall move
The trembling leaves, and thro' the close boughs breath
Still music, whilst we rest our selves beneath
Their dancing shade : till a soft murmur, sent
From souls entranced in amorous languishment,
    Rouse us, and shoot into our veins fresh fire,
    Till we in their sweet ecstasy expire.

Then, as the empty Bee, that lately bore
Into the common treasure all her store,
Flies 'bout the painted field with nimble wing,
Deflow'ring the fresh virgins of the Spring—
So will I rifle all the sweets that dwell
In thy delicious Paradise, and swell
My bag with honey, drawn forth by the power
Of fervent kisses from each spicy flower.
I'll seize the Rose-buds in their perfumed bed,
The violet knots, like curious mazes spread
O'er all the garden ; taste the ripened cherries,
The warm firm apple, tipp'd with coral berries.
Then will I visit with a wand'ring kiss
The Vale of lilies, and the Bower of bliss ;
And where the beauteous region doth divide
Into two milky ways, my lip shall slide
Down those smooth alleys, wearing as they go
A track for lovers on the printed snow ;
Thence climbing o'er the swelling *Apennine,*
Retire into the grove of Eglantine :
Where I will all those ravished sweets distil
Through Love's alembic, and with chymic skill
 From the mixed mass one sovereign balm derive,
 Then bring the great Elixir to thy hive.

 Now in more subtle wreaths I will entwine
My sinewy limbs, my arms and legs, with thine.
Thou like a sea of milk shalt lie display'd,
Whilst I the smooth calm ocean will invade,
With such a tempest, as when *Jove* of old
Fell down on *Danæ* in a stream of gold ;
Yet my tall pinnace shall in th' *Cyprian* strait
Ride safe at anchor, and unload her freight :
My rudder with thy bold hand, like a tried
And skilful pilot, thou shalt steer, and guide
 My Bark into Love's channel, where it shall
 Dance, as the bounding waves do rise or fall.

Then shall thy circling arms embrace and clip
My naked body, and thy balmy lip
Bathe me in juice of kisses, whose perfume
Like a religious incense shall consume,
And send up holy vapours to those powers
That bless our loves and crown our sportful hours
That with such *Halcyon* calmness fix our souls
In steadfast peace, that no annoy controuls.
There no rude sounds fright us with sudden starts
No jealous ears, when we unrip our hearts,
Suck our discourse in ; no observing spies
This blush, that glance traduce ; no envious eyes
Watch our close meetings : nor are we betray'd
To rivals, by the bribed Chambermaid.
No wedlock bonds unwreath our twisted love ;
We seek no midnight Arbour nor dark grove,
To hide our kisses : there the hated name
Of husband, wife, chaste, modest, lust or shame,
Are vain and empty words, whose very sound
Was never heard in the *Elizian* ground.
All things are lawful there, that may delight
Nature or unrestrained appetite :
  Like and enjoy : to will and act is one :
  We only sin when Love's rites are not done.

  The Roman *Lucrece* there reads the divine
Lectures of Love's great master, *Aretine*,
And knows as well as *Lais* how to move
Her pliant body in the act of love.
Tarquin.] To quench the burning Ravisher, she hurls
Her limbs into a thousand winding curls,
And studies artful postures, such as be
Carved on the bark of every neighbouring tree,
By learned hands, that so adorned the rind
Of those fair plants, which, as they lay entwined,
Penelope.] Have fann'd their glowing fires. The Grecian da
That in her endless Web toil'd for a name,

As fruitless as her work, doth now display
Her self before the youth of *Ithaca*,
And th' amorous sport of gamesome nights prefer
Before dull dreams of the lost Traveller.   [*Odysseus.*
Daphne hath broke her bark, and that swift foot
Which th' angry Gods had fast'ned with a root
To the fix'd earth, doth now unfetter'd run
To meet th' embraces of the youthful Sun.   [*Phœbus.*
She hangs upon him, like his *Delphic* Lyre ;
Her kisses blow the old, and breathe new, fire ;
Full of her God, she sings inspired lays,
Sweet Odes of love, such as deserve the Bays,
Which she herself was.   Next her, *Laura* lies
In *Petrarch's* learned arms, drying those eyes
That did in such sweet smooth-paced numbers flow,
As made the world enamour'd of his woe.
These, and ten thousand Beauties more, that died
Slave to the Tyrant, now enlarged deride   [*i.e.* Hono
    His cancell'd laws, and for their time mis-spent
    Pay into Love's Exchequer double rent.

    Come then, my *Celia*, we'll no more forbear
To taste our joys, struck with a Panic fear,
But will depose from his imperious sway
This proud Usurper, and walk free as they,
With necks unyoked ; nor is it just that he
Should fetter your soft sex with chastity,
Whom Nature made unapt for abstinence ;
When yet this false Impostor can dispense
With human Justice and with sacred Right,
And (maugre both their laws) command me fight
With Rivals, or when emulous Lovers dare
Equal with thine their Mistress' eyes or hair.
    If thou complain'st of wrong, and call my sword
To carve out thy revenge, upon that word
He bids me fight and kill ; or else he brands
With marks of infamy my coward hands.

And yet Religion bids from blood-shed fly,
And damns me for that act.   Then tell me why
  This goblin 'Honour,' whom the world enshrined,
  Should make men Atheists, and not women Kind

THE SECOND RAPTURE.

NO, worldling, no ; 'tis not thy gold,
      Which thou dost use but to behold,
Nor fortune, honour, nor long life,
Children, or friends, or a good wife,
That makes thee happy : these things be
But shadows of felicity.
Give me a wench above thirteen,
Already voted to the Queen
Of Love, and lovers ; whose soft hair
Fann'd with the breath of gentle air,
O'er-spreads her shoulders like a tent,
And is her veil and ornament ;
Whose tender touch will make the blood
Wild in the aged and the good ;
Whose kisses, fast'ned to the mouth
= Sloth.] Of three-score years and longer slouth,
Renew the age ; and whose bright eye
Obscures those 'lesser lights' of sky ;
Whose snowy breasts (if we may call
That snow, that never melts at all,)
Makes *Jove* invent a new disguise,
In spite of *Juno's* jealousies ;
Whose every part doth re-invite
The old decayed appetite :
And in whose sweet embraces I
May melt my self to love, and die.
      This is true bliss, and I confess
      There is no other happiness.

Epitaph on the Lady *Mary Villiers*.

THE Lady *Mary Villiers* lies
    Under this stone ; with weeping eyes
The parents that first gave her birth,
And their sad friends, laid her in earth.
If any of them, Reader, were
Known unto thee, shed a tear ;
Or if thyself possess a gem
As dear to thee, as this to them ;
Though a stranger to this place,
Bewail in theirs thine own hard case :
    For thou, perhaps, at thy return
    Mayest find thy Darling in an urn.

Another.

THE purest Soul, that e'er was sent
    Into a clayey tenement,
Inform'd this dust ; but the weak mould
Could the great guest no longer hold :
The substance was too pure, the flame
Too glorious that thither came.
Ten thousand *Cupids* brought along
A Grace on each wing, that did throng
For place there, till they all oppress'd
The seat in which they sought to rest :
    So the fair Model broke, for want
    Of room to lodge th' Inhabitant.

Another.

THIS little vault, this narrow room,
    Of Love and Beauty is the tomb ;
The dawning beam, that 'gan to clear
Our clouded sky, lies dark'ned here,

For ever set to us : by death
Sent to enflame the world beneath.
  'Twas but a bud, yet did contain
More sweetness than shall spring again ;
A budding Star, that might have grown
Into a sun when it had blown.
This hopeful beauty did create
New life in Love's declining state ;
But now his empire ends, and we
From fire and wounding darts are free ;
    His brand, his bow, let no man fear :
    The flames, the arrows, all lie here.

EPITAPH ON LADY S[ALTER] :

WIFE OF SIR *W.* S[ALTER].

THE harmony of colours, features, grace,
  Resulting airs (the magic of a face)
Of musical sweet tunes, all which combined
To crown one Sovereign Beauty, lies confined
To this dark vault. She was a cabinet
Where all the choicest stones of price were set :
Whose native colours and pure lustre lent
Her eye, cheek, lip, a dazzling ornament ;
Whose rare and outward beauties did express
Her inward virtues, and mind's fairer dress.
The constant diamond, the wise chrysolite,
The devout sapphire, emerald, apt to write
Records of memory, cheerful agate, grave
And serious onyx, topaz, that doth save
The brain's calm temper, witty amethyst ;
This precious quarry, or what else the list
On *Aaron's* Ephod planted had, she wore :
One only Pearl was wanting to her store,
    Which in her Saviour's book she found express'd
    To purchase that, she sold Death all the rest.

THE INSCRIPTION ON THE TOMB OF

LADY *MARY WENTWORTH.*

MARIA WENTWORTH, ILLUSTRISSIMI THOMÆ COMITIS CLEVELAND
FILIA, PRÆ MORTUÆ PRIMA ANIMAM VIRGINEAM EXHALUIT:
JANU: ANNO DOMINI 1632. ÆTATIS SUÆ 18.

AND here the precious dust is laid,
    Whose purely temper'd clay was made
So fine, that it the guest betray'd.

Else, the soul grew so fast within
It broke the outward shell of sin,
And so was hatch'd a Cherubin.

In height it soar'd to God above ;
In depth, it did to knowledge move,
And spread in breadth to general love.

Before, a pious duty shined
To parents ; courtesy behind ;
On either side, an equal mind.

Good to the Poor, to kindred dear,
To servants kind, to friendship clear :
To nothing but her self severe.

So, though a virgin, yet a Bride
To every grace, she justified
A chaste Polygamy, and died.

Learn from hence, Reader, what small trust
We owe the world : where virtue must,
Frail as our flesh, crumble to dust.

INSCRIPTION ON THE TOMB OF THE

'DUKE OF *BUCKINGHAM.*

BEATISSIMIS MANIBUS CHARISSIMI VIRI ILLUSTRISSIMA
CONJUNX MOERENS SIC PARENTAVIT.

WHEN in the brazen leaves of Fame
    The life, the death of *Buckingham*
Shall be recorded,—if Truth's hand
Incize the story of our land—
Posterity shall see a fair
Structure, by the studious care
Of two kings raised, that did no less
Their wisdom than their power express.

    By blinded zeal (whose doubtful light
Made Murder's scarlet robe seem white ;
Whose vain deluding phantoms charm'd

Felton.]   A clouded sullen Soul, and arm'd
A desperate hand, thirsty of blood,)
Torn from the fair earth where it stood :
So the majestic fabric fell.

    His actions let our Annals tell ;
We write no chronicle ; this pile
Wears only Sorrow's face and style :
Which even the envy that did wait
Upon his flourishing estate,
Turn'd to soft pity of his death,
Now pays his Hearse : but that cheap breath
    Shall not blow here, nor th' impure brine
    Puddle those streams that bathe this shrine.

    These are the pious Obsequies
Dropp'd from his chaste Wife's pregnant eyes
In frequent showers, and were alone
By her congealing sighs made stone ;

culptor.]   On which the Carver did bestow
These forms and characters of woe :
    So he the fashion only lent,
    Whilst she wept all the Monument.

The other Inscription on the same Tomb.

SISTE HOSPES, SIVE INDIGENA, SIVE ADVENA, VICISSITUDINIS
RERUM MEMOR, PAUCA PELLEGE.

READER, when these dumb stones have told
 In borrow'd speech what Guest they hold,
Thou shalt confess the vain pursuit
Of human glory yields no fruit
But an untimely grave. If Fate
Could constant happiness create,
Her ministers, Fortune and Worth,
Had here that miracle brought forth :
They fixed this Child of Honour where
No room was left for hope or fear,
Of more or less ; so high, so great
His growth was, yet so safe his seat.
Safe in the circle of his friends,
Safe in his loyal heart, and ends ;
Safe in his native valiant spirit,
By favour safe, and safe by merit ;
Safe by the stamp of Nature, which
Did strength with shape and grace enrich ;
Safe in the cheerful courtesies
Of flowing gestures, speech, and eyes ; ·
Safe in his bounties, which were more
Proportion'd to his mind, than store :
Yet, though for Virtue he becomes
Involved himself in borrow'd sums,
  Safe in his care, he leaves betray'd
  No friend engaged, no debt unpaid.

 But though the stars conspire to shower
Upon one head th' united power
Of all their graces, if their dire
Aspects must other breasts inspire
With vicious thoughts, a Murderer's knife   [*John*
May cut—as here—their Darling's life.
  Who can be happy then, if Nature must
  To make one happy man, make all men just ?

Four Songs, by way of Chorus to a Play.

AT AN ENTERTAINMENT OF THE KING AND QUEEN,
BY MY LORD CHAMBERLAIN [AT WHITEHALL, 1633].

THE FIRST SONG, OF JEALOUSY: IN DIALOGUE.

Question.

'FROM whence was first this Fury hurl'd,
    This Jealousy, into the World?
Came she from Hell?' *Answer.* 'No, there doth reign
Eternal hatred, with Disdain;
But she the daughter is of Love,
Sister of Beauty.' *Questioner.* 'Then above
She must derive, from the third sphere,
Her heavenly offspring?' *Answer.* 'Neither there,
    From those immortal flames, could she
    Draw her cold frozen pedigree.'

Question. 'If nor from Heaven nor Hell, where then
Had she her birth?' *Answer.* 'In th' hearts of men.
Beauty and Fear did her create,
Younger than Love, elder than Hate,
Sister to both; by Beauty's side
To Love, by Fear to Hate, allied.
Despair her issue is, whose race
Of fruitful mischiefs drowns the space
    Of the wide earth in a swol'n flood
    Of wrath, revenge, spite, rage, and blood.'

Question. 'Ah, how can such a spurious line
Proceed from parents so divine?'
Answer. 'As streams which from their crystal spring
Do sweet and clear their waters bring,
Yet, mingling with the brackish main,
Nor taste nor colour they retain.'

Question. 'Yet Rivers 'twixt their own banks flow
Still fresh ; can Jealousy do so ? '
   Answer. 'Yes, whilst she keeps the steadfast ground
     Of Hope and Fear, her equal bound.

'Hope sprung from favour, worth, or chance,
Towards the fair object doth advance ;
Whilst Fear, as watchful Sentinel,
Doth the invading foe repel :
And Jealousy, thus mixed, doth prove
The season[ing] and the salt of Love.
But when Fear takes a larger scope,
(Stifling the child of Reason, Hope,)
Then, sitting on th' usurped throne,
She like a Tyrant rules alone :
   As the wild Ocean unconfined
   And raging as the Northern wind.'

SONG II.—OF FEMININE HONOUR.

IN what esteem did the gods hold
   Fair Innocence and the chaste bed,
When scandal'd Virtue might be bold
   Bare-foot upon sharp coulters, spread
O'er burning coals, to march ; yet feel
Nor scorching fire nor piercing steel !

Why, when the hard-edged Iron did turn
   Soft as a bed of roses blown,
When cruel flames forgot to burn
   Their chaste pure limbs, should man alone
'Gainst female Innocence conspire
Harder than steel, fiercer than fire ?

Oh, hapless sex ! Unequal sway
   Of partial honour ! Who may know
Rebels, from subjects that obey ;
   When malice can on Vestals throw
Disgrace, and Fame fix high repute
On the close shameless Prostitute ?

p. 45.]   Vain Honour ! thou art but disguise,
 A cheating voice, a juggling art ;
No judge of Virtue, whose pure eyes
 Court her own image in the heart,
More pleased with her true figure there
Than her false echo in the ear.

Song III.—Separation of Lovers.

STOP the chafed Boar, or play
 With the Lion's paw, yet fear
 From the Lover's side to tear
Th' idol of his soul away.

Though Love enter by the sight
 To the heart, it doth not fly
 From the mind, when from the eye
The fair objects take their flight.

But since want provokes desire,
 When we lose what we before
 Have enjoy'd, as we want more,
So is Love more set on fire.

Love doth with an hungry eye
 Gloat on Beauty ; and you may
 Safer snatch the Tiger's prey,
Than *his* vital food deny.

Yet though absence for a space
 Sharpen the keen appetite,
 Long continuance doth quite
All Love's characters efface :

For the sense, not fed, denies
 Nourishment unto the mind :
 Which, with expectation pined,
Love of famine quickly dies.

Song IV.—Incommunicability of Love.

Question.

' B Y what power was Love confined
      To one object? Who can bind,
Or fix a limit to a free-born mind?'

> *Answer.*—'Nature : for as bodies may
>   Move at once but in one way,
> So nor can minds to more than one love stray.'

> *Questioner.*—'Yet I feel a double smart,
>   Love's twinn'd flame, his forked dart.'
> *Answer.*—'Then hath wild lust, not love, possess'd thy
>   heart.'

> *Question.*—'Whence springs Love?' *Ans.*—'From
>   Beauty.' *Question.*—'Why
> Should th' effect not multiply
> As fast i' th' heart, as doth the cause i' th' eye?'

> *Answer.*—'When two Beauties equal are
>   Sense preferring neither fair,
> Desire stands still, distracted 'twixt the pair.

> 'So in equal distance lay
>   Two fair lambs in the wolf's way,
> The hungry beast will starve ere choose his prey.

> 'But where one is chief, the rest
>   Cease : and that's alone possess'd,
> Without a rival, monarch of the breast.'

Other Songs in the Play.

I.—A Lover, in the Disguise of an Amazon,
is dearly Beloved of his Mistress.

CEASE, thou afflicted Soul, to mourn,
　　Whose love and faith are paid with scorn;
For I am starved, that feel the blisses
Of dear embraces, smiles, and kisses
　　　From my soul's Idol, yet complain
　　　Of equal love more than disdain.

Cease, Beauty's exile, to lament
The frozen shades of banishment;
For I in that fair bosom dwell
That is my Paradise and Hell:
　　　Banish'd at home, at once, from ease,
　　　In the safe port, and toss'd on seas.

Cease in cold jealous fears to pine,
Sad wretch, whom Rivals undermine;
For though I hold lock'd in mine arms
My life's sole joy, a traitor's charms
　　　Prevail: whilst I may only blame
　　　My self, that mine own Rival am.

Another Song [The Princess's].

II.—A Lady, rescued from death by a Knight
who in the instant leaves her,
complains thus:

OH, whither is my fair Sun fled
　　Bearing his light, not heat, away?
If thou repose' in the moist bed
　　Of the Sea Queen, bring back the day
To our dark clime, and thou shalt lie
Bathed in the sea, flows from mine eye.

Upon what whirlwind dost thou ride
  Hence, yet remain'st fix'd in my heart?
From me, and to me; fled and tied?
  Dark riddles of the amorous art!
Love lent thee wings to fly, so he
Unfeather'd now must rest with me.

Help, help, brave youth! I burn, I bleed!
  The cruel God with bow and brand
Pursues that life thy valour freed.
  Disarm him with thy conquering hand;
And that thou may'st the wild Boy tame,
Give me his dart, keep thou his flame.

To Ben Jonson.

PON OCCASION OF HIS ODE OF DEFIANCE ANNEXED
  TO HIS PLAY OF 'THE NEW INN,' 1631.

'TIS true, dear *BEN*, thy just chastising hand
    Hath fix'd upon the 'sotted Age a brand,
To their swol'n pride and empty scribbling due;
It can nor judge, nor write: and yet 'tis true
Thy Comic Muse, from the exalted line
Touch'd by thy '*Alchemist*,' doth since decline   [1610.
From that her zenith, and foretells a red
And blushing evening, when she goes to bed;
Yet such as shall outshine the glimmering light
With which all stars shall gild the following night.
Nor think it much, since all thy Eaglets may
Endure the Sunny trial, if we say
'This hath the stronger wing,' or, 'that doth shine
Trick'd up in fairer plumes;' since all are thine.

Who hath his flock of cackling geese compar'd
With thy tuned choir of swans ? or who hath dared
To call thy births deform'd ? but if thou bind
By City-Custom or by *Gavel-kind*
In equal shares thy love on all thy race,
We may distinguish of their sex and place ;
 Though one hand shape them, and though on
  brain strike
 Souls into all, they are not all alike.

 Why should the follies, then, of this dull Age
Draw from thy pen such an immodest rage,
As seems to blast thy else-immortal Bays,
When thine own tongue proclaims thy itch of praise ?
Such thirst will argue drought.   No, let be hurl'd
Upon thy works by the detracting world
What malice can suggest : let the Rout say,
' The running sands that—ere thou make a play—
sands.] Count the slow minutes, might a *Goodwin* frame,
To swallow when th' hast done thy shipwreck'd name.
Let them the dear expense of oil upbraid,
Suck'd by thy watchful lamp, ' that hath betray'd
To theft the blood of martyr'd authors, spilt
Into thy ink, whilst thou growest pale with guilt.'
Repine not at thy thrifty taper's waste,
That sleeks thy terser poems ; nor is haste
Praise, but excuse ; and if thou overcome
A knotty writer, bring thy booty home,
Nor think it theft, if the rich spoils so torn
From conquer'd authors be as Trophies worn.
Let others glut on the extorted praise
Of vulgar breath ; trust thou to after days :
Thy labour'd ' Works' shall live, when Time devours
Th' abortive offspring of their hasty hours.
Thou art not of their rank, the quarrel lies
Within thine own verge : then let this suffice—
 The wiser world doth greater Thee confess
 Than all men else, than Thy self only less.

An Hymeneal Dialogue.

BRIDE AND GROOM.

Groom.

'TELL me, my Love, since *Hymen* tied
The holy knot, hast thou not felt
A new infused spirit slide
Into thy breast, whilst mine did melt?'

Bride.—' First tell me, Sweet, whose words were those?
For though your voice the air did break,
Yet did my soul the sense compose,
And through your lips my heart did speak.'

Groom.—' Then I perceive, when from the flame
Of Love my scorch'd soul did retire,
Your frozen heart in her place came,
And sweetly melted in that fire.'

Bride.—' 'Tis true, for when that mutual change
Of souls was made, with equal gain,
I straight might feel diffused a strange
But gentle heat through every vein.

Chorus.—' O blest disunion! that doth so
Our bodies from our souls divide;
As two do one, and one four grow:
Each by contraction multiplied.'

Bride.—' Thy bosom then I'll make my nest,
Since there my willing soul doth perch.'
Groom.—' And for my heart, in thy chaste breast,
I'll make an everlasting search.'

Chorus.—' O blest disunion, that doth so
Our bodies from our souls divide;
As two do one, and one four grow:
Each by contraction multiplied.'

The Comparison.

(*ON THE PERFECTION OF HIS MISTRESS.*)

DEAREST, thy tresses are not threads of gold,
    Nor thine eyes diamonds ; nor do I hold
Thy lips for rubies ; thy fair cheeks to be
Fresh roses, nor thy teeth of ivory :
The skin that doth thy dainty body sheathe
Not alabaster is, nor dost thou breathe
Arabian odours : those the earth brings forth :
Compare with which would but impair thy worth.
    Such may be others' Mistresses, but mine
    Holds nothing earthly : She is all divine.

Thy tresses are those rays that do arise
Not from one sun, but two ; such are thy eyes :
Thy lips congealed nectar are, and such
As (but a deity) there's none dare touch. .
The perfect crimson that thy cheek doth clothe
(But only that it far excels them both,)
Aurora's blush resembles, or the red
That *Iris* frisks in when her mantle's spread.
Thy teeth in white do *Leda's* swan exceed ;
Thy skin's a heavenly and immortal weed ;
And when thou breathest, winds are ready straight
To filch it from thee, and do therefore wait
Close at thy lips, and snatching it from thence,
Bear it to heaven, where 'tis *Jove's* frankincense.

Fair Goddess, since thy feature makes thee one,
Yet be not such for these respects alone ;
    But, as you are divine in outward view,
    So be within as fair, as good, as true.

The Enquiry.

[Rightly attributed to Robert Herrick.] [*Cf.* p. 73.

A MONGST the myrtles as I walk'd,
   Love and my sighs thus inter-talk'd :
'Tell me,' said I, in deep distress,
'Where may I find my Shepherdess?'

'Thou fool !' said Love, 'know'st thou not this ?
In every thing that's good she is :
In yonder Tulip go and seek,
There thou may'st find her lip, her cheek ;

'In you enamell'd Pansy by,
There thou shalt have her curious eye ;
In bloom of Peach, in rosy Bud,
There wave the streamers of her blood ;

'In brightest Lily, that there stands,
The emblem of her whiter hands :—
On yonder rising Hill, there smell
Such sweets as in her bosom dwell.'

''Tis true !' said I ; and thereupon
I went to pluck them, one by one,
To make of parts a union :
But, on a sudden, all was gone.

With that I stopp'd. Said Love, 'These be,
Fond man ! resemblances of thee ;
And as these flowers, thy joys shall die,
Even in the twinkling of an eye :
   And all thy hopes of her shall wither,
   Like those short sweets thus knit together.'

The Spark.

M Y First Love, whom all beauties did adorn,
   Firing my heart, suppress'd it with her scorn,
Sunlike, to tinder ; in my breast it lies,
By every sparkle made a sacrifice.

E

Each wanton eye now kindles my desire,
And that is free to all that was entire.
Desiring more, by thee desire I lost,
As those that in consumptions hunger most ;
And now my wand'ring thoughts are not confine
Unto one woman, but to woman-kind.
This for her shape I love, that for her face,
This for her gesture, or some other grace ;
And where I none of these do use to find,
I choose thereby the kernel, not the rind.
And so I hope, since my first hopes are gone,
To find in many what I lost in one ;
And, like to Merchants after some great loss,
Trade by retail, that cannot now in gross.

Cf. p. 73.] The fault is her's, who made me go astray :
He needs must wander that hath lost his way.
Guiltless I am : she did this change provoke,
And made that charcoal which at first was oak.
And as a Looking-glass, to the aspect,
Whilst it is whole, doth but one face reflect,
But, being crack'd or broken, there are shown
Many half-faces—which at first were one ;
So Love unto my heart did first prefer
Her image, and there planted none but her :
But since 'twas broke, and martyr'd by her scorn
Many less faces are in her seat borne.

Thus, like to tinder, am I prone to catch
Each falling sparkle, fit for any match.

LOVE'S COMPLEMENT.

O MY Dearest, I shall grieve thee,
    When I swear (yet, Sweet, believe me :)
By thine eyes, the tempting book
On which even crabbed old men look,—
    I swear to thee, though none abhor them,
    Yet I do not love thee for them.

I do not love thee for that fair
Rich fan of thy most curious hair ;
Though the wires thereof be drawn
Finer than the threads of lawn,
 And are softer than the leaves
 On which the subtle spinner weaves.

I do not love thee for those flowers
Growing on thy cheeks—Love's bowers ;
Though such cunning hath them spread,
None can part their white and red ;
 Love's golden arrows thence are shot :
 Yet for them I love thee not.

I do not love thee for those soft
Red coral lips I've kiss'd so oft ;
Nor teeth of pearl, the double guard
To speech, whence music still is heard :
 Though from those lips a kiss being taken
 Would Tyrants melt, and Death awaken.

I do not love thee, O my fairest !
For that richest—for that rarest
Silver pillar which stands under
Thy round head, that globe of wonder :
 Though that neck be whiter far
 Than towers of polish'd ivory are.

I do not love thee for those mountains
Hill'd with snow ; whence milky fountains
(Sugar'd sweets, as sirup'd berries,)
Must one day run, through pipes of cherries :
 O how much those breasts do move me !
 Yet for them I do not love thee.

I do not love thee for that belly,
Sleek as satin, soft as jelly ;
Though within that crystal Mound
Heaps of treasure may be found,
    So rich, that for the least of them
    A king might leave his diadem.

I do not love thee for those thighs,
Whose alabaster rocks do rise
So high and even, that they stand
Like sea-marks to some happy land :
    Happy they, whose eyes have seen them,
    But happier he that sails between them.

I love thee not for thy moist palm,
Though the dew thereof be balm ;
Nor for thy pretty leg and foot,
Although it be the precious root
    On which this goodly cedar grows :
    Sweet, I love thee not for those.

Nor for thy wit, though pure and quick,
Whose substance no arithmetic
Can number down ; nor for the charms
Thou makest with thy embracing arms :
    Though in them one night to lie,
    Dearest, I would gladly die.

I love not for those eyes, nor hair,
Nor cheeks, nor lips, nor teeth so rare,
Nor for thy speech, thy neck, nor breast,
Nor for thy belly, nor the rest ;
    Nor for thy hand nor foot so small :
    But, would'st thou know, dear sweet ?—for All

A Song.

ASK me no more where *Jove* bestows,
　　When *June* is past, the fading rose?
For in your Beauty's orient deep
These flowers, as in their causes, sleep.

　Ask me no more, whither do stray
The golden atoms of the day?
For in pure love heaven did prepare
Those powders to enrich your hair.

　Ask me no more, whither doth haste
The Nightingale, when *May* is past?
For in your sweet dividing throat
She winters, and keeps warm her note.

　Ask me no more, where those stars 'light,
That downwards fall in dead of night?
For in your eyes they sit, and there
Fixed become, as in their sphere.

　Ask me no more, if east or west
The Phœnix builds her spicy nest?
For unto you at last she flies,
And in your fragrant bosom dies.

On sight of a Gentlewoman's Face, in the Water.

STAND still, you floods! do not deface
　　That image which you bear;
So votaries from every place
　　To you shall altars rear.

No winds but Lovers' sighs blow here,
　　To trouble these glad streams,
On which no star from any sphere
　　Did ever dart such beams.

To crystal then in haste congeal,
　　Lest you should lose your bliss ;
And to my cruel Fair reveal
　　How cold, how hard she is !

But if the envious Nymphs shall fear
　　Their beauties will be scorn'd,
And hire the ruder winds to tear
　　That face which you adorn'd,—

Then rage and foam amain, that we
　　Their malice may despise ;
When from your froth we soon shall see
　　A second *Venus* rise.

Song.

WOULD you know what's soft ?　I dare
　　Not bring you to the down, or air ;
Nor to stars, to show what's bright ;
Nor to snow, to teach you white.

　Nor, if you would Music hear,
Call the Orbs to take your ear ;
Nor, to please your sense, bring forth
Bruised Nard, or what's more worth.

　Or, on food were your thoughts placed,
Bring you Nectar for a taste :
Would you have all these in one ?
Name my Mistress, and 'tis done.

THE HUE AND CRY.

[See p. 179.

IN Love's name you are charged hereby
　　To make a speedy 'Hue and Cry'
After a face, which, t'other day,
Stole my wand'ring heart away.
　　　To direct you, these, in brief,
　　　Are ready marks to know the Thief.

Her hair a net of beams would prove
Strong enough to captive *Jove*,
In his Eagle's shape ; her brow
Is a comely field of snow ;
Her eye so rich, so pure a grey,
Every beam creates a day :
　　　And, if she but sleep (not when
　　　The sun sets), 'tis Night again.

In her cheeks are to be seen
Of flowers both the King and Queen,
Thither by the Graces led,
And freshly laid in nuptial bed ;
On whose lips, like-Nymphs do wait,
Who deplore their virgin state :
　　　Oft they blush, and blush for this,
　　　That they one another kiss.

But observe, besides the rest,
You shall know this Felon best
By her tongue ; for if your ear
Once a heavenly music hear,
Such as neither gods nor men—
But from that voice—shall hear again,
That, that is she.　O ! straight surprise,
And bring her unto Love's Assize.
If you let her go, she may
Ante-date the Latter Day,
　　　Fate and Philosophy controul,
　　　And leave the world without a soul.

SONG.

To his Mistress confined.

O THINK not, *Phœbe*, 'cause a cloud
    Doth now thy silver brightness shroud,
        My wand'ring eye
Can stoop to common beauties of the sky.
    Rather be kind, and this eclipse
    Shall neither hinder eye nor lips ;
        For we shall meet
Within our hearts, and kiss, and none shall see't.

Nor can'st thou in thy prison be
Without some living sign of me ;
        When thou dost spy
A sunbeam peep into the room, 'tis I :
    For I am hid within a flame,
    And thus into thy chamber came,
        To let thee see
In what a martyrdom I burn for thee.

When thou do'st touch thy Lute, thou mayest
Think on my heart, on which thou playest ;
        When each sad tone
Upon the strings doth show my deeper groan :
    When thou dost please, they shall rebound
    With nimble airs, struck to the sound
        Of thy own voice :
O think, how much I tremble and rejoice !

There's no sad picture that doth dwell
Upon thy Arras-wall, but well
        Resembles me ;
No matter though our age do not agree.
    Love can make old, as well as Time ;
    And he that doth but twenty climb,
        If he dare prove
As true as I, shows four-score years in love.

The Primrose.

[*Attributed, with 'The Enquiry,' to* Robert Herrick.] [p. 65.

ASK me why I send you here
   This firstling of the infant Year?
Ask me why I send to you
This Primrose, all be-pearl'd with dew?
   I straight whisper to your ears,
    'The sweets of Love are wash'd with tears.'

Ask me why this flower does show
So yellow-green, and sickly too?—
Ask me why the stalk is weak,
And bending, yet it doth not break?
   I must tell you, 'These discover
    What doubts and fears are in a Lover.'

The Tinder.

[*Cf.* p. 66.

OF what mould did Nature frame me?
   Or was it her intent to shame me?
That no woman can come near me,
Fair, but her I court to hear me?
Sure that Mistress, to whose beauty
First I paid a Lover's duty,
Burn'd in rage my heart to tinder:
That nor prayers nor tears can hinder,
But where ever I do turn me,
Every spark let fall doth burn me.
   Women, since you thus inflame me,
   Flint and steel I'll ever name ye.

A Song.

IN her fair cheeks two pits do lie,
 To bury those slain by her eye ;
So, spite of Death, this comforts me,
That fairly buried I shall be :
My grave with rose and lily spread !
O 'tis a life to be so dead !
    Come then, and kill me with thy eye :
    For, if thou let me live, I die.

When I behold those lips again—
Reviving, what those eyes have slain,
With kisses sweet, whose balsam pure
Love's wounds, as soon as made, can cure—
Methinks 'tis sickness to be sound,
And there's no health to such a wound.
    Come then, and kill me with thy eye :
    For, if thou let me live, I die.

When in her chaste breast I behold
Those downy mounts of snow, ne'er cold ;
And those blest hearts, her Beauty kills,
Revive by climbing those fair hills :
Methinks there's life in such a death,
And so t' expire inspires new breath.
    Come then, and kill me with thy eye :
    For, if thou let me live, I die.

Nymph, since no death is deadly, where
Such choice of Antidotes is near,
And your keen eyes but kill in vain
Those that are sound, as soon as slain ;
That I no longer dead survive,
Your way 's to bury me alive
In *Cupid's* Cave : where happy I
May dying live, and living die.
    Come then, and kill me with thy eye :
    For, if thou let me live, I die.

The Carver.

TO HIS MISTRESS.

A CARVER, having loved too long in vain, [*i.e.* Sculptor.
  Hew'd out the portraiture of *Venus'* sun
In marble rock, upon the which did rain
  Small drizzling drops, that from a fount did run ;
Imagining the drops would either wear
  His fury out, or quench his living flame :
But when he saw it bootless did appear,
  He swore the water did augment the same.
So I, that seek in verse to carve thee out,
  Hoping thy Beauty will my flame allay,
Viewing my lines impolish'd all throughout,
  Find my will rather to my love obey :
That with the Carver I my work do blame,
Finding it still th' augmenter of my flame.

To the Painter.

F OND man, that hopest to catch that face
  With those false colours, whose short grace
Serves but to show the lookers-on
The faults of thy presumption ;
Or, at the least, to let us see
That is divine, but yet not she :
Say, you could imitate the rays
Of those eyes that outshine the days,
Or counterfeit in red and white
That most uncounterfeited light
Of her complexion ; yet can'st thou,
Great master though thou be, tell how
    To paint a Virtue ?   Then desist,
    This Fair your artifice hath miss'd.

You should have mark'd how she begins
To grow in virtue, not in sins :
Instead of that same rosy dye,
You should have drawn out Modesty,
    Whose beauty sits enthroned there,
    And learn'd to look and blush at her.

Or can you colour just the same,
When virtue blushes, or when shame ?
When sickness, and when innocence,
Shows pale or white unto the sense ?
Can such coarse varnish e'er be said
To imitate her white and red ?
This may do well elsewhere, in *Spain*,
Among those faces dyed in grain ;
    So you may thrive, and what you do
    Prove the best picture of the two.

Besides, if all I hear be true,
'Tis taken ill by some that you
Should be so insolently vain,
As to contrive all that rich gain
Into one Tablet, which alone
May teach us superstition :
Instructing our amazed eyes
To admire and worship Imag'ries,
Such as quickly might outshine
Some new Saint, were 't allow'd a shrine,
    And turn each wand'ring looker-on
    Into a new *Pygmaleon*.

Yet your art cannot equalise
This picture in her Lover's eyes ;
His eyes the pencils are which limn
Her truly, as her's copy him :

His heart the Tablet, which alone
Is for that portrait th' truest stone.
If you would a truer see,
Mark it in their posterity :
    And you shall read it truly there,
    When the glad world shall see their Heir.

LOVE'S COURTSHIP : TO *CELIA.*

K ISS, lovely *Celia*, and be kind ;
    Let my desires freedom find !
        Sit thee down,
And we will make the Gods confess
Mortals enjoy some happiness.

Mars would disdain his Mistress' charms
If he beheld thee in my arms,
        And descend,
Thee his mortal Queen to make :
Or live as mortal for thy sake.

Venus must lose her title now,
And leave to brag of *Cupid's* bow ;
        Silly Queen !
She hath but one, but I can spy
Ten thousand *Cupids* in thy eye.

Nor may the Sun behold our bliss,
For sure thy eyes do dazzle his ;
        If thou fear
That he'll betray thee with his light,
Let me eclipse thee from his sight !

And while I shade thee from his eye,
Oh ! let me hear thee gently cry,
        ' *Celia* yields ! '
Maids often lose their maidenhead,
Ere they set foot in nuptial bed.

On a Damask Rose,

WORN UPON A LADY'S BREAST.

LET pride grow big, my Rose, and let the clear
 And damask colour of thy leaves appear ;
Let scent and looks be sweet, and bless that hand
That did transplant thee to thy sacred land.
 O happy thou ! that in such garden rests,
 That Paradise between a Lady's breasts !

There's an eternal Summer ; thou shalt lie
Betwixt two Lily mounts, and never die.
There shalt thou spring, amongst the fertile valleys,
By buds, like thee, that grow in 'midst of Lilies.
There none dare pluck thee : for that place is such,
That—but a good Divine—none dare to touch.
If any but approach, straight doth arise
A blushing light'ning flash, and blasts his eyes.
There, 'stead of rain, shall living fountains flow ;
For wind, her fragrant breath for ever blow :
 Nor now, as erst, one Sun shall on thee shine,
 But those two glorious suns, her eyes divine.

O then, what Monarch would not think 't a grace
To leave his regal throne to have thy place ?
 My self, to gain thy blessed seat, do vow,
 Would be transform'd into a Rose, as thou.

The Protestation.

A SONNET.

NO more shall meads be deck'd with flowers,
 Nor sweetness dwell in rosy bowers,
Nor greenest buds on branches spring,
Nor warbling birds delight to sing,
 Nor *April* violets paint the grove,
 If I forsake my *Celia's* love.

The fish shall in the ocean burn,
And fountains sweet shall bitter turn ;
The humble oak no flood shall know,
When floods shall highest hills o'er-flow :
  Black *Lethe* shall oblivion leave,
  If e'er my *Celia* I deceive.

Love shall his bow and shaft lay by,
And *Venus'* doves want wings to fly ;
The Sun refuse to show his light,
And day shall then be turn'd to night :
  And in that night no star appear,
  If once I leave my *Celia* dear.

Love shall no more inhabit Earth,
Nor lovers more shall love for worth,
Nor joy above in heaven dwell,
Nor pain torment poor souls in hell ;
  Grim Death no more shall horrid prove :
  If e'er I leave bright *Celia's* love.

THE TOOTH-ACHE CURED BY A KISS.

FATE 's now grown merciful to men,
 Turning disease to bliss ;
For had not kind rheum vext me, then,
 I might not *Celia* kiss.
Physicians, you are now my scorn,
 For I have found a way
To cure diseases—when forlorn
 By your dull art—which may
Patch up a body for a time :
 But can restore to health
No more than 'chymists can sublime
 True Gold, the *Indies'* wealth.
That Angel sure, that used to move
 The Pool men so admired,   [*Bethesda.*
Hath to her lip, the seat of Love,
 As to his heaven, retired.

The Dart.

OFT when I look I may descry
　　A little face peep through that eye ;
Sure, that's the Boy, who wisely chose
His throne among such beams as those,
　　Which, if his quiver chance to fall,
　　May serve for darts to kill withal.

The Mistake.

WHEN on fair *Celia* I did spy
　　A wounded heart of stone,
The wound had almost made me cry,
　　'Sure this heart is my own !'

But when I saw it was enthroned
　　In her celestial breast,
O then I it no longer own'd,
　　For mine was ne'er so blest.

Yet, if in highest heavens do shine
　　Each constant Martyr's heart,
Then she may well give rest to mine,
　　That for her sake doth smart ;

Where, seated in so high a bliss,
　　Though wounded, it shall live ;
Death enters not in Paradise :
　　The place free life doth give.

Or if the place less sacred were,
　　Did but her saving eye
Bathe my sick heart in one kind tear,
　　Then should I never die.

Slight balms may heal a slighter sore,
　　No medicine less divine
Can ever hope for to restore
　　A wounded heart like mine.

To his Jealous Mistress.

ADMIT, thou darling of mine eyes,
　I have some Idol lately framed,
That under such a false disguise
　Our true loves might the less be famed :
Can'st thou, that knowest my heart, suppose
I'll fall from thee, and worship those ?

Remember, Dear, how loth and slow
　I was to cast a look or smile,
Or one love-line to misbestow,
　Till thou had'st changed both face and style :
And art thou grown afraid to see
That mask put on, thou madest for me.

I dare not call those childish fears,
　Coming from Love, much less from thee ;
But wash away, with frequent tears,
　This counterfeit Idolatry :
And henceforth kneel at ne'er a shrine,
To blind the world, but only thine.

On the Marriage of T[homas] K[illigrew] and C[ecilia] C[rofts] : the morning stormy.

SUCH should this day be, so the Sun should hide
　His bashful face, and let the conquering Bride
Without a rival shine, whilst he forbears
To mingle his unequal beams with hers ;
Or if sometimes he glance his squinting eye
Between the parting clouds, 'tis but to spy,
Not emulate, her glories ; so comes drest
In veils, but as a Masquer to the feast.
Thus heaven should lour, such stormy gusts should blow,
Not to denounce ungentle fates, but show
　The cheerful Bridegroom to the clouds and wind
　Hath all his tears and all his sighs assign'd.

F

Let tempests struggle in the air, but rest
Eternal calms within thy peaceful breast,
Thrice happy youth ! but ever sacrifice
To that fair hand that dried thy blubber'd eyes,—
That crown'd thy head with roses, and turn'd all
The plagues of love into a cordial,—
When first it join'd her virgin snow to thine :
Which, when to-day the Priest shall re-combine,
From the mysterious holy touch such charms
Will flow, as shall unlock her wreathed arms,
　　And open a free passage to that fruit
　　Which thou hast toil'd for with a long pursuit.

　　But ere thou feed, that thou may'st better taste
Thy present joys, think on thy torments past ;
Think on the mercy freed thee ; think upon
Her virtues, graces, beauties, one by one :
So shalt thou relish all, enjoy the whole
Delights of her fair body and pure soul.
Then boldly to the fight of Love proceed !
'Tis mercy not to pity, though she bleed.
We'll strew no nuts, but change that ancient form,
For till to-morrow we'll prorogue this storm ;
　　Which shall confound, with its loud whistling nois
　　　Her pleasing shrieks, and fan thy panting joys.

UPON MY LORD CHIEF JUSTICE [SIR *JOHN FINCH*
　　HIS ELECTION OF MY LADY A[*NN*] *W*[*ENTWORTH*],
　　　FOR HIS MISTRESS.

I.

HEAR this, and tremble, all
　　　Usurping Beauties, that create
A Government tyrannical,
　　In Love's free state !
Justice hath to the sword of your edged eyes
His equal balance join'd ; his sage head lies
In Love's soft lap, which must be just and wise.

II.

Hark ! how the stern Law breathes
  Forth amorous sighs, and now prepares
No fetters, but of silken wreaths,
  And braided hairs ;
His dreadful Rods and Axes are exiled,
Whilst he sits crown'd with roses : Love hath filed
His native roughness : Justice is grown mild.

III.

The Golden Age returns !
  Love's bow and quiver useless lie ;
His shaft, his brand, nor wounds nor burns,
  And cruelty
Is sunk to Hell : the Fair shall all be kind :
Who loves shall be beloved, the froward mind
To a deformed shape shall be confined.

IV.

Astræa hath possess'd
  An earthly seat, and now remains
In *Finch's* heart, but *Wentworth's* breast
  That guest contains ;
With her she dwells, yet hath not left the skies,
Nor lost her sphere : for, new enthroned, she cries
' I know no Heaven but fair *Wentworth's* eyes.'

HYMENEAL SONG, ON THE NUPTIALS OF THE
LADY *ANN WENTWORTH* AND THE LORD *LOVELACE.*

B REAK not the slumbers of the Bride,
    But let the sun in triumph ride,
      Scattering his beamy light ;
When she awakes, he shall resign
His rays : and she alone shall shine
      In glory all the night.

For she, till day return, must keep
An amorous Vigil, and not steep
Her fair eyes in the dew of sleep.

Yet gently whisper, as she lies,
And say 'her Lord waits her uprise,
  The Priests at the Altar stay :
With flowery wreaths the Virgin crew
Attend, while some with roses strew,
  And myrtles trim the way.'

Now to the Temple and the Priest
See her convey'd, thence to the Feast ;
Then back to bed, though not to rest.

For now, to crown his faith and truth,
We must admit the noble youth
  To revel in Love's sphere ;
To rule, as chief Intelligence,
That Orb, and happy time dispense
  To wretched Lovers here.

For they are exalted far above
All hope, fear, change ; or they do move
The wheel that spins, the Fates of Love.

They know no night, nor glaring noon,
Measure no hours of Sun or Moon,
  Nor mark Time's restless glass ;
Their kisses measure as they flow
Minutes, and their embraces show
  The hours as they pass.

Their motions the Year's circle make,
And we from their conjunctions take
Rules to make Love an Almanack.

[*This 'Hymeneal Song,' on the Lady Ann Wentworth'
Nuptials, was first printed in the* 1642 *edition. See note, i*
Appendix.]

A Married Woman.

WHEN I shall marry, if I do not find
    A wife thus moulded, I'll create this kind :
Nor from her noble birth, nor ample dower,
Beauty, nor wit, shall she derive a power
To prejudice my Right ; but if she be
A subject born, she shall be so to me.
  As to the soul the flesh, so Appetite
To Reason is ; which shall our wills unite,
In habits so confirm'd, as no rough sway
Shall once appear, if she but learns t' obey.
For in habitual virtues sense is wrought
To that calm temper, as the body's thought
To have nor blood nor gall, if wild and rude
Passions of Lust and Anger are subdued ;
When 'tis the fair obedience to the soul
Doth in the birth those swelling Acts controul.
If I in Murder steep my furious rage,
Or with Adult'ry my hot lust assuage,
Will it suffice to say, 'My sense—the Beast—
Provoked me to 't ?' Could I my soul divest,
My plea were good. Lions and bulls commit
Both freely, but man must in judgment sit,
And tame this Beast ; for *Adam* was not free
When in excuse he said, '*Eve* gave it me !'
    Had he not eaten, she perhaps had been
    Unpunish'd : his consent made her's a sin.

A Divine Love.

WHY should dull Art, which is wise Nature's ape,
    If she produce a Shape
So far beyond all patterns that of old
    Fell from her mould,
As thine, admired *Lucinda !* not bring forth   [*Cf.* p. 99.
An equal wonder to express that worth
    In some new way, that hath
Like her great work no print of vulgar path ?

Is it because the rapes of Poetry,
   Rifling the spacious sky
Of all its fires, light, beauty, influence,
   Did those dispense
On aëry Creations, that surpass'd
The real works of Nature ; she at last,
   To prove their raptures vain,
Show'd such a light as Poets could not feign.

Or is it 'cause the factious wits did vie
   With vain Idolatry,
Whose Goddess was supreme, and so had hurl'd
   Schism through the world,
Whose Priest sung sweetest lays,—thou did'st appear,
A glorious mystery, so dark, so clear,
   As Nature did intend
All should confess, but none might comprehend.

Perhaps all other beauties share a light
   Proportion'd to the sight
Of weak mortality ; scattering such loose fires
   As stir desires,
And from the brain distil salt amorous rheumes ;
Whilst thy immortal flame such dross consumes,
   And from the earthy mould
With purging fires severs the purer gold ?

If so, then why in Fame's immortal scroll
   Do we their names enroll,
Whose easy hearts and wanton eyes did sweat
   With sensual heat ?
If *Petrarch's* unarm'd bosom catch a wound
From a light glance, must *Laura* be renown'd ?
   Or both a glory gain,
He from ill-govern'd Love, she from Disdain ?

Shall he more famed in his great Art become,
      For wilful martyrdom ?
Shall she more title gain, too chaste and fair,
      Through his despair ?
Is *Troy* more noble 'cause to ashes turn'd,
Than virgin cities that yet never burn'd ?
      Is fire, when it consumes
Temples, more fire, than when it melts perfumes ?

'Cause *Venus* from the Ocean took her form,
      Must Love needs be a storm ?
'Cause she her wanton shrines in Islands rears,
      Through seas of tears ;—
O'er rocks and gulfs, with our own sighs for gale,
Must we to *Cyprus* or to *Paphos* sail ?
      Can there no way be given,
But a true Hell, that leads to her false Heaven ?

LOVE'S FORCE.

IN the first ruder Age, when Love was wild,
  Nor yet by Laws reclaim'd, not reconciled
To order, nor by Reason mann'd, but flew
Full-summ'd by Nature, on the instant view,
Upon the wings of Appetite, at all
The eye could fair or sense delightful call ;
Election was not yet : but as their cheap
Food from the oak, or the next acorn-heap—
As water from the nearest spring or brook—
So men their undistinguish'd females took
By chance, not choice. But soon the heavenly spark,
That in man's bosom lurk'd, broke through this dark
    Confusion : then the noblest breast first felt
    It self, for its own proper object melt.

A Fancy.

MARK how this polish'd Eastern sheet
 Doth with our Northern tincture meet !
For though the paper seem to sink,
Yet it receives and bears the Ink ;
And on her smooth soft brow these spots
Seem rather ornaments than blots :
Like those you Ladies use to place
Mysteriously about your face,
Not only to set off and break
Shadows and eye-beams, but to speak
To the skill'd Lover, and relate
Unheard his sad or happy fate.
 Nor do their characters delight
As careless works of black and white ;
But 'cause you underneath may find
A sense that can inform the mind ;
Divine or moral Rules impart,
Or Raptures of Poetic Art :
  So what at first was only fit
  To fold up silks, may wrap up wit.

To his Mistress.

GRIEVE not, my *Celia*, but with haste
 Obey the fury of thy fate ;
'Tis some perfection to waste
 Discreetly out our wretched state :
To be obedient in this sense
Will prove thy virtue, though offence.

Who knows but Destiny may relent ?
 For many miracles have been :
Thou proving thus obedient
 To all the griefs she plunged thee in :
And then, the certainty she meant
Reverted is, by accident.

But yet, I must confess, 'tis much,
  When we remember what hath been :
Thus parting, never more to touch,
  To let eternal absence in :
Though never was our pleasure yet
So pure, but chance distracted it.

What, shall we then submit to Fate,
  And die to one another's love ?
No, *Celia*, no, my soul doth hate
  Those Lovers that inconstant prove.
Fate may be cruel, but if you decline,
The crime is yours, and all the glory mine.
    Fate, and the Planets, sometimes bodies part :
    But canker'd nature only alters th' heart.

SONG.

COME, my *Celia*, let us prove,
  While we may, the sports of Love ;
Time will not be ours for ever,
He at length our good will sever.

  Spend not then his gifts in vain,
Suns that set may rise again,
But if once we lose this light,
'Tis with us perpetual night.

  Why should we defer our joys ?
Fame and rumour are but toys.
Cannot we delude the eyes
Of a few poor household spies ?

  Or his easier ears beguile,
So removed, by our wile ?
'Tis no sin Love's Fruit to steal,
But the sweet theft to reveal.
    To be taken, to be seen :
    These have crimes accounted been.

In Praise of his Mistress.

YOU that will a wonder know,
    Go with me !
Two Suns in a Heaven of Snow
    Both burning be :
All they fire, that do but eye them,
But the snow 's unmelted by them.

Leaves of Crimson Tulips met,
    Guide the way
Where two Pearly rows be set,
    As white as day :
When they part themselves asunder,
She breathes Oracles of wonder.

Hills of milk, with azure mix'd,
    Swell beneath ;
Waving sweetly, yet still fix'd,
    While she doth breathe :
From those hills descends a valley,
Where all fall, that dare to dally.

Fair as under Statues stand,
    Pillars two ;
Whiter than the silver Swan
    That swims in *Po :*
If at any time they move her,
Every step begets a Lover.

All this but the Casket is,
    Which contains
Such a Jewel, as to miss
    Breeds endless pains ;
That's her Mind : and they that know it,
May admire, but cannot show it.

To *CELIA*, ON LOVE'S UBIQUITY.

A S one that strives, being sick, and sick to death,
   By changing places to preserve a breath,
A tedious restless breath ; removes, and tries
A thousand rooms, a thousand policies,
     To cozen pain, when he thinks to find ease :
     At last he finds all change, but his disease.

So, like a Ball with fire and powder fill'd,
I restless am, yet live, each minute kill'd :
And, with that moving, torture must retain—
With change of all things else—a constant pain.

So I stay with you, presence is to me
Nought but a light to show my misery ;
And partings are as Racks to plague Love on :
The further stretch'd, the more affliction.

Go I to *Holland*, *France*, or farthest *Ind*,
I change but only countries, not my mind ;
And though I pass through air and water free,
Despair and hopeless fate still follow me.

Whilst in the bosom of the waves I reel,
My heart I'll liken to the tottering Keel,
The Sea to my own troubled fate, the Wind
To your disdain, sent from a soul unkind.

But when I lift my sad looks to the skies,
Then shall I think I see my *Celia's* eyes ;
And when a cloud or storm appears between,
I shall remember what her frowns have been.
     Thus, whatsoever course my Fates allow,
     All things but make me mind my business : You.

The good things that I meet, I think streams be,
From you, the Fountain ; but when bad I see,
' How vile and cursed is that thing ! ' think I,
' That to such goodness is so contrary ! '

My whole life is 'bout you, the Centre Star ;
But a perpetual Motion Circular.
I am the Dial's hand, still walking round ;
You are the Compass : and I never sound
　　Beyond your circle, neither can I show
　　Aught, but what first expressed is in you.

Thus, wheresoe'er my tears do cause me move,
My fate still keeps me bounded with your love ;
Which, ere it die, or be extinct in me,
Time shall stand still, and moist waves flaming be.
Yet, being gone, think not on me : I am
A thing too wretched for thy thoughts to name :
　　But when I die, and wish all comforts given,
　　I'll think on you, and by you think on heaven.

On his Mistress Going to Sea.

Cf. p. 104.]　　(*Music composed to it by Henry Lawes.*)

FAREWELL, fair Saint ! may not the sea and win
　　Swell like the hearts and eyes you leave behind
But calm and gentle, as the looks you bear,
Smile in your face, and whisper in your ear

Let no bold billow offer to arise,
That it may nearer gaze upon your eyes :
Lest wind and wave, enamour'd of your form,
Should throng and crowd themselves into a storm.

But if it be your fate, vast Seas ! to love,
Of my becalmed breast learn how to move ;
Move then, but in a gentle Lover's pace :
No wrinkle, nor no furrow, in your face.

And you, fierce Winds, see that you tell your tale
In such a breath as may but fill her Sail ;
So, whilst you court her, each your several way,
You may her safely to her Port convey,
　　And loose her, by the noblest way of Wooing :
　　Whilst both contribute to your own undoing.

To A[NN] D[ORIS], UNREASONABLE,
DISTRUSTFUL OF HER OWN BEAUTY.

FAIR *Doris*, break thy glass! it hath perplex'd
  With a dark comment Beauty's clearest text;
It hath not told thy face's story true,
But brought false copies to thy jealous view.
No colour, feature, lovely air or grace,
That ever yet adorn'd a beauteous face,
But thou may'st read in thine; or justly doubt
Thy glass hath been suborn'd to leave it out.
But if it offer to thy nice survey
A spot, a stain, a blemish, or decay,
      It not belongs to thee: the treacherous light
      Or faithless stone abuse thy credulous sight.

  Perhaps the magic of thy face hath wrought
Upon th' enchanted Crystal, and so brought
Fantastic shadows to delude thine eyes,
With airy repercussive sorceries;
Or else th' enamour'd Image pines away
For love of the fair object, and so may
Wax pale and wan, and though the substance grow
Lively and fresh, that may consume with woe:
      Give then no faith to the false specular stone,
      But let thy beauties by th' effects be known.

  Look, sweetest *Doris*, on my love-sick heart,
In that true mirror see how fair thou art!   `
There, by Love's never-erring pencil drawn,
Shalt thou behold thy face, like th' early dawn,
Shoot through the shady covert of thy hair,
Enamelling and perfuming the calm air
With pearls and roses, till thy suns display
Their lids, and let out the imprison'd day;
Whilst *Delphic* priests, enlight'ned by their theme,
In amorous numbers count thy golden beam:
      And from Love's altars clouds of sighs arise
      In smoking incense, to adore thine eyes.

If, then, Love flow from Beauty, as th' effect,
How can'st thou the resistless cause suspect ?
Who would not brand that Fool, who should contend
There was no fire, where smoke and flames ascend ?
Distrust is worse than scorn : not to believe
My harms, is greater wrong than not to grieve.
What cure can for my fest'ring sore be found,
Whilst thou believest thy Beauty cannot wound ?
-Such humble thoughts more cruel tyrants prove
Than all the pride that e'er usurp'd in Love,
For Beauty's herald here denounceth war :
There are false spies betray me to a snare.
If fire, disguised in balls of snow, were hurled,
It unsuspected might consume the world ;
Where our prevention ends, danger begins,
So wolves in sheep's—lions in asses' skins—
  Might far more mischief work, because less fear'd :
  Those the whole flock, these might kill all the herd.

Appear then as thou art, break through this cloud,
Confess thy beauty, though thou thence grow proud ;
Be fair, though scornful ; rather let me find
Thee cruel, than thus mild and more unkind :
Thy cruelty doth only me defy,
But these dull thoughts thee to thy self deny.
  Whether thou mean to barter, or bestow,
  Thy self, 'tis fit thou thine own value know.

I will not cheat thee of thy self, nor pay
Less for thee than thou'rt worth ; thou shalt not say
'That is but brittle glass,' which I have found
By strict enquiry a firm diamond.
I'll trade with no such *Indian* fool, who sells
Gold, pearls, and precious stones, for beads and bells ;
Nor will I take a present from your hand,
Which you or prize not, or not understand.
It not endears your bounty that I do
Esteem your gift, unless you do so too :
  You undervalue me, when you bestow
  On me what you nor care for, nor yet know.

‘ No, lovely *Doris*, change thy thoughts, and be
In love first with thy self, and then with me.
You are afflicted that you are not fair,
And I as much tormented that you are.
What I admire, you scorn ; what I love, hate ;
Through different faiths, both share an equal fate ;
    Fast to the truth, which you renounce, I stick :
    I die a Martyr, you an Heretic.

To a Lady, that desired I would Love her.

I.

NOW you have freely given me leave to love,
        What will you do ?
Shall I your mirth or passion move
        When I begin to woo ?
Will you torment, or scorn, or love me too ?

II.

Each petty Beauty can disdain, and I,
        ’Spite of your hate,
Without your leave can see, and die.
        Dispense a nobler fate !
’Tis easy to destroy : you may create.

III.

Then give me leave to love, and love me too :
        Not with design
To raise, as Love’s curst rebels do,
        When puling poets whine,
Fame to their Beauty, from their blubber’d eyne.

IV.

Grief is a puddle, and reflects not clear
        Your Beauty’s rays ;
Joys are pure streams : your eyes appear
        Sullen in sadder lays :
In cheerful numbers they shine bright with praise,

v.

Which shall not mention to express, you Fair !
　　　　　Wounds, flames, and darts,
Storms in your brow, nets in your hair,—
　　　　　Suborning all your parts,
Or to betray, or torture captive hearts.

vi.

I'll make your eyes like morning suns appear,
　　　　　As mild and fair ;
Your brow as crystal smooth and clear ;
　　　　　And your dishevell'd hair
Shall flow like a calm region of the air.

vii.

Rich Nature's store, which is the Poet's treasure,
　　　　　I'll spend to dress
Your beauties, if your mine of pleasure
　　　　　In equal thankfulness
You but unlock : so we each other bless.

For a Picture, where a Queen Laments over the Tomb of a Slain Knight.

BRAVE Youth, to whom Fate in one hour
　Gave death and conquest, by whose power
Those chains about my heart are wound,
With which the Foe my kingdom bound :
Freed and captived by thee, I bring
For either act an offering.
For Victory, this wreath of Bay ;
In sign of thraldom, down I lay
Sceptre and crown : take from my sight
Those Royal robes, since Fortune's spite
　　　Forbids me live thy Virtue's prize
　　　I'll die thy Valour's sacrifice.

A New Year's Gift.

I.—*TO THE KING.*

L OOK back, old *Janus*, and survey
   From Time's birth till this new-born day,
All the successful season bound
With laurel wreaths, and trophies crown'd ;
Turn o'er the Annals past, and where
Happy auspicious days appear,
Mark'd with the whiter stone, that cast
On the dark brow of th' ages past
A dazzling lustre, let them shine
In this succeeding circle's twine,
Till it be round with glories spread,
Then with it crown our *Charles* his head :
   That we th' ensuing years may call
   One great continued festival.

   Fresh joys, in varied forms, apply
To each distinct captivity.
Season his cares by day with nights
Crown'd with all conjugal delights ;
May the choice beauties that enflame
His Royal breast be still the same ;
   And he still think them such, since more
   Thou can'st not give from Nature's store.

   Then as a Father let him be
With numerous issue blest, and see
The fair and god-like offspring grown
From budding stars to suns full blown.
Circle with peaceful olive boughs
And conquering bays his Regal brows ;
Let his strong virtues overcome
And bring him bloodless Trophies home ;
Strew all the pavements where he treads
With loyal hearts or rebels' heads :
   But, *Bifront*, open thou no more   [*See* App.
   In his blest reign thy Temple door.

G

A New Year's Gift.

II.—*TO THE QUEEN.*

THOU great Commandress, that do'st move
　　Thy sceptre o'er the crown of Love,
And through his empire, with the awe
Of thy chaste beams, dost give the law ;
From his profaner altars we
Turn to adore thy deity.
He only can wild lust provoke ;
Thou those impurer flames can'st choke ;
　　And where he scatters looser fires,
　　Thou turn'st them into chaste desires.

His kingdom knows no rule but this :
'*Whatever pleaseth, lawful is :*'
Thy sacred lore shows us the path
Of Modesty and constant Faith,
Which makes the rude Male satisfied
With one fair Female by his side :
Doth either sex to each unite,
And form Love's pure hermaphrodite.
To this thy faith, behold the wild
Satyrs already reconciled,
　　Who from the influence of thine eye
　　Have suck'd the deep divinity.

O free them then, that they may teach
The Centaur, and the Horse-man preach
To beasts and birds, sweetly to rest,
Each in his proper lair and nest ;
They shall convey it to the flood,
Till there thy law be understood :
　　So shall thou with thy pregnant fire
　　The water, earth, and air inspire.

Tò the New Year.

III.—*FOR THE COUNTESS OF CARLISLE.*

[LADY *LUCY HAY*, BORN *PERCY: VIDUA*, 1636.] [*Ob.* 1660.

GIVE *Lucinda* pearl nor stone ;
Lend them light who else have none :
Let her beauties shine alone.

Gums nor spice bring from the East ;
For the Phœnix, in her breast
Builds his funeral pile and nest.

No attire thou can'st invent
Shall to grace her form be sent :
She adorns all ornament.

Give her nothing : but restore
Those sweet smiles, which heretofore
In her cheerful eyes she wore.

Drive those envious clouds away ;
Veils that have o'er-cast my day,
And eclipsed her brighter ray.

Let the royal *Goth* mow down
This year's harvest with his own
Sword, and spare *Lucinda's* frown.

Janus, if when next I trace
Those sweet lips, I in her face
Read the Charter of my grace,

Then from bright *Apollo's* tree
Such a garland wreath'd shall be,
As shall crown both her and thee.

To my Lord Admiral,

[*George Villiers*, Duke of *Buckingham*,]

Aug. 1628.]   on his late sickness and recovery.

WITH joy like ours, the *Thracian* youth invade
    Orpheus returning from th' Elysian shade,
Embrace the Hero, and his stay implore;
Make it their public suit he would no more
Desert them so, and for his Spouse's sake,
His vanish'd love, tempt the *Lethœan* Lake.
The Ladies too, the brightest of that time,
Ambitious all his lofty bed to climb,
Their doubtful hopes with expectation feed,
Which shall the fair *Euridice* succeed ;
Euridice ! for whom his numerous moan
Makes list'ning Trees and savage Mountains groan.
Through all the air his sounding strings dilate
Sorrow, like that which touch'd our hearts of late ;
Your pining sickness, and your restless pain,
At once the Land affecting, and the Main.

l. 28, 1618.]When the glad news that you were Admiral
Scarce through the Nation spread, 'twas fear'd by all
That our great *Charles*, whose wisdom shines in you,
Should be perplexed how to choose a new :
So more than private was the joy and grief,
That, at the worst, it gave our souls relief,
    That in our Age such sense of virtue lived :
    They joy'd so justly, and so justly grieved.

    Nature, her fairest light eclipsed, seems
Herself to suffer in these sad extremes ;
While not from thine alone thy blood retires,
Villiers, But from those cheeks which all the world admires.
ess Bu. The stem thus threat'ned, and the sap, in thee,
Droop all the branches of that noble Tree ;
Their beauties they, and we our love, suspend ;
Nought can our wishes save thy health intend :

As lilies over-charged with rain, they bend
Their beauteous heads, and with high heaven contend ;
Fold thee within their snowy arms, and cry,
' He is too faultless and too young to die ! '
    So, like Immortals round about thee, they
    Sit, that they fright approaching Death away.

    Who would not languish, by so fair a train
To be lamented and restored again ?
Or thus with-held, what hasty soul would go,
Though to the Blest ? O'er young *Adonis* so
Fair *Venus* mourn'd, and with the precious shower
Of her warm tears cherish'd the springing flower.
The next support, fair hope of your great name,   [*Cf.* p. 110, *Christopher.*
And second Pillar of that noble frame,
    By loss of thee would no advantage have,
    But, step by step, pursues thee to thy grave.

    And now relentless Fate, about to end
The line, which backward doth so far extend,
That Antique stock, which still the world supplies   [*Villiers.*
With bravest spirit and with brightest eyes,
Kind *Phœbus* interposing, bade me say—
' Such storms no more shall shake that house ; but they
Like *Neptune* and his sea-born niece, shall be
The shining glories of the Land and Sea :
    With courage guard, and beauty warm our Age,
    And lovers fill with like Poetic rage.'   [*Qu.* by Waller

THE RETIRED BLOOD EXHORTED TO RETURN,
IN THE CHEEKS OF THE PALE SISTERS, MISTRESS
KATHERINE AND MISTRESS *MARY NEVILLE.*

STAY, coward blood, and do not yield
    To thy pale sister beauty's field,
Who, there displaying all her white
Ensigns, hath usurp'd thy right ;

Invading thy peculiar throne,
The lip, where thou should'st rule alone ;
And on the cheek, where Nature's care
Allotted each an equal share,
    The spreading Lily only grows,
    Whose milky deluge drowns thy Rose.

Quit not the field, faint blood, nor rush
In the short sally of a blush
Upon thy sister foe, but strive
To keep an endless war alive :
    Though peace do petty states maintain,
    Here war alone makes Beauty reign.

UPON A MOLE IN *CELIA'S* BOSOM.

THAT lovely spot, which thou dost see
    In *Celia's* bosom, was a Bee
Who built her amorous spicy nest
In th' *Hyblas* of her either breast.
  But from those ivory hives she flew
To suck the aromatic dew,
Which from the neighbour vale distils,
Which parts those two twin-sister hills.
  There feasting on ambrosial meat,
A rolling file of balmy sweet
(As in soft murmurs before death
Swan-like she sung), choked up her breath :
    So she in water did expire,
    More precious than the Phœnix fire.

Yet still her shadow there remains,
Confined to those Elysian plains,
With this strict law, that who shall lay
His bold lips on that milky way,
    The sweet and smart from thence shall bring
    Of the bee's honey and her sting.

METHODUS AMANDI.

' Written by Mr. T. C., of his Majesty's Bed-Chamber.'

A DIALOGUE.

I.

TELL me, *Lucretia,*—since my fate,   [' *Eutresia.*
    And thy more powerful form, decrees
My heart an Immolation at thy Shrine,
Where it is ever to incline,—
How I must love, and at what rate ;
    And by what steps, and what degrees,
I shall my hopes enlarge, or my desires confine.

[SHE REPLIES.]

    First, when thy flames begin,
        See they burn all within ;
And so, as lookers-on may not descry
Smoke in a sigh, or sparkle in an eye.
    I'd have thy love a good while there,
        Ere thine own heart should be aware :
And I my self would choose to know it,
First by thy care and cunning not to show it.

II.

[HE PLEADS.]

When my flame, thine own way, is thus betray'd,
        Must it be still afraid ?
May it not be sharp-sighted too, as well,
And know thou know'st, that which it dares not tell ?
        And, by that knowledge, find it may
        Tell itself o'er, a louder way ?

[*HER TRUCE.*]

Let me alone, a while !
For so thou mayest beguile
My heart to a consent,
Long ere it meant.
For while I dare not disapprove,
Lest that betray a knowledge of thy love,
I shall be so accustom'd to allow,
That I shall not know how
To be displeased, when thou shalt it avow.

III.

[*HE ARGUES.*]

When by Love's powerful secret sympathy
Our Souls are got thus nigh,
And that, by one another seen,
There needs no breath to go between ;
Though in the main agreement of our breasts,
Our *Hearts* subscribe as *Interests,*
Will it not need
The Tongues sign too, as *Witness* to the deed ?

[*SHE YIELDS.*]

Speak, then ! but when you whisper out the tale,
Of what you ail,
Let it be so disorder'd that I may
Guess only thence what you would say :
Then to be able to speak sense
Were an offence :
And 'twill thy passion tell the subtlest way,
Not to know what to say !

T. C.

[*Note.*—There is some doubt as to the authorship of this
'Dialogue,' equally with song (*vide* p. 92), 'On his Mistress
Going to Sea,' beginning, 'Farewell, fair Saint, may not the
seas and wind,' to which Henry Lawes composed the music.

Henry Lawes printed it, with the words, in his *Ayres and Dialogues,* Book I. p. 10, 1653 (mentioning, in the Table of Contents, that the song had been 'written by Mr. *Thomas Cary,* son to the Earl of *Monmouth').* This '*Methodus Amandi*' is given, with a Latin version by Sir Richard Fanshawe, among his own 'Miscellaneous Poems,' at the end of his translation of Guarini's '*Pastor Fido,*' 1648. The present lines are there described as ' *Written by Mr. T. C.,* of his Majesty's Bed-Chamber.' Fanshawe's Latin version, '*Ex Linguâ Anglicanâ,*' begins thus :—

> ' *Dic, quonian Fatumque meum, tuaque optima Forma,*
> *Fato omni major, cor hoc tibi destinat olim,*' etc.

George Ellis (in his admirable '*Specimens of the Early English Poets,*' 1801, vol. iii. 144-146) reprints this English 'Dialogue,' without hesitation, amongst the poems written by Thomas Carew, giving entire (from Malone Coll., MS. 13, formerly at the Bodleian Library,) the version beginning, 'Tell me, *Utrechia,*' i.e. '*Eutrechia:*' Fanshawe's reads '*Eutresia,*' but the Index rectifies the typographical blunder, if a blunder it were, by reading '*Lucretia,*' which we follow.

It is scarcely probable that Henry Lawes could be mis-informed concerning the authorship of the song, 'Farewell, dear Saint,' but he certainly makes a distinct difference in his mention of our '*Thomas Carew, Gentleman of the Privy Chamber:*' rightly attributing to him, in the same Table, six other songs, to which Lawes had composed music, *viz.,* 'Give me more love' (p. 10); 'He that loves a rosy cheek' (p. 16); 'If when the Sun at noon displays his brighter rays' (p. 5); 'When on the altar of my hand' (p. 37); 'When thou, poor Excommunicate' (p. 13); and the Dialogue, 'When *Celia* rested in the shade' (p. 39). He gives 'Ask me why I send you here' (The Primrose, p. 73) to Herrick. In his *Second Book of Ayres,* 1655, Lawes gives as Thomas Carew's three others, 'Know, *Celia,* since thou art so proud' (p. 15); 'Weep not,' (p. 44); and 'Fear not, dear Love, that I'll reveal' (p. 9). Of the other song (p. 92), Fanshawe's Latin version begins—

> ' *O Diva, O Formosa vale ;*
> *Non ventus, et Æquor,*' etc.

Obsequies.

To the Lady *Anne Hay.*

[DAUGHTER OF *HONORA*, LADY *HAY*,
THE FIRST WIFE OF *JAMES*, LORD *HAY*, OF *SAWLEY*,
WHO, IN SEPT. 1622, BECAME THE EARL OF *CARLISLE*.]

I HEARD the Virgins sigh, I saw the sleek
   And polish'd Courtier channel his fresh cheek
With real tears ; the new-betrothed Maid
Smiled not that day ; the graver Senate laid
Their business by : of all the Courtly throng
Grief seal'd the heart, and silence bound the tongue.
I, that ne'er more of private sorrow knew
Than from my pen some froward Mistress drew,
And for the public woe had my dull sense
So sear'd with ever-adverse influence,
As the invader's sword might have unfelt
Pierced my dead bosom, yet began to melt :
Grief's strong instinct did to my blood suggest
In the unknown loss peculiar interest.
But when I heard the noble *Carlisle's* gem,
The fairest branch of *Dennye's* ancient stem,
   Was from that casket stol'n, from this trunk torn,
   I found just cause why they—why I—should mourn.

   But who shall guide my artless pen, to draw
Those blooming beauties, which I never saw ?
How shall posterity believe my story,
If I her crowded graces, and the glory
Due to her riper virtues, shall relate
Without the knowledge of her mortal state ?

Shall I (as once *Apelles*), here a feature,
There a grace steal, and rifling so whole Nature
Of all the sweets a learned eye can see,
Figure one *Venus,* and say, 'Such was she ?'
Shall I her Legend fill, with what of old
Hath of the Worthies of her Sex been told ;
And what all pens and times to us dispense,
Re-strain to her, by a prophetic sense ?
Or shall I to the moral and divine
Exactest laws shape, by an even line,
A life so straight, as it should shame the square
Left in the rules of *Catherine* or *Clare,*
And call it hers ? say, 'So did she begin,
And, had she lived, such had her progress been.'
These are dull ways, by which base pens for hire
Daub glorious Vice, and from *Apollo's* choir
  Steal holy ditties, which profanely they
  Upon the hearse of every strumpet lay.

  We will not bathe thy corpse with a forced tear,
Nor shall thy train borrow the blacks they wear ;
Such vulgar spice and gums embalm not thee :
Thou art the theme of Truth, not Poetry.
Thou shalt endure a trial by thy peers :
Virgins of equal birth, of equal years,
  Whose virtues held with thine an emulous strife,
  Shall draw thy picture, and record thy life.

  One shall ensphere thine eyes ; another shall
Impearl thy teeth ; a third, thy white and small
Hand shall be-snow ; a fourth, incarnadine
Thy rosy cheek : until each beauteous line,
Drawn by her hand in whom that part excells,
Meets in one centre, where all Beauty dwells.
  Others, in task, shall thy choice virtues share,
Some shall their birth, some their ripe growth declare.
Though niggard Time left much unhatch'd by deeds,
They shall relate how thou had'st all the seeds

[*S. Cath.* of
Siena, S. C

Of every virtue, which, in the pursuit
Of time, must have brought forth admired fruit.

Thus shalt thou from the mouth of Envy raise
A glorious Journal of thy thrifty days :
Like a bright star shot from his sphere, whose race
In a continued line of flames we trace.
This, if survey'd, shall to the view impart
How, little more than late, thou wert, thou art.
This shall gain credit with succeeding times,
When, nor by bribed pens, nor partial rhymes
Of engaged kindred, but the sacred truth
Is storied by the partners of thy youth :
   Their breath shall Saint thee, and be this thy pride,
   Thus even by Rivals to be deified.

To the Countess of *Anglesey*.

Upon the Death of her Husband,

[*Christopher Villiers, obiit* 1630,]

By her immoderately lamented.

MADAM, men say, you keep with dropping eyes
   Your sorrows fresh, watering the rose, that lies
Fall'n from your cheeks, upon your dear Lord's hearse.
Alas ! those odours now no more can pierce
His cold pale nostril, nor the crimson dye
Present a graceful blush to his dark eye.
Think you that flood of pearly moisture hath
The virtue fabled of old *Æson's* bath ?
You may your beauties and your youth consume
Over his Urn, and with your sighs perfume
The solitary Vault, which, as you groan,
In hollow echoes shall repeat your moan ;
   There you may wither, and an Autumn bring
   Upon your self, but not call back his Spring.

Forbear your fruitless grief, then, and let those
Whose love was doubted, gain belief with shows
To their suspected faith. You, whose whole life
In every act crowned you a constant Wife,
May spare the practice of that vulgar trade,
Which superstitious custom only made.
Rather, a Widow now, of wisdom prove
The pattern ; as, a Wife, you were of love.
Yet since you surfeit on your Grief, 'tis fit
I tell the world upon what cates you sit
    Glutting your sorrows ; and at once include
    His story, your excuse, my gratitude.

You, that behold how yond' sad Lady blends
Those ashes with her tears, lest, as she spends
Her tributary sighs, the frequent gust
Might scatter up and down the noble dust—
Know, when that heap of atoms was with blood
Kneaded to solid flesh, and firmly stood
On stately pillars, the rare form might move
The froward *Juno's* or chaste *Cinthia's* love.
In motion, active grace ; in rest, a calm
Attractive sweetness : brought both wound and balm
To every heart. He was composed of all
The wishes of ripe Virgins, when they call
    For *Hymen's* rites, and in their fancies wed
    A shape of studied beauties to their bed.

Within this curious palace dwelt a soul
Gave lustre to each part, and to the whole :
This dress'd his face in courteous smiles, and so
From comely gestures sweeter manners flow ;
This, courage join'd to strength ; so the hand bent
Was Valour's : open'd, Bounty's instrument :
Which did the scale and sword of Justice hold :
Knew how to brandish steel and scatter gold.
This taught him, not to engage his modest tongue
In suits of private gain, though public wrong ;

Nor misemploy (*as is the Great Man's use,*)
His credit with his Master to traduce,
Deprave, malign, and ruin Innocence,
In proud revenge of some mis-judged offence :
　　But all his actions had the noble end
　　To advance desert, or grace some worthy friend.

He chose not in the active stream to swim,
Nor hunted Honour, which yet hunted him ;
But like a quiet eddy, that hath found
Some hollow creek, there turns his waters round,
And in continual circles dances free
From the impetuous Torrent ; so did he
Give others leave to turn the wheel of State,
(Whose restless motion spins the subject's fate,)
Whilst he, retired from the tumultuous noise
Of Court, and suitors' press, apart enjoys
Freedom and mirth, himself, his time, and friends,
And with sweet relish tastes each hour he spends.
　　I could remember how his noble heart
First kindled at your beauties ; with what art
He chased his game through all opposing fears,
When I his sighs to you, and back your tears
Convey'd to him ; how loyal then, and how
Constant he proved since, to his marriage-vow ;
So as his wand'ring eyes never drew in
One lustful thought to tempt his soul to sin :
　　But that I fear such mention rather may
　　Kindle new grief, than blow the old away.

Cf. pp. 54, 100.] Then let him rest, join'd to great *Buckingham*,
And with his Brother's mingle his bright flame.
Look up, and meet their beams, and you from thence
May chance derive a cheerful influence.
Seek him no more in dust, but call again
Your scatter'd beauties home ; and so the pen,
　　Which now I take from this sad Elegy,
　　Shall sing the Trophies of your conquering eye.

AN ELEGY UPON THE DEATH OF DR. *DONNE,*
DEAN OF *S. PAUL'S.* [1631.]

CAN we not force from widow'd Poetry,
    Now thou art dead, great *Donne,* one Elegy,
To crown thy Hearse ? Why yet did we not trust,
Though with unkneaded dough-baked prose, thy dust ;
Such as the unsizar'd Lecturer, from the flower
Of fading Rhetoric, short-lived as his hour,
Dry as the sand that measures it, might lay
Upon the ashes on the funeral day ?
Have we nor tune nor voice ? Did'st thou dispence [=exhaust.
Through all our language both the words and sense ?
'Tis a sad truth. The pulpit may her plain
And sober Christian precepts still retain ;
Doctrines it may, and wholesome Uses, frame,
Grave Homilies and Lectures ; but the flame
Of thy brave soul—that shot such heat and light,
As burn'd our earth, and made our darkness bright,
(Committed holy rapes upon the will ;
Did through the eye the melting heart distil :
And the deep knowledge of dark truths so teach,
As sense might judge, where fancy could not reach,)
Must be desired for ever. So the fire,
That fills with spirit and heat the *Delphic* choir,
Which—kindled first by thy *Promethean* breath,
Glow'd here awhile—lies quench'd now in thy death.
    The Muses' Garden, with pedantic weeds
O'erspread, was purged by thee ; the lazy seeds
Of servile Imitation thrown away,
And fresh invention planted ; thou did'st pay
The debts of our penurious bankrupt Age :
Licentious thefts, that make poetic rage
A mimic fury, when our souls must be
Possess'd—or with *Anacreon's* ecstasy,
Or *Pindar's,* not their own ; the subtle cheat
Of sly exchanges, and the juggling feat

Of two-edged words, or whatsoever wrong
By ours was done the Greek or Latin tongue,
Thou hast redeem'd, and open'd as a mine
Of rich and pregnant fancy ; drawn a line   .
Of masculine expression : which, had good
Old *Orpheus* seen, or all the ancient brood
Our superstitious fools admire, and hold
Their lead more precious than thy burnish'd gold,
      Thou had'st been their Exchequer, and no more
qu. dross ?]   They each in other's dross had search'd for ore.

    Thou shalt yield no precedence, but of Time ;
And the blind fate of Language, whose tuned chime
More charms the outward sense : yet thou may'st claim
From so great disadvantage greater fame,
Since to the awe of thy imperious wit   \
Our troublesome language bends, made only fit
With her tough thick-ribb'd hoops to gird about
Thy giant Fancy, which had proved too stout
For their soft melting phrases.   As in time
They had the start, so did they cull the prime
Buds of invention many a hundred year,
And left the rifled fields, besides the fear
To touch their harvest : yet from those bare lands,
Of what was only thine, thy only hands
      (And that their smallest work,) have gleaned more
      Than all those times and tongues could reap before.

    But thou art gone, and thy strict laws will be
Too hard for Libertines in Poetry.
They will recall the goodly exiled train
Of Gods and Goddesses, which in thy just reign
Was banish'd nobler poems ; now with these,
The silenced tales i' th' *Metamorphoses,*
Shall stuff their lines, and swell the windy page :
Till verse, refined by thee in this last Age,
      Turn Ballad-rhyme, or those old idols be
      Adored again with new apostacy.

O pardon me, that break with untuned verse
The reverend silence that attends thy Hearse :
Whose solemn awful murmurs were to thee,
More than these rude lines, a loud Elegy,
That did proclaim in a dumb eloquence
The death of all the Arts : whose influence,
Grown feeble, in these panting numbers lies,
Gasping short-winded accents, and so dies.
  So doth the swiftly-turning wheel not stand
In th' instant we withdraw the moving hand ;
But some short time retain a faint weak course,
By virtue of the first impulsive force :
And so, whilst I cast on thy funeral pile
Thy Crown of Bays, O let it crack awhile,
      And spit disdain, till the devouring flashes
      Suck all the moisture up, then turn to ashes.

  I will not draw thee envy, to engross
All thy perfections, or weep all the loss ;
Those are too numerous for one Elegy,
And this too great to be express'd by me.
Let others carve the rest ; it shall suffice
I on thy grave this Epitaph incize :—

      '*Here lies a King that ruled, as he thought fit,*
      The Universal Monarchy of wit ;
      Here lie two Flamens, *and both these the best :*
      Apollo's *first, at last the true* God's *Priest.*'

In answer to an Elegiacal Letter,
(from *Aurelian Townsend*,)
Upon the Death of the King of *Sweden* [1632]
inviting me to write on that subject.

W HY dost thou sound, my dear *Aurelian*,
    In so shrill accents from thy *Barbican*
A loud alarum to my drowsy eyes,
Bidding them wake in tears and elegies

Gustavus ⎤ For mighty *Sweden's* fall? Alas! how may
Adolphus.⎦ My lyric feet—that of the smooth soft way
Of Love and Beauty only know the tread—
In dancing paces celebrate the dead
Victorious King, or his majestic Hearse
Profane with th' humble touch of their low verse?
Virgil, nor *Lucan*, no, nor *Tasso*—more

Cf. p. 111.] Than both; not *Donne*, worth all that went before—
With the united labour of their wit,
Could a just poem to this subject fit.
His actions were too mighty to be raised
Higher by verse: let him in prose be praised,
In modest faithful story, which his deeds
Shall turn to Poems. When the next Age reads
Of *Frankfort, Leipzig, Wurzburg*, of the *Rhine*,
The *Lech*, the *Danube, Tilly, Wallenstein*,
Bavaria, Pappenheim, or *Lutzen*-field, where he
Gain'd after death a posthume victory,
They'll think his acts things rather feign'd than done,
Like our romances of ' The Knight o' th' Sun.'
    Leave we him, then, to the grave Chronicler,
Who, though to Annals he can not refer
His too-brief story, yet his Journals may
Stand by the *Cæsar's* years; and, every day
Cut into minutes, each shall more contain
Of great designments than an Emperor's reign.
And, since 'twas but his church-yard, let him have
For his own ashes now no narrower grave

Than the whole *German* continent's vast womb,
Whilst all her cities do but make his tomb.
    Let us to supreme Providence commit
The fate of Monarchs, which first thought it fit
To rend the Empire from the *Austrian* grasp ;   *[Ferdin. II.*
And next from *Sweden's*, even when he did clasp
Within his dying arms the sovereignty
Of all those provinces, that men might see
The Divine wisdom would not leave that land
Subject to any one King's sole command.
        Then let the Germans fear, if *Cæsar* shall,
        Or the United Princes, rise and fall.

    But let us, that in myrtle bowers sit
Under secure shades, use the benefit
Of peace and plenty, which the blessed hand
Of our good King gives this obdurate land ;   *[Charles I.*
Let us of Revels sing, and let thy breath,
(Which filled Fame's trumpet, with *Gustavus'* death,
Blowing his name to heaven), gently inspire
Thy Pastoral Pipe, till all our swains admire
Thy song and subject, whilst thou dost comprise
The beauties of the SHEPHERD'S PARADISE.   [*W. M.'s.*
For who like thee, whose loose discourse is far
More neat and polish'd than our Poems are—
Whose very gait's more graceful than our dance—
In sweetly-flowing numbers may advance
That glorious night when, not to act foul rapes
Like birds or beasts, but in their Angel shapes,
A troop of Deities came down to guide
Our steerless barks in Passion's swelling tide
By Virtue's 'Card,' and brought us from above
A pattern of their own Celestial Love.
    Nor lay it in dark sullen precepts drown'd,
But with rich fancy and clear action crown'd,
Through a mysterious Fable—that was drawn,
Like a transparent veil of purest lawn,
        Before their dazzling beauties—the divine
        Venus did with her heavenly *Cupid* shine.

The story's curious web, the masculine style,
The subtle sense, did Time and Sleep beguile ;
Pinion'd and charm'd they stood to gaze upon
Th' angelic forms, gestures and motion ;
To hear those ravishing sounds, that did dispense
Knowledge and pleasure to the soul and sense.
It fill'd us with amazement to behold
Love made all spirit ; his corporeal mould
Dissected into atoms, melt away
To empty air, and from the gross allay
Of mixtures and compounding accidents
Refined to immaterial elements.
But when the Queen of Beauty did inspire
The air with perfumes, and our hearts with fire,
Breathing from her celestial organ sweet
Harmonious notes, our souls fell at her feet,
    And did with humble reverend duty more
    Her rare perfections than high state adore.

These harmless pastimes let my *Townsend* sing
To rural tunes ; not that thy Muse wants wing
To soar a loftier pitch, for she hath made
A noble flight, and placed th' Heroic shade
Above the reach of our faint flagging rhyme ;
But these are subjects proper to our clime.
Tourneys, Masques, Theatres, better become
Our Halcyon days : What though the German drum
Bellow for freedom and revenge, the noise
Concerns not us, nor should divert our joys ;
Nor ought the thunder of their carabines
Drown the sweet airs of our tuned violins.
Believe me, friend, if their prevailing powers
Gain them a calm security like ours,
    They'll hang their arms upon the Olive bough,
    And dance and revel then, as we do now.

COMMENDATORY VERSES.

To my Worthy Friend Master *George Sandys*,

on his Translation of the Psalms.

[1638.]

I PRESS not to the Choir, nor dare I greet
   The holy Place with my unhallow'd feet ;
My unwash'd Muse pollutes not things divine,
Nor mingles her profaner notes with thine ;
Here list'ning humbly at the Porch she stays,
And with glad ears sucks in thy Sacred Lays.
  So devout Penitents of old were wont
Some without door, and some beneath the Font,
To stand and hear the Church's Liturgies,
Yet not assist the Solemn Exercise.
  Sufficeth her, that she a Lay-place gain,
To trim thy vestments, or but bear thy train ;
Though nor in tune nor wing she reach thy Lark,
Her lyric feet may dance before the Ark.
  Who knows, but that her wand'ring eyes, that run
Now hunting Glow-worms, may adore the Sun ;
A pure flame may, shot by Almighty Power
Into my breast, the earthy flame devour ?
    My eyes in penitential dew may steep
    That brine, which they for sensual love did weep.

  So, tho' 'gainst Nature's course, fire may be quench'd
With fire, and water be with water drench'd,

Perhaps my restless Soul, tired with pursuit
Of mortal beauty, seeking without fruit
Contentment there—which hath not, when enjoy'd,
Quench'd all her thirst, nor satisfied, though cloy'd :
    Weary of her vain search below, above
    In the first Fair may find th' immortal Love.

Prompted by thy example then, no more
In moulds of clay will I my GOD adore ;
But tear those Idols from my heart, and write
What his blest Spirit, not fond Love, shall indite.
Then I no more shall court the verdant Bay,
But the dry leafless trunk on *Golgotha :*
    And rather strive to gain from thence one Thorn,
    Than all the flourishing Wreaths by Laureats worn.

TO MY MUCH HONOURED FRIEND, *HENRY*, LORD *CAREY*,

OF *LEPPINGTON* : ON HIS TRANSLATION OF *MALVEZZI*.

[*ROMULUS AND TARQUIN*, 1638.]

MY LORD.   In every trivial work, 'tis known,
    Translators must be masters of their own
And of their Author's language ; but your task
A greater latitude of skill did ask ;
For your *Malvezzi* first required a man
To teach him speak vulgar *Italian.*
His matter's so sublime, so now his phrase
So far above the style of *Bembo's* days,
L' Ercolano.] Old *Varchi's* rules, or what the *Crusca* yet
For current *Tuscan* mintage will admit :
As I believe your Marquess, by a good
Part of his natives, hardly understood.
    You must expect no happier fate ; 'tis true,
He is of noble birth ; of nobler you :
So nor your thoughts nor words fit common ears :
He writes, and you translate, both to your Peers.

To my Honoured Friend, Master *Thomas May:*

UPON HIS COMEDY 'THE HEIR.' [1633.]

'THE HEIR' being born, was in his tender age
   Rock'd in the Cradle of a Private Stage ;
Where, lifted up by many a willing hand,
The Child did from the first day fairly stand ;
Since, having gather'd strength, he dares prefer
His steps into the public Theatre,
The World : where he despairs not but to find
A doom from men more able, not less kind.
   I but his Usher am, yet if my word
May pass, I dare be bound he will afford
Things must deserve a welcome, if well known,
Such as best writers would have wish'd their own.

   You shall observe his words in order meet,
And softly stealing on with equal feet,
Slide into even numbers with such grace
As each word had been moulded for that place.
   You shall perceive an amorous passion spun
Into so smooth a web, as, had the Sun
When he pursued the swiftly flying Maid,   *[Daphne.*
Courted her in such language, she had stay'd.
   A love so well express'd must be the same
   The Author felt himself from his fair flame.

   The whole Plot doth alike itself disclose
Through the five Acts, as doth the Lock that goes
With letters : for, till every one be known,
The Lock's as fast as if you had found none :
   And where his sportive Muse doth draw a thread
   Of mirth, chaste Matrons may not blush to read.

   Thus have I thought it fitter to reveal
My want of art, dear Friend, than to conceal
My love. It did appear I did not mean
So to commend thy well wrought Comic Scene,

As men might judge my aim rather to be
To gain praise to my self, than give it thee :
　　Though I can give thee none but what thou hast
　　Deserv'd, and what must my faint breath out-last.

Yet was this garment (though I skill-less be
To take thy measure), only made for thee ;
　　And if it prove too scant, 'tis 'cause the stuff
　　Nature allow'd me is not large enough.

To my Worthy Friend, Master *D'Avenant*,

UPON HIS EXCELLENT PLAY, 'THE JUST ITALIAN.' [1630.]

I'LL not mis-spend in praise the narrow room
　　I borrow in this lease ; the Garlands bloom
From thine own seeds, that crown each glorious page
Of thy triumphant works ; the sullen Age
Requires a Satire.　What star guides the soul
Of these our froward times, that dare controul,
Yet dare not learn to judge ?　When did'st thou fly
From hence, clear candid Ingenuity ?
　　I have beheld when, perch'd on the smooth brow
Of a fair modest troop, thou did'st allow
Applause to slighter works ; but then the weak
Spectator gave the knowing leave to speak.
　　Now noise prevails, and he is tax'd for drouth
Of wit, that with ' the cry' spends not his mouth.
Yet ask him reason why he did not like ?—
Him, why he did ? their ignorance will strike
Thy soul with scorn and pity.　Mark the places
Provoke their smiles, frowns, or distorted faces ;
When they admire, nod, shake the head :—they'll be
A scene of mirth, a double comedy.
But thy strong fancies (raptures of the brain,
Dress'd in poetic flames,) they entertain
　　As a bold impious reach ; for they'll still slight
　　All that exceeds *Red-Bull* and *Cock-pit* flight.

These are the men in crowded heap that throng
To that adulterate Stage, where not a tongue
Of th' untuned Kennel can a line repeat
Of serious sense ; but like-lips meet like-meat :
Whilst the true brood of Actors, that alone
Keep natural unstrain'd action in her throne,
 Behold their benches bare, though they rehearse
 The terser *Beaumont's* or great *Jonson's* verse.

Repine not thou, then, since this churlish fate
Rules not the Stage alone ; perhaps the State
Hath felt this rancour, where men great and good
Have by the Rabble been misunderstood.
 So was thy Play, whose clear yet lofty strain
 Wise men, that govern Fate, shall entertain.

To the Reader of Master *William Davenant's*

Play. ['*The Wits, a Comedy.*' 1636.]

IT hath been said of old, that Plays be Feasts,
 Poets the cooks, and the Spectators guests ;
The Actors, waiters.   From this simile
Some have derived an unsafe liberty,
To use their judgments as their tastes, which choose
Without controul this dish, and that refuse.
But Wit allows not this large privilege :
Either you must confess, or feel its edge.
Nor shall you make a current inference,
If you transfer your reason to your sense :
 Things are distinct, and must the same appear
 To every piercing eye or well-tuned ear.

Tho' sweets with yours, sharps best with my taste meet ;
Both must agree this meat's or sharp or sweet :
But if I scent a stench or a perfume,
Whilst you smell nought at all, I may presume
You have that sense imperfect : So you may
Affect a sad, merry, or humourous Play ;

If, though the kind distaste or please, the Good
And Bad be by your judgment understood.
But if, as in this Play, where with delight
I feast my Epicurean appetite,
With relishes so curious, as dispense
The utmost pleasure to the ravish'd sense,
You should profess that you can nothing meet
That hits your taste either with sharp or sweet,
But cry out, ''Tis insipid!' your bold tongue
May do its Master, not the Author, wrong.
  For men of better palate will by it `
  Take the just elevation of your Wit.

To *WILL. DAVENANT*, MY FRIEND.

(*f. Notes.*]   [*ON HIS POEM OF 'MADAGASCAR.'* 1636.]

WHEN I behold, by warrant from thy pen,
  A Prince rigging our fleets, arming our men,
Conducting to remotest shores our force,
Without a *Dido* to retard his course ;
And thence repelling in successful fight
Th' usurping Foe, whose strength was all his right,
By two brave Heroes (whom we justly may
By *Homer's Ajax* or *Achilles* lay) :
I doubt the author of the 'Tale of *Troy*,'
Virgil.] With him that makes his Fugitive enjoy
The *Carthage* Queen ; and think thy Poem may
Impose upon posterity, as they
Have done on us. What though Romances lie
Thus blended with more faithful History ;
We of th' adulterate mixture not complain,
But thence more Characters of Virtue gain ;
More pregnant Patterns of transcendent worth,
Than barren and insipid Truth brings forth :
  So oft the Bastard nobler fortune meets
  Than the dull Issue of the lawful sheets.

UPON MASTER W[ALTER] MONTAGUE,

HIS RETURN FROM TRAVEL.

LEAD the black bull to slaughter, with the boar
    And lamb ; then 'purple with their mingled gore
The Ocean's curled brow, that so we may
The Sea-Gods for their careful waftage pay :
Send grateful incense up in pious smoke
To those mild Spirits, that cast a curbing yoke
Upon the stubborn winds, that calmly blew
To the wish'd shore our long'd-for *Mountague.*
Then, whilst the aromatic odours burn
In honour of their darling's safe return,
    The Muses' Choir shall thus with voice and hand
    Bless the fair gale that drove his ship to land :—

    Sweetly breathing Vernal air,
    That with kind warmth do'st repair
    Winter's ruins ; from whose breast
    All the gums and spice of th' East
    Borrow their perfumes ; whose eye
    Gilds the morn and clears the sky ;
    Whose dishevell'd tresses shed
    Pearls upon the violet bed ;
    On whose brow, with calm smiles dress'd,
    The Halcyon sits and builds her nest :
        Beauty, youth, and endless Spring
        Dwell upon thy rosy wing.

    Thou, if stormy *Boreas* throws
    Down whole forests when he blows,
    With a pregnant flowery birth
    Can'st refresh the teeming earth ;
    If he nip the early bud—
    If he blast what's fair and good,
    If he scatter our choice flowers,
    If he shake our hills or bowers,

If his rude breath threaten us—
Thou can'st stroke great *Æolus*,
        And from him the grace obtain
        To bind him in an iron chain.

Thus, whilst you deal your body 'mongst your friends,
And fill their circling arms, my glad Soul sends
        This her embrace : Thus we of *Delphos* greet :
        As Laymen clasp their hands, we join our feet.

To Master *W[ALTER]* Montague.

SIR, I arrest you at your Country's suit,
        Who, as a debt to her, requires the fruit
Of that rich stock, which she by Nature's hand
Gave you in trust, to th' use of this whole land.
        Next, she indicts you of a felony,
=*proprius.*] For stealing what was her propriety—
Your self—from hence : so seeking to convey
The public treasure of the State away.
        More, you're accused of Ostracism, the fate
Imposed of old by the *Athenian* state
On eminent virtue ; but that curse, which they
Cast on their men, you on your country lay.
For, thus divided from your noble parts,
This kingdom lives in exile, and all hearts
        That relish worth or honour, being rent
        From your perfections, suffer banishment.

These are your public injuries ; but I
Have a just private quarrel, to defy,
And call you Coward, thus to run away
When you had pierced my heart, not daring stay
Till I redeem'd my honour : but I swear,
By *Celia's* eyes, by the same force to tear
        Your heart from you, or not to end this strife
        Till I or find revenge, or lose my life.

But as in single fights it oft hath been
In that unequal 'equal trial' seen,
That he who had received the wrong at first
Came from the Combat too oft with the worst ;
    So, if you foil me when we meet, I'll then
    Give you fair leave to wound me so again.

To my Friend *G*[ILBERT] *N*[EVILLE] ;

From *Wrest* [PARK, BEDFORDSHIRE.]

I BREATHE, sweet *Ghib*, the temperate air of *Wrest*,
    Where I, no more with raging storms oppress'd,
Wear the cold nights out by the banks of *Tweed*,
On the bleak mountains, where fierce tempests breed,
And everlasting Winter dwells ; where mild
Favonius, and the vernal winds, exiled
    Did never spread their wings : but the wild North
    Brings sterile fern, thistles, and brambles forth.

Here, steep'd in balmy dew, the pregnant Earth
Sends forth her teeming womb a flowery birth ;
And, cherish'd with the warm sun's quickening heat,
Her porous bosom doth rich odours sweat ;
Whose perfumes through the ambient air diffuse
Such native aromatics, as we use :
No foreign gums, nor essence fetch'd from far,
No volatile spirits, nor compounds that are
    Adulterate ; but at Nature's cheap expense
    With far more genuine sweets refresh the sense.

Such pure and uncompounded beauties bless
This mansion with an useful comeliness,
Devoid of art : for here the architect
Did not with curious skill a pile erect
Of carved marble, or tough porphyry,
But built a house for Hospitality ;

No sumptuous chimney-piece of shining stone
Invites the stranger's eye to gaze upon,
And coldly entertains his sight, but clear
And cheerful flames cherish and warm him here ;
No Doric or Corinthian pillars grace
With imagery this structure's naked face.
    The Lord and Lady of this place delight
    Rather to be, in act, than seen in sight.

    In stead of statues, to adorn their wall,
They throng with living men their merry Hall ;
Where, at large tables fill'd with wholesome meats,
The servant, tenant, and kind neighbour eats.
Some of that rank, spun of a finer thread,
Are with the women, steward, and Chaplain, fed
With daintier cates ; others of better note,
Whom wealth, parts, office, or the Herald's coat
Have sever'd from the common, freely sit
At the Lord's table, whose spread sides admit
A large access of friends, to fill those seats
Of his capacious circle, fill'd with meats
    Of choicest relish, till his oaken back
    Under the load of piled up dishes crack.

    Nor think, because our pyramids, and high
Exalted towers threaten not the sky,
That therefore *Wrest* of narrowness complains,
Or strait'ned walls ; for she more numerous trains
Of noble guests daily receives, and those
Can with far more conveniency dispose,
Than prouder piles : where the vain builder spent
More cost in outward gay embellishment
Than real use, which was the sole design
Of our contriver, who made things not fine,
But fit for service. *Amalthea's* Horn
Of Plenty is not in effigy worn,
Without the gate, but she, within the door
Empties her free and unexhausted store.

Nor, crown'd with wheaten wreaths, doth *Ceres* stand
In stone, with a crook'd sickle in her hand ;
Nor on a marble tun, his face besmear'd
With grapes, is curl'd unscissor'd *Bacchus* rear'd :
We offer not in emblems to the eyes,
But to the taste, those useful deities :
    We press the juicy God, and drink his blood,
    And grind the yellow Goddess into food.

Yet we decline not all the work of Art ;
But where more bounteous Nature bears a part,
And guides her handmaid, if she but dispense
Fit matter, she with care and diligence
Employs her skill ; for where the neighbour source
Pours forth her waters, she directs their course,
And entertains the flowing streams in deep
And spacious channels, where they slowly creep
In snaky windings, as the shelving ground
Leads them in circles, till they twice surround
This Island Mansion, which, i' th' centre placed,
Is with a double crystal heaven embraced :
In which our watery constellations float,
Our fishes, swans, our water-man, and boat :
Envy'd by those above, who wish to slake
Their star-burn'd limbs in our refreshing Lake ;
But they stick fast, nail'd to the barren sphere,
Whilst ours increase, in fertile waters here,
    Disport and wander freely where they please,
    Within the circuit of our narrow seas.

With various trees we fringe the water's brink,
Whose thirsty roots the soaking moisture drink ;
And whose extended boughs in equal ranks
Yield fruit, and shade, and beauty to the banks.
On this side young *Vertumnus* sits, and courts
His ruddy-cheek'd *Pomona ; Zephyr* sports
On th' other, with loved *Flora*, yielding there
Sweets for the smell, sweets for the palate here.

But did you taste the high and mighty drink
Which from that fountain flows, you 'ld clearly think
The God of Wine did his plump clusters bring,
And crush the *Falerne* grape into our spring ;
Or else, disguis'd in watery robes, did swim
To *Ceres* bed, and make her big of him,
Begetting so himself on her : for know
Our Vintage here in *March* doth nothing owe
    To theirs in Autumn, but our fire boils here
    As lusty liquor, as the Sun makes there.

Thus I enjoy my self, and taste the fruit
Of this blest Peace ; whilst, toil'd in the pursuit
    Of bucks and stags, emblems of War, you strive
    To keep the memory of our arms alive.

Coelvm Britannicvm.

A Masqve,

At White-Hall in the Banquetting-House,

On Shrove-Tuesday Night, the 18 of February
1633.

1633.]

LONDON:

Printed for *Thomas Walkley*, and are to be Sold
at his Shop, neare *White-Hall.*

1634

I

[*Non habet ingenium; Cæsar sed jussit; habebo:*
Cur me posse negem, posse quid ille putat?

THE INVENTORS OF THE MASQUE:
Thomas Carew. Inigo Jones.

THE MASQUE:

COELUM BRITANNICUM.

The Description of the Scene.

THE first thing that presented itself to the sight, was a rich Ornament, that enclosed the Scene. In the upper part of which were great branches of Foliage, growing out of leaves and husks, with a Coronice at the top ; and in the midst was placed a large compartment, composed of Grotesque work, wherein were Harpies, with wings and lion's claws, and their hinder parts converted into leaves and branches : over all was a broken Frontispice, [*sic*. wrought with scrolls and mask-heads of Children ; and within this a Table, adorned with a lesser compartment, with this inscription, COELUM BRITANNICUM. The two sides of this ornament were thus ordered : First, from the ground arose a square Basement, and on the Plinth stood a great Vase of gold, richly enchased, and beautified with sculptures of Great Relief, with fruitages hanging from the upper part. At the foot of this sat two Youths, naked, in their natural colours ; each of these with one arm supported the Vase, on the cover of which stood two young Women, in draperies, arm in arm : the one figuring the Glory of Princes, and the other Mansuetude [gentleness] : their other arms bore up an Oval, in which, to the King's Majesty, was this Impress—A Lion, with [Impr. = *effigy*. an imperial crown on his head : the word [motto], *Animum sub pectore forti*. On the other side was the like composition, but the design of the Figures varied ;

131

and in the Oval on the top, being borne up by Nobility
and Fecundity, was this Impress, to the Queen's Majesty,
a Lily growing with branches and leaves, and three lesser
Lilies springing out of the stem ; the word, *Semper
inclita Virtus.* All this Ornament was heightened with
gold, and for the invention and various composition
was the newest and most gracious that hath been done
in this place.

By *Inigo
Jones.*]

The curtain was watchet, and a pale yellow in panes ;
which, flying up on the sudden, discovered the Scene,
representing old arches, old palaces, decayed walls,
parts of Temples, Theatres, Basilicas, and Thermæ,
with confused heaps of broken columns, bases, coronices,
and statues, lying as under ground ; and altogether
resembling the ruins of some great City of the ancient
Romans or civilized *Britons.* This strange prospect
detained the eyes of the spectators some time, when,
to a loud music, *Mercury* descends ; on the upper part
of his chariot stands a Cock, in action of crowing. His
habit was a coat of flame colour, girt to him, and a
white mantle trimmed with gold and silver ; upon his
head a wreath, with small falls of white feathers, a
Caduceus in his hand, and wings at his heels. Being
come to the ground, he dismounts, and goes up to the
State.

*Watchet =
pale blue.*]

B

= Throne.]

Mercury.

FROM the high Senate of the Gods, to You,
      Bright glorious Twins of Love and Majesty,
Before whose throne three warlike Nations bend
Their willing knees : on whose Imperial brows
The Regal Circle prints no awful frowns
To fright your Subjects, but whose calmer eyes
Shed joy and safety on their melting hearts,
That flow with cheerful loyal reverence,
Come I, *Cyllenius, Jove's* Ambassador ;
Not, as of old, to whisper amorous tales
Of wanton love into the glowing ear
Of some choice beauty in this numerous train :

Hermes.]

Those days are fled, the rebel flame is quench'd
In heavenly breasts ; the gods have sworn by *Styx*,
Never to tempt yielding mortality
To loose embraces.   Your exemplar' life
Hath not alone transfus'd a zealous heat
Of imitation through your virtuous Court—
By whose bright blaze your Palace is become
The envy'd pattern of this under-world—
But th' aspiring flame hath kindled heaven ;
Th' immortal bosoms burn with emulous fires,
Love rivals your great virtues, Royal sir,
And *Juno*, Madam, your attractive grace :
He his wild lusts, her raging jealousies
She lays aside, and through th' Olympic hall,
As yours doth here, their great Example spreads.
And though of old, when youthful blood conspired
With his new Empire, prone to heats of lust,
He acted incests, rapes, adulteries,
On earthly beauties which his raging Queen,
Swoln with revengeful fury, turn'd to beasts,
And in despite he re-transform'd to Stars,
Till he had fill'd the crowded Firmament
With his loose Strumpets, and their spurious race,
Where the eternal records of his shame
Shine to the world in flaming Characters ;
When in the Crystal mirror of your reign
He view'd him self, he found his loathsome stains :
And now, to expiate the infectious guilt
Of those detested luxuries, he'll chase
The infamous lights from their usurped Sphere,
And drown in the *Lethæan* flood their curst
Both names and memories.   In whose vacant rooms
First you succeed ; and of the wheeling Orb   [*Charl. I.*
In the most eminent and conspicuous point,
With dazzling beams and spreading magnitude,
Shine the bright Pole-star of this hemisphere.
Next, by your side, in a triumphant Chair,   [*Q. Hen. Mar.*
And crown'd with *Ariadne's* diadem,

Sits the fair Consort of your heart and throne.
Diffused about you, with that share of light,
As they of virtue have derived from you,
He'll fix this Noble train, of either sex ;
So to the *British* stars this lower Globe
    Shall owe its light, and they alone dispense
    To th' world a pure refined influence.

Enter *Momus*, attired in a long darkish robe, all wrought
over with poniards, Serpents' tongues, eyes, and
ears ; his beard and hair parti-coloured, and upon
his head a wreath stuck with Feathers, and a
Porcupine in the forepart.

Momus.

By your leave, Mortals. Good-den, Cousin *Hermes !*
your pardon, good my Lord Ambassador. I found the
tables of your Arms and Titles in every Inn betwixt
this and *Olympus*, where your present expedition is
registered your nine thousandth nine hundred ninety-
ninth Legation. I cannot reach the policy why your
master breeds so few Statesmen ; it suits not with his
dignity that in the whole empyræum there should not
be a god fit to send on these honourable errands but
your self, who are not yet so careful of his honour or
your own, as might become your quality, when you are
itinerant : the Hosts upon the high-way cry out with
open mouth upon you, for support pilfery in your
train ; which, though as you are the god of petty
larceny, you might protect, yet you know it is directly
against the new orders, and opposes the Reformation in
Diameter.

    Mercury.—Peace, Railer ! bridle your licentious
        tongue,
And let this Presence teach you modesty.

    Momus.—Let it, if it can ; in the mean time I will
acquaint it with my condition. Know, gay people,
that though your Poets, (who enjoy by Patent a parti-
cular privilege to draw down any of the Deities, from

en,' *passim.*]

t. larclnry.]

Twelfth-night till Shrove-tuesday, at what time there is annually a most familiar intercourse between the two Courts,) have as yet never invited me to these Solemnities ; yet it shall appear by my intrusion this night, that I am a very considerable Person upon these occasions, and may most properly assist at such entertainments. My name is *Momus-ap-Somnus-ap-Erebus-ap-Chaos-ap-Demogorgon-ap-Eternity*. My offices and titles are, the supreme Theomastix, Hypercritic of manners, Protonotary of abuses, Arch-Informer, Dilator-General, Universal Calumniator, Eternal Plaintiff, and perpetual Foreman of the Grand Inquest. My privileges are an ubiquitary, circumambulatory, speculatory, interrogatory, redargutory immunity over all the privy lodgings, behind hangings, doors, curtains, through key-holes, chinks, windows, about all Venerial Lobbies, Sconces, or Redoubts : though it be to the surprise of a *perdu* Page or Chambermaid ; in and at all Courts of civil and criminal judicature, all counsels, consultations, and Parliamentary Assemblies, where, though I am but a Wool-sack god, and have no vote in the sanction of new laws, I have yet a Prerogative of wresting the old to any whatsoever interpretation, whether it be to the behoof or prejudice of *Jupiter* his crown and dignity, for and against the Rights of either houses of Patrician or Plebeian gods. My natural qualities are to make *Jove* frown, *Juno* pout, *Mars* chafe, *Venus* blush, *Vulcan* glow, *Saturn* quake, *Cynthia* pale, *Phœbus* hide his face, and *Mercury* here take his heels. My recreations are witty mischiefs, as when *Saturn* gelt his father ; the Smith caught his wife and her Bravo in a net of cob-web-iron ; and *Hebe*, through the lubricity of the pavement tumbling over the Half-pace, presented the emblem of the forked tree, and discover'd to the tanned *Ethiops* the snowy cliffs of *Calabria* with the Grotto of *Puteoli*. But that you may arrive at the perfect knowledge of me by the familiar illustration of a Bird of mine own feather, old *Peter Aretine*, who reduced all the sceptres and mitres of that age tributary to his wit, was my Parallel ; and *Frank Rab'lais* suck'd much of my milk too ; but your modern French Hospital of Oratory is mere counterfeit, an arrant Mountebank ; for, though fearing no other tortures than his Sciatica, he discourse of Kings and Queens with as little reverence as of Grooms and Chambermaids, yet he wants their fang-teeth and scorpion's tail : I mean that fellow who, to add to his stature thinks it a greater grace to dance on his tiptoes like a Dog in a doublet, than to walk like other men on the soles of his feet.

Malherbe ?]

> *Mercury.*—No more, impertinent Trifler ! you disturb
> The great Affair with your rude scurrilous chat :
> What doth the knowledge of your abject state
> Concern *Jove's* solemn Message ?

Momus.—Sir, by your favour, though you have a more especial Commission of employment from *Jupiter*, and a larger entertainment from his Exchequer, yet as a free-born god I have the liberty to travel at mine own charges, without your pass or countenance Legatine ; and that it may appear a sedulous acute observer may know as much as a dull phlegmatic Ambassador, and wears a triple key to unlock the mysterious Cyphers of your dark secrecies, I will discourse the politic state of Heaven to this trim Audience.—

> At this the Scene changeth, and in the heaven is dis-covered a Sphere, with Stars placed in their several Images, borne up by a huge naked Figure (only a piece of Drapery hanging over his thigh), kneeling and bowing forwards, as if the great weight lying on his shoulders oppressed him ; upon his head a Crown : by all which he might easily be known to be *Atlas.*

—You shall understand that *Jupiter*, upon the inspec-tion of I know not what virtuous precedents, extant, as they say, here in this Court (but, as I more probably

guess, out of the consideration of the decay of his
natural abilities), hath before a frequent convocation
of the Superlunary Peers in a solemn Oration recanted,
disclaimed, and utterly renounced, all the lascivious
extravagancies and riotous enormities of his forepast
licentious life ; and taken his oath on *Juno's* Breviary,
religiously kissing the two-leaved Book, never to stretch
his limbs more betwixt adulterous sheets : and hath
with pathetical remonstrances exhorted, and under strict
penalties enjoined, a respective conformity in the several
subordinate Deities. And because the Libertines of
Antiquity, the Ribald Poets, to perpetuate the memory
and example of their triumphs over chastity to all
future imitation, have in their immoral songs celebrated ['immortal.'
the martyrdom of those Strumpets under the persecu-
tion of the wives, and devolved to posterity the pedigrees
of their whores, bawds, and bastards ; it is therefore
by the authority aforesaid enacted, that this whole
Army of Constellations be immediately disbanded and
cashiered, so to remove all imputation of impiety from
the Celestial Spirits, and all lustful influence upon
terrestrial bodies ; and, consequently, that there be
an Inquisition erected to expunge in the Ancient, and
suppress in the modern and succeeding Poems and
Pamphlets, all past, present, and future mention of
those abjured heresies, and to take particular notice of
all ensuing incontinencies, and punish them in their
high Commission Court. Am not I in election to be
a tall Statesman, think you, that can repeat a passage
at a Council-table thus punctually ?

Mercury.—I shun in vain the importunity
With which this snarler vexeth all the gods ;
Jove cannot 'scape him. Well, what else from heaven ?

Momus.—Heaven ! Heaven is no more the place it
was : a cloister of Carthusians, a monastery of converted
gods ; *Jove* is grown old and fearful, apprehends a
subversion of his Empire, and doubts lest Fate should

introduce a legal succession in the legitimate heir, by repossessing the *Titanian* line : and hence springs all this innovation.   We have had new orders read in the Presence Chamber by the Vi'-President of *Parnassus*, too strict to be observed long : Monopolies are called in, sophistication of wars punished, and rates imposed on Commodities.   Injunctions are gone out to the Nectar Brewers, for the purging of the heavenly Beverage of a narcotic weed which hath rend'red the Ideas confused in the Divine intellects, and reducing it to the composition used in *Saturn's* reign.   Edicts are made for the restoring of decayed house-keeping, prohibiting the repair of Families to the Metropolis ; but this did endanger an *Amazonian* mutiny, till the females put on a more masculine resolution of soliciting businesses in their own persons, and leaving their husbands at home for stallions of hospitality. *Bacchus* hath commanded all Taverns to be shut, and no liquor drawn after ten at night. *Cupid* must go no more so scandalously naked, but is enjoined to make him breeches, though of his mother's petticoats. *Gani-mede* is forbidden the Bed-chamber, and must only minister in public.   The gods must keep no Pages, nor Grooms of their Chamber, under the age of 25, and those provided of a competent stock of beard. *·Pan* may not pipe, nor *Proteus* juggle, but by special permission. *Vulcan* was brought to an *Ore-tenus*, and fined, for driving in a plate of iron into one of the Sun's chariot-wheels, and frost-nailing his horses upon the fifth of *November* last, for breach of a penal Statute prohibiting work upon Holydays, that being the annual celebration of the *Gygantomachy*.   In brief, the whole state of the Hierarchy suffers a total reformation, especially in the point of reciprocation of conjugal affection. *Venus* hath confessed all her adulteries, and is received to grace by her husband ; who, conscious of the great disparity betwixt her perfections and his deformities, allows those levities as

= By word of mouth : *Star-Chamber.*

Gunpowder Plot.

an equal counterpoise ; but it is the prettiest spectacle to see her stroking with her ivory hand his collied cheeks, and with her snowy fingers combing his sooty beard. *Jupiter* too begins to learn to lead his own wife ; I left him practising in the milky way ; and there is no doubt of an universal obedience, where the Law-giver himself in his own person observes his decrees so punctually : who, besides, to eternize the memory of that great example of Matrimonial union which he derives from hence, hath on his bed-chamber door and ceiling, fretted with stars in capital letters, engraven the inscription of *CARLO MARIA.* This is as much, I am sure, as either your knowledge or Instructions can direct you to, which I having in a blunt round tale, without State-formality, politic inferences, or suspected Rhetorical elegancies, already delivered, you may now dexteriously proceed to the second part of your charge, which is the raking-up of yon heavenly sparks in the embers, or reducing the Ætherial lights to their primitive opacity and gross dark substance ; they are all unrivetted from the Sphere, and hang loose in their sockets, where they but attend the waving of your Caduce, and immediately they re-invest their pristine shapes, and appear before you in their own natural deformities.

    Mercury.—*Momus,* thou shalt prevail, for since thy
        bold
Intrusion hath inverted my resolves,
I must obey necessity, and thus turn
My face, to breáthe the Thunderer's just decree
'Gainst this adulterate Sphere, which first I purge
Of loathsome Monsters and mis-shapen forms :
Down from the azure concave thus I charm
The *Lyrnœan* Hydra, the rough unlick'd Bear,
The watchful Dragon, the storm-boding Whale,
The Centaur, the horn'd Goat-fish Capricorn,
The Snake-head Gorgon, and fierce Sagittar.
' Divested of your gorgeous starry robes,

Fall from the circling Orb ! and e'er you suck
Fresh venom in, measure this happy earth :
    Then to the fens, caves, forests, deserts, seas,
    Fly, and resume your native qualities ! '

They dance, in these monstrous shapes, the first Anti-
masque, of natural deformity.

Momus.—Are not these fine companions, trim play-
fellows for the Deities? Yet these and their fellows
have made up all our conversation for some thousands
of years. Do not you, fair Ladies, acknowledge your
selves deeply engaged now to those Poets, your servants,
that, in the height of commendation, have raised your
beauties to a parallel with such society? Hath not
the consideration of these inhabitants rather frighted
your thoughts utterly from the contemplation of the
place? But now that those heavenly Mansions are to
be void, you that shall hereafter be found unlodged
will become inexcusable ; especially since Virtue alone
shall be sufficient title, fine, and rent : yet if there be
a Lady, not competently stock'd that way, she shall
not on the instant utterly despair, if she carry a
sufficient pawn of handsomeness ; for however the
letter of the Law runs, *Jupiter*, notwithstanding his
age and present austerity, will never refuse to stamp
Beauty, and make it current with his own Impression ;
but to such as are destitute of both, I can afford but
small encouragement. Proceed, Cousin *Mercury* ; what
follows ?

Merc.—Look up, and mark where the broad Zodiac
Hangs like a Belt about the breast of heaven ;
On the right shoulder, like a flaming Jewel,
His shell with nine rich topazes adorn'd,
Lord of this Tropic, sits the scalding *Crab :*
He, when the Sun gallops in full career
His annual race, his ghastly claws uprear'd,
Frights at the confines of the torrid Zone,
The fiery team, and proudly stops their course,

Making a solstice, till the fierce Steeds learn
His backward paces, and so retrograde
Post down-hill to th' opposed *Capricorn.*
Thus I depose him from his haughty Throne :
'Drop from the Sky into the briny flood ;
There teach thy motion to the ebbing Sea !
But let those fires that beautified thy shell
    Take human shapes, and the disorder show
    Of thy regressive paces here below !'

The second Anti-masque is danced in retrograde paces,
expressing obliquity in motion.

Momus.—This *Crab,* I confess, did ill become the
heavens ; but there is another that more infests the
Earth, and makes such a solstice in the politer Arts
and Sciences, as they have not been observed for many
Ages to have made any sensible advance. Could you
but lead the learned squadrons with a masculine
resolution past this point of retrogradation, it were a
benefit to mankind, worthy the power of a God, and to
be paid with Altars ; but that not being the work of
this night, you may pursue your purposes. What now
succeeds ?

Mercury.—Vice that, unbodied, in the Appetite
Erects his Throne, hath yet in bestial shapes,
Branded by Nature with the character
And distinct stamp of some peculiar ill,
Mounted the sky, and fix'd his Trophies there :
As fawning Flattery in the Little Dog,
I' th' Bigger, churlish Murmur ; Cowardice
I' th' timorous Hare ; Ambition in the Eagle ;
Rapine and Avarice in th' adventurous Ship
That sail'd to *Colchis* for the golden fleece.
Drunken distemper in the Goblet flows ;
I' th' Dart and Scorpion, biting Calumny ;
In *Hercules* and Lion, furious rage ;
Vain Ostentation in *Cassiopeia* :

All these I to eternal exile doom,
But to this place their emblem'd figures summon,
　　Clad in their proper Figures, by which best
　　Their incorporeal nature is express'd.

The third Anti-masque is danced of these several Vices,
expressing the deviation from Virtue.

Momus.—From henceforth it shall be no more said
in the Proverb, when you would express a riotous
Assembly, That hell—but heaven—is broke loose.
This was an arrant Gaol-delivery ; all the prisons of
your great Cities could not have vomited more corrupt
matter ; but, Cousin *Cylleneus,* in my judgment it is
not safe that these infectious persons should wander
here, to the hazard of this Island ; they threat'ned less
danger when they were nailed to the Firmament.   I
should conceive it a very discreet course, since they are
provided of a tall vessel of their own, ready rigg'd, to
embark them all together in that good Ship called the
Argo, and send them to the plantation in *New-England,*
which hath purged more virulent humours from the
politic body, than Guiacum and all the West-Indian
drugs have from the natural bodies of this kingdom.
Can you devise how to dispose them better ?

Mercury.—They cannot breathe this pure and
　　temperate Air,
Where Virtue lives ; but will, with hasty flight,
'Mongst fogs and vapours, seek unsound abodes.
Fly after them, from your usurped seats,
You foul remainders of that viperous brood !
　　Let not a Star of the luxurious race
　　With his loose blaze stain the sky's crystal face.

All the Stars are quenched, and the Sphere is darkened.

Before the entry of every Anti-masque, the Stars in
　　those figures in the Sphere which they were to
　　represent, were extinct ; so, by the end of the Anti-
　　masques in the Sphere, no more Stars were to be seen.

Momus.—Here is a total Eclipse of the eighth Sphere, which neither *Booker, Allestre,* nor any of your prognosticators, no, nor their great master, *Tycho,* were aware of ; but yet, in my opinion, there were some innocent, and some generous Constellations, that might have been reserved for noble uses ; as the Scales and Sword to adorn the statue of Justice, since she resides here on Earth only in picture and effigy. The Eagle had been a fit present for the *Germans,* in regard their bird hath mew'd most of her feathers lately. The Dolphin, too, had been most welcome to the *French ;* [*Dauphin.* and then, had you but clap'd *Perseus* on his *Pegasus,* brandishing his Sword, the Dragon yawning on his back under the horse's feet, with *Python's* dart through his throat, there had been a divine St. *George* for this Nation ! but since you have improvidently shuffled them altogether, it now rests only that we provide an immediate succession ; and to that purpose I will instantly proclaim a free Election.

> *O yes, O yes, O yes,*
> *By the Father of the gods,*
> *and the King of Men.*

Whereas we having observed a very commendable practice taken into frequent use by the Princes of these latter Ages, of perpetuating the memory of their famous enterprizes, sieges, battles, victories, in Picture, Sculpture, Tapistry, Embroideries, and other manufactures, wherewith they have embellished their public Palaces, and taken into Our more distinct and serious consideration the particular Christmas hanging of the Guard-Chamber of this Court, wherein the Naval Victory of '88 is, to the eternal glory of this Nation, exactly delineated ; and whereas We likewise, out of a prophetical imitation of this so laudable custom, did, for many thousand years before, adorn and beautify the eighth room of Our Celestial Mansion, commonly called the Star-Chamber, with the military adventures, stratagems, achievements, feats, and defeats, performed in Our Own person, whilst yet Our Standard was erected, and We a Combatant in the Amorous Warfare : it hath, notwithstanding, after mature deliberation and long debate—held first in our own inscrutable bosom, and afterwards communicated with Our Privy Council—seemed meet to Our Omnipotency, for causes to Our self best known, to unfurnish and dis-array our 'fore-said Star-Chamber of all those Ancient Constellations which have for so many Ages been sufficiently notorious, and to admit into their vacant places such Persons only as shall be qualified, with exemplar' Virtue and eminent Desert, there to shine in indelible characters of glory to all Posterity. It is therefore Our divine will and pleasure, voluntarily, and out of Our own free and proper motion, mere grace and special favour, by these presents, to specify and declare to all Our loving People, that it shall be lawful for any Person whatsoever, that conceiveth him or her self to be really endued with any Heroical Virtue or transcendent Merit, worthy so high a calling and dignity, to bring their several pleas and pretences before Our Right trusty and well-beloved Cousin and Counsellor, Don *Mercury* and god *Momus*, &c., our peculiar Delegates for that affair ; upon whom We have Transferr'd an absolute power to conclude and determine, without Appeal or Revocation, accordingly as to their wisdoms it shall in such cases appear behooveful and expedient. Given at Our Palace in *Olympus* the first day of the first month, in the first year of the Reformation.

Plutus enters, an old man full of wrinkles, a bald head, a thin white beard, spectacles on his nose, with a bunched back, and attired in a Robe of Cloth of Gold.

               Plutus appears.

Mercury.—Who 's this appears ?

Momus.—This is a subterranean fiend, *Plutus*, in this dialect term'd Riches, or the God of Gold ; a Poison hid by Providence, in the bottom of seas and navel of the

earth, from man's discovery ; where, if the seeds began
to sprout above-ground, the excrescence was carefully
guarded by Dragons ; yet at last, by human curiosity,
brought to light to their own destruction, this being
the true *Pundora's* box, whence issued all those
mischiefs that now fill the universe.

Plutus.—That I prevent the message of the gods
Thus with my haste, and not attend their summons,
Which ought in Justice call me to the place
I now require of Right, is not alone
To show the just precedence that I hold
Before all earthly, next th' immortal Powers ;
But to exclude the hope of partial Grace
In all Pretenders, who, since I descend
To equal trial, must by my example,
Waiving your favour, claim by sole Desert,
   If Virtue must inherit, she's my slave ;
I lead her captive in a golden chain,
About the world ; she takes her form and being
From my creation ; and those barren seeds
That drop from Heaven, if I not cherish them
With my distilling dews and fotive heat,   [nourishing.
They know no vegetation ; but, exposed
To blasting winds of freezing Poverty,
Or not shoot forth at all, or budding wither.
Should I proclaim the daily sacrifice
Brought to my Temples by the toiling rout,
Not of the fat and gore of abject Beasts
But human sweat and blood pour'd on my Altars,
I might provoke the envy of the gods.
Turn but your eyes, and mark the busy world,
Climbing steep Mountains for the sparkling stone,
Piercing the Centre for the shining Ore,
And th' Ocean's bosom to rake pearly sands :
Crossing the torrid and the frozen Zones,
'Midst rocks and swallowing Gulfs, for gainful trade :
And through opposing swords, fire, murd'ring cannon,
Scaling the walled Town for precious spoils.

Plant, in the passage to your heavenly seats,
These horrid dangers, and then see who dares
Advance his desperate foot; yet am I sought,
And oft in vain, through these and greater hazards :
I could discover how your Deities
Are for my sake slighted, despised, abused ;
Your temples, shrines, altars, and images,
Uncover'd, rifled, robb'd and disarray'd
By sacrilegious hands ; yet is this treasure
To th' golden Mountain, where I sit adored,
With superstitious solemn rites convey'd,
And becomes sacred there ; the sordid wretch
Not daring touch the consecrated Ore,
Or with profane hands lessen the bright heap :
But this might draw your anger down on mortals,
For rend'ring me the homage due to you ;
Yet what is said may well express my power,
Too great for Earth, and only fit for Heaven,
    Now, for your pastime, view the naked root
Which, in the dirty earth and base mould drown'd,
Sends forth this precious Plant and golden fruit.
You lusty Swains, that to your grazing flocks
Pipe amorous roundelays ; you toiling Hinds,
That barb the fields, and to your merry teams
Whistle your passions ; and you mining Moles,
That in the bowels of your Mother-earth
Dwell, the eternal burden of her womb,
      Cease from your labours, when Wealth bids you
        play,
      Sing, dance, and keep a cheerful holyday.

*They dance the fourth Anti-masque, consisting of Country
    people, music, and measures.*

    Mercury.—*Plutus*, the gods know and confess your
      power,
Which feeble Virtue seldom can resist ;
Stronger than Towers of brass or Chastity :

Jove knew you when he courted *Danae*,
And *Cupid* wears you on that arrow's head
That still prevails.   But the gods keep their Thrones
To install Virtue, not her Enemies.
They dread thy force, which even themselves have felt :
Witness Mount *Ida*, where the Martial Maid
And frowning *Juno* did to mortal eyes
Naked for gold their sacred bodies show !
Therefore for ever be from heaven banish'd :
But since with toil from undiscover'd Worlds
Thou art brought hither, where thou first did'st breathe
The thirst of Empire into Regal breasts,
And frightedst quiet Peace from her meek Throne,
Filling the World with tumult, blood, and war ;
Follow the Camps of the contentious earth,
And be the Conqu'ror's slave : but he that can
    Or conquer thee, or give thee Virtue's stamp,
    Shall shine in heaven a pure immortal Lamp.

Momus.—Nay, stay, and take my benediction along
with you !   I could, being here a Co-Judge, like others
in my place, now that you are condemned, either rail
at you, or break jests upon you ; but I rather choose to
loose a word of good counsel, and entreat you to be
more careful in your choice of company ; for you are
always found either with Misers, that not use you at
all, or with Fools, that know not how to use you well.
Be not hereafter so reserved and coy to men of worth
and parts, and so you shall gain such credit, as at the
next Sessions you may be heard with better success.
But till you are thus reform'd, I pronounce this
positive sentence, That wheresoever you shall choose
to abide, your society shall add no credit or reputation
to the party, nor your discontinuance or total absence
be matter of discouragement to any man ; and who-
soever shall hold a contrary estimation of you, shall be
condemn'd to wear perpetual Motley, unless he recant
his opinion.   Now you may void the Court.

=Poverty.] *Pœnia* enters, a woman of a pale colour, large brims of a hat upon her head, through which her hair started up like a fury; her Robe was of a dark colour, full of patches; about one of her hands was tied a Chain of Iron, to which was fastened a weighty stone, which she bore up under her arm.

Pœnia enters.

Mercury.—What Creature 's this ?

Momus.—The Antipodes to the other : they move like two buckets, or as two nails drive out one another. If Riches depart, Poverty will enter.

> *Poverty.*—I nothing doubt, Great and Immortal Powers,
> But that the place your Wisdom hath denied
> My foe, your Justice will confer on me ;
> Since that which renders him incapable
> Proves a strong plea for me. I could pretend,
> Even in these rags, a larger Sovereignty
> Than gaudy Wealth in all his pomp can boast ;
> For mark how few they are that share the world ;
> The numerous Armies, and the swarming Ants
> That fight and toil for them, are all my Subjects,
> They take my wages, wear my Livery :
> Invention too and Wit are both my creatures,
> And the whole race of Virtue is my offspring :
> As many mischiefs issue from my womb,
> And those as mighty, as proceed from Gold.
> Oft o'er his Throne I wave my awful Sceptre,
> And in the bowels of his state command,
> When, midst his heaps of coin and hills of gold,
> I pine and starve the avaricious Fool.
> But I decline those titles, and lay claim
> To heaven by right of Divine Contemplation :
> She is my Darling, I in my soft lap

Free from disturbing cares, bargains, accounts,
Leases, rents, stewards, and the fear of thieves
That vex the rich, nurse her in calm repose,
And with her all the Virtues speculative,
Which but with me find no secure retreat.
For entertainment of this hour, I'll call
A race of people to this place, that live
At Nature's charge, and not importune heaven
To chain the winds up, or keep back the storms,
To stay the thunder, or forbid the hail
To thresh the unreap'd ear, but to all weathers,
Both chilling frost and scalding sun, expose
Their equal face. Come forth, my swarthy train !
In this fair circle dance, and as you move,
Mark and foretell happy events of Love.

They dance the fifth Anti-masque, of Gipsies.

Momus.—I cannot but wonder, that your perpetual
conversation with Poets and Philosophers hath fur-
nished you with no more Logic, or that you should
think to impose upon us so gross an inference, as
because *Plutus* and you are contrary, therefore what-
soever is denied of the one must be true of the other ;
as if it should follow of necessity, because he is not
Jupiter, you are. No, I give you to know, I am better
versed in cavils with the gods than to swallow such a
fallacy ; for though you two cannot be together in one
place, yet there are many places that may be without
you both, and such is heaven, where neither of you [is]
likely to arrive : therefore let me advise you to marry
your self to Content, and beget sage Apophthegms and
goodly moral Sentences, in dispraise of Riches, and
contempt of the world.

Mercury.—Thou dost presume too much, poor needy
  wretch,
To claim a station in the Firmament,
Because thy humble Cottage or thy Tub

Nurses some lazy or pedantic virtue,
In the cheap sun-shine or by shady springs,
With roots and pot-herbs ; where thy rigid hand,
Tearing those human passions from the mind,
Upon whose stocks fair blooming virtues flourish,
Degradeth Nature, and benumbeth sense,
And *Gorgon*-like, turns active men to stone.

Nota bene.] We not require the dull society
Of your necessitated Temperance,
Or that unnatural stupidity
That knows nor joy nor sorrow ; nor your forced
Falsely exalted passive Fortitude
Above the active.   This low abject brood,

Total Abst.] That fix their seats in mediocrity,
Become your servile minds ; but we advance
Such virtues only as admit excess :
Brave bounteous Acts, Regal Magnificence,
All-seeing Prudence, Magnanimity
That knows no bound, and that Heroic virtue
For which Antiquity hath left no name,
But patterns only, such as *Hercules,*
Achilles, Theseus.   Back to thy loath'd cell !

And when thou seëst the new enlighten'd Sphere,
Study to know but what those Worthies are.   (

Tiche [*Opportunity* or *Fortune*] enters : her head bald
behind, and one great lock before ; wings at her
shoulders, and in her hand a wheel ; her upper
parts naked, and the skirt of her garment wrought
all over with crowns, sceptres, books, and such
other things as express both her greatest and
smallest gifts.

Momus.—See where Dame *Fortune* comes ; you may
know her by her wheel, and that veil over [her] eyes ;
s. = hooded.] with which she hopes, like a seeled Pigeon, to mount
above the Clouds, and perch in the Eighth Sphere.
Listen ! she begins.

Fortune.—I come not here, you gods, to plead the
    right
By which Antiquity assign'd my Deity,
(Though no peculiar station 'mongst the Stars,
Yet general power to rule their Influence ;)
Or boast the title of Omnipotent,
Ascribed me then, by which I rivall'd *Jove*,
Since you have cancell'd all those old records :
But, confident in my good cause and merit,
Claim a succession in the vacant Orb.
For since *Astræa* fled to heaven, I sit
Her Deputy on Earth ; I hold her scales,
And weigh men's fates out, who have made me blind,
Because themselves want eyes to see my causes ;
Call me inconstant, 'cause my works surpass
The shallow fathom of their human reason ;
Yet here, like blinded Justice, I dispense
With my impartial hands their constant lots :
And if desertless impious men engross
My best rewards, the fault is yours, you gods,
That scant your graces to mortality,
And, niggards of your good, scarce spare the world
One virtuous for a thousand wicked men.
It is no error to confer dignity,
But to bestow it on a vicious man ;
I gave the dignity, but you made the vice :
Make you men good, and I'll make good men happy.

That *Plutus* is refused, dismays me not ;
He is my Drudge, and the external pomp
In which he decks the world proceeds from me,
Not him ; like Harmony, that not resides
In strings or notes, but in the hand and voice.
The revolutions of Empires, States,
Sceptres and Crowns, are but my game and sport,
Which as they hang on the events of War,
So these depend upon my turning wheel.

You warlike Squadrons, who, in battle join'd,
Dispute the Right of Kings, which I decide,
    Present the model of that martial frame,
    By which, when Crowns are staked, I rule the game!

They dance the sixth Anti-masque, being the representation of a battle.

Momus.—Madam, I should censure you, *pro falso clamore,* — for preferring a scandalous cross-bill of recrimination against the gods ; but your blindness shall excuse you. Alas ! what would it advantage you, if Virtue were as universal as vice is ? It would only follow that, as the world now exclaims upon you for exalting the vicious, it would then rail as fast at you for depressing the virtuous ; so they would still keep their tune, though you changed the ditty.

Mercury.—The mists in which future events are
        wrapp'd,
= *against.*] That oft succeed beside the purposes
Of him that works (his dull eyes not discerning
The first great Cause), offer'd thy clouded shape
To his enquiring search ; so in the dark
The groping world first found thy Deity,
And gave thee rule over contingencies,
Which to the piercing eye of Providence
Being fixed and certain, where past and to-come
Are always present, thou do'st disappear,
Losest thy being, and art not at all.
Be thou then only a deluding Phantom,
At best a blind guide, leading blinder fools :
Who, would they but survey their mutual wants,
And help each other, there were left no room
For thy vain aid. Wisdom, whose strong-built plots
Leave nought to hazard, mocks thy futile power !
Industrious Labour drags thee by the locks,
Bound to his toiling Car, and, not attending
Till thou dispense, reaches his own reward.

Only the lazy sluggard yawning lies
Before thy threshold, gaping for thy dole,
And licks the easy hand that feeds his sloth ;
The shallow, rash, and unadvised man
Makes thee his stale, disburdens all the follies
Of his mis-guided actions on thy shoulders.
Vanish from hence, and seek those idiots out
　　That thy fantastic god-head hath allow'd,
　　And rule that giddy superstitious crowd.

Hedone [Pleasure], a young woman with a shining face,
　　in a light lascivious habit, adorn'd with silver and
　　gold ; her temples crown'd with a garland of Roses,
　　and over that a Rainbow encircling her head down
　　to her shoulders.

Hedone enters.

Mercury.—What wanton 's this ?
Momus.—This is the sprightly Lady *Hedone ;* a merry
gamester : this people call her Pleasure.

[*a. l.* 1634,
'youngster.'

Pleasure.—The reasons (equal Judges) here alleged
By the dismiss'd Pretenders, all concur
To strengthen my just title to the Sphere.
Honour or Wealth, or the contempt of both,
Have in themselves no simple real good,
But as they are the means to purchase Pleasure :
The paths that lead to my delicious Palace.
They for my sake, I for mine own, am prized.
Beyond me nothing is ; I am the Goal,
The journey's end, to which the sweating world
And wearied Nature travel.　For this the best
And wisest sect of all Philosophers　　　　　　　[*Epicureans.*
Made me the seat of supreme happiness ;
And though some, more austere, upon my ruins　　[*Stoics.*
Did to the prejudice of Nature raise
Some petty low-built virtues, 'twas because
They wanted wings to reach my soaring pitch.

] Had they been Princes born, themselves had proved
] Of all mankind the most luxurious.
For those delights, which to their low condition
Were obvious, they with greedy appetite
Suck'd and devour'd : from offices of State,
From cares of family, children, wife, hopes, fears,
Retired, the churlish Cynic in his Tub
Enjoy'd those pleasures which his tongue defamed.
Nor am I rank'd 'mongst the superfluous goods ;
My necessary offices preserve
Each single man, and propagate the kind.
    Then am I universal, as the light,
Or common air we breathe ; and since I am
The general desire of all mankind,
Civil Felicity must reside in me.
Tell me what rate my choicest pleasures bear
When, for the short delight of a poor draught
Of cheap cold water, great *Lysimachus*
Rend'red himself slave to the Scythians ?
Should I the curious structure of my seats,
The art and beauty of my several objects,
Rehearse at large, your bounties would reserve
For every sense a proper constellation ;
But I present their Persons to your eyes.
    Come forth, my subtle Organs of Delight !
        With changing figures please the curious eye,
        And charm the ear with moving Harmony.

They dance the seventh Anti-masque, of the Five Senses

Mercury.—Bewitching Syren, gilded rottenness !
Thou hast with cunning artifice display'd
Th' enamel'd outside and the honied verge
Of the fair Cup, where deadly poison lurks :
Within, a thousand sorrows dance the round ;
And like a shell, Pain circles thee without.
Grief is the shadow waiting on thy steps,
Which, as thy joys 'gin tow'rds their West decline,
Doth to a Giant's spreading form extend

Thy Dwarfish stature. Thou thy self art Pain ;
Greedy, intense Desire, and the keen edge
Of thy fierce Appetite oft strangles thee,
And cuts thy slender thread ; but still the terror
And apprehension of thy hasty end
Mingles with Gall thy most refined sweets :
   Yet thy *Circean* charms transform the world.
Captains, that have resisted war and death,
Nations, that over Fortune [oft] have triumph'd,
Are by thy magic made effeminate :
Empires, that knew no limit but the Poles,
Have in thy wanton lap melted away.
Thou wert the Author of the first excess
That drew this reformation on the gods.
Can'st thou then dream, those Powers that from heaven have
   have
Banish'd th' effect, will there enthrone the cause ?
     To thy voluptuous den, fly, Witch, from hence !
     There dwell, for ever drown'd in brutish sense.

Momus.—I concur : and am grown so weary of these tedious pleadings, as I'll pack up too and be gone. Besides, I see a crowd of other suitors pressing hither ; I'll stop 'em, take their petitions, and prefer 'em above; and as I came in bluntly, without knocking, and nobody bade me welcome, so I'll depart as abruptly, without taking leave, and bid nobody farewell.

Mercury.—These, with forced reasons and strain'd
   arguments,
Urge vain pretences, whilst your Actions plead,
And with a silent importunity
Awake the drowsy Justice of the gods,
To crown your deeds with immortality.
The growing Titles of your ancestors,
These Nations' glorious Acts, join'd to the stock
Of your own Royal virtues, and the clear
Reflex they take from th' imitation

Of your famed Court, make Honour's story full,
And have to that secure fix'd state advanced
Both you and them, to which the labouring world—
Wading through streams of blood—sweats to aspire.
Those Ancient Worthies of these famous Isles,
That long have slept, in fresh and lively shapes
Shall straight appear, where you shall see your self
Circled with modern Heroes, who shall be
In Act, whatever elder times can boast,
Noble or Great, as they in Prophecy
Were all but what you are.   Then shall you see
The sacred hand of bright Eternity
Mould you to Stars, and fix you in the Sphere.

The Queen,]   To you, your Royal half, to them she'll join
her ladies.]   Such of this Train, as with industrious steps
In the fair prints your virtuous feet have made,
Though with unequal paces, follow you.
This is decreed by *Jove,* which my return
Shall see perform'd ; but first behold the rude
And old Abiders here, and in them view
The point from which your full perfections grew.
You naked, ancient, wild Inhabitants,
That breathed this air and press'd this flowery Earth,
    Come from those shades where dwells eternal night,
    And see what wonders Time hath brought to light !

Atlas and the Sphere vanish, and a new Scene appears,
of Mountains, whose eminent height exceed the
Clouds, which pass beneath them ; the lower parts
are wild and woody : out of this place comes forth
a more grave Anti-masque of *Picts,* the natural
Inhabitants of this Isle, ancient *Scots* and *Irish :*
these dance a *Pyrrhica,* or martial dance.

B

text, 'Perica.']

[*They dance the eighth Anti-masque : a* Pyrrhic *dance.*]

When this Anti-masque was past, there began to arise
out of the earth the top of a hill, which, by little
and little, grew to be a huge Mountain, that covered
all the Scene ; the under-part of this was wild and
craggy, and above somewhat more pleasant and
flourishing ; about the middle part of this Moun-
tain were seated the three kingdoms of *England,*
Scotland, and *Ireland,* all richly attired in regal
habits, appropriated to the several Nations, with
Crowns on their heads, and each of them bearing
the ancient Arms of the kingdoms they represented.
At a distance above these, sate a young man in
a white embroidered robe ; upon his fair hair an
olive garland, with wings at his shoulders, and
holding in his hand a Cornucopia filled with
corn and fruits, representing the Genius of these
kingdoms.

THE FIRST SONG.

GENIUS.

Raise from these rocky cliffs your heads,
Brave Sons, and see where Glory spreads
Her glittering wings ; where Majesty,
Crown'd with sweet smiles, shoots from her eye
Diffusive joy ; where Good and Fair
United sit in Honour's chair.
Call forth your aged Priests, and crystal streams,
To warm their hearts and waves in these bright beams !

KINGDOMS.

1. *From your consecrated woods,*
   Holy Druids ; 2. *Silver floods,*
   From your channels fringed with flowers,
3. *Hither move ; forsake your bowers—*
1. *Strew'd with hallowed Oaken leaves,*
   Deck'd with flags and sedgy sheaves—
2. *And behold a wonder.* 3. *Say,*
   What do your duller eyes survey ?

CHORUS OF DRUIDS AND RIVERS.

We see at once, in dead of night,
A Sun appear, and yet a bright
Noon-day springing from Star-light.

GENIUS.

Look up, and see the darkened Sphere
Deprived of light! her eyes shine Here!

CHORUS.

These are more sparkling than those were.

KINGDOMS.

1. *These shed a milder influence;*
2. *These by a pure intelligence*
   Of more transcendent Virtue move;
3. *These first feel, then kindle love;*
1, 2. *From the bosoms they inspire,*
   These receive a mutual fire:
1, 2, 3. *And where their flames impure return,*
   These can quench, as well as burn.

GENIUS.

Here the fair victorious eyes
Make Worth only Beauty's prize;
Here the hand of Virtue ties
'Bout the heart Love's amorous chain:
Captives triumph, Vassals reign,
And none live here but the slain.

CHORUS.

These are th' Hesperian bowers, whose fair trees bear
Rich golden fruit, and yet no Dragon near.

GENIUS.

Then from your impris'ning womb,
Which is the cradle and the tomb
Of British Worthies, fair Sons ! send
A troop of Heroes, that may lend
Their hands to ease this loaden grove,
And gather the ripe fruits of Love.

KINGDOMS.

1, 2, 3. *Open thy stony entrails wide,*
And break, old Atlas, *that the pride*
Of Three famed Kingdoms may be spied.

CHORUS.

Pace forth, thou mighty British Hercules,
With thy choice band, for only thou and these
May revel here in LOVE'S Hesperides.

At this, the under-part of the Rock opens, and out of a
Cave are seen to come the Masquers, richly attired
like ancient Heroes, the colours yellow, embroidered
with silver, their antique Helms curiously wrought,
and great plumes on the top ; before them a troop
of young Lords and Noblemen's sons, bearing [*Cf.* p. 168.
torches of virgin-wax. These were apparelled
after the old *British* fashion in white Coats, em-
broidered with silver, girt, and full gathered, cut
square-collared, and round caps on their heads,
with a white feather wreathen about them. First
these dance with the lights in their hands, after
which the Masquers descend into the room, and
dance their entry.

The dance being past, there appears in the further part
of the heaven coming down a pleasant Cloud, bright
and transparent ; which, coming softly downwards
before the upper part of the mountain, embraceth
the Genius, but so as through it all his body is seen.

Then the Cloud, rising again with a gentle motion,
  bears up the Genius of the Three Kingdoms, and
  being past the Airy Region, pierceth the heavens,
  and is no more seen ; at that instant, the Rock
  with the three kingdoms on it sinks, and is hidden
  in the earth.   This strange spectacle gave great
  cause of admiration, but especially how so huge a
  machine, and of that great height, could come from
  under the Stage, which was but six foot high.

THE SECOND SONG.

KINGDOMS.

1. *Here are shapes form'd fit for heaven ;*
2. *These move gracefully and even.*
3. *Here the Air and paces meet,*
    So just, as if the skilful feet
    Had struck the Viols.—1, 2, 3. So the ear
    Might the tuneful footing hear.

CHORUS.

And had the Music silent been,
The eye a moving tune had seen.

GENIUS.

These must in the unpeopled sky
Succeed, and govern Destiny :
Jove is tempering purer fire,
And will with brighter flames attire
These glorious lights.   I must ascend,
And help the Work.

KINGDOMS.

                    1. *We cannot lend*
Heaven so much treasure.   2. Nor that pay,
But rend'ring what it takes away.
Why should they, that here can move
So well, be ever fix'd above ?

CHORUS.

Or be to one eternal posture tied,
That can into such various figures slide?

GENIUS.

Jove shall not, to enrich the Sky,
Beggar the Earth: their Fame shall fly
From hence alone, and in the Sphere
Kindle new Stars, whilst they rest here.

KINGDOMS.

1, 2, 3. *How can the shaft stay in the quiver,*
Yet hit the mark?

GENIUS.

Did not the River
Eridanus the grace acquire
In Heaven and Earth to flow:
Above in streams of golden fire,
In silver waves below?

KINGDOMS.

, 2, 3. *But shall not we, now thou art gone*
Who wert our Nature, wither,
Or break that triple Union
Which thy soul held together?

GENIUS.

In Concord's pure immortal spring
I will my force renew,
And a more active Virtue bring
At my return.   Adieu.

KINGDOMS. *Adieu.*—CHORUS. *Adieu.*

L

The Masquers dance their main dance; which done, the Scene again is varied into a new and pleasant prospect, clean differing from all the other; the nearest part shewing a delicious garden, with several walks and parterras set round with low trees, and on the sides, against these walks, were fountains and grots, and in the farthest part a Palace, from whence went high walks upon Arches, and above them open Terraces planted with Cypress trees; and all this together was composed of such Ornaments as might express a Princely Villa.

From hence the Chorus, descending into the room, goes up to the State.

THE THIRD SONG.

BY THE CHORUS GOING UP TO THE QUEEN.

Whilst thus the darlings of the Gods
  From Honour's Temple, to the Shrine
Of Beauty, and these sweet abodes
  Of Love, we guide, let thy Divine
Aspects, bright Deity! with fair
And Halcyon *beams becalm the air.*

We bring Prince Arthur, *or the brave*
  St. George *himself, great Queen! to you :*
You'll soon discern him; and we have
  A Guy, *a* Bevis, *or some true*
Round-Table Knight, as ever fought
For Lady, to each Beauty brought.

Plant in your martial hands, War's *seat,*
  Your peaceful pledges of warm snow,
And, if a speaking touch repeat
  In Love's known language tales of woe,
Say, in soft whispers of the Palm,
'As Eyes shoot darts, so Lips shed balm.'

For though you seem, like Captives, led
　In triumph by the Foe away,
Yet on the Conqu'ror's neck you tread,
　And the fierce Victor proves your prey ;
What heart is then secure from you,
That can, though vanquish'd, yet subdue ?

The Song done, they retire, and the Masquers dance the
　Revels with the Ladies, which continued a great
　part of the night.

The Revels being past, and the King's Majesty seated
　under the State by the Queen, for Conclusion to
　this Masque there appears coming forth from one
　of the sides, as moving by a gentle wind, a great
　Cloud, which, arriving at the middle of the heaven,
　stayeth ; this was of several colours, and so great,
　that it covered the whole Scene. Out of the farther
　part of the heaven, began to break forth two other
　Clouds, differing in colour and shape ; and being
　fully discovered, there appeared sitting in one of
　them Religion, Truth, and Wisdom. Religion was
　apparelled in white, and part of her face was
　covered with a light veil, in one hand a book, and
　in the other a flame of fire : Truth in a Watchet [*Blue.*
　Robe, a Sun upon her fore-head, and bearing in
　her hand a Palm ; Wisdom in a mantle wrought
　with eyes and hands, golden rays about her head,
　and *Apollo's* Cithera in her hand. In the other [*Lyre,* or *Lute.*
　Cloud sate Concord, Government, and Reputation.
　The habit of Concord was Carnation, bearing in
　her hand a little faggot of sticks bound together,
　and on the top of it a heart, and a garland of corn
　on her head. Government was figured in a coat
　of Armour, bearing a shield, and on˜it a *Medusa's*
　head ; upon her [own] head a plumed helm, and
　in her right hand a Lance. Reputation, a young

man in a purple robe wrought with gold, and
wearing a laurel wreath on his head. These being
come down in an equal distance to the middle part
of the Air, the great Cloud began to break open,
out of which struck beams of light ; in the midst,
suspended in the Air, sate Eternity on a Globe ;
his garment was long, of a light blue, wrought all
over with Stars of gold, and bearing in his hand
a Serpent bent into a circle, with his tail in his
mouth.   In the firmament about him was a troop
of fifteen stars, expressing the stellifying of our
British Heroes ; but one more great and eminent
than the rest, which was over his head, figured his
Majesty. And in the lower part was seen, afar off,
the prospect of *Windsor* Castle, the famous seat of
the most honourable Order of the Garter.

The Fourth Song.

Eternity, Eusebeia, Aletheia, Sophia, Homonoia,
Dicæarche, Euphemia.

Eternity.

Be fixed, you rapid Orbs, that bear
The changing seasons of the year
On your swift wings, and see the old
Decrepit Sphere grown dark and cold ;
Nor did Jove *quench her fires : these bright*
Flames have eclipsed her sullen light :
This Royal Pair, for whom Fate will
Make Motion cease, and Time stand still :
Since Good is here so perfect, as no Worth
Is left for After-Ages to bring forth.

Eusebeia.

Mortality cannot with more
Religious zeal the Gods adore.

ALETHEIA.

My Truths, from human eyes conceal'd,
Are naked to their sight reveal'd.

SOPHIA.

Nor do their Actions from the guide
Of my exactest precepts slide.

HOMONOIA.

And as their own pure Souls entwined,
So are their Subjects' hearts combined.

DICÆARCHE.

So just, so gentle is their sway,
As it seems Empire to obey.

EUPHEMIA.

And their fair Fame, like incense hurl'd
On Altars, hath perfum'd the world.

SOPH., *Wisdom :*—ALETH., *Truth :*—EUSE., *Pure Adoration :*
HOM., *Concord:*—DICÆ., *Rule :*—EUPHEM., *Clear Reputation :*

CHORUS.

Crown this King, this Queen, this Nation !

CHORUS.

Wisdom, truth, pure adoration,
Concord, rule, clear reputation :
Crown this King, this Queen, this Nation !

ETERNITY.

Brave Spirits, whose advent'rous feet
  Have to the Mountain's top aspired,
Where fair Desert and Honour meet,
  Here from the toiling press retired,
Secure from all disturbing evil,
For ever in my Temple revel.

With wreaths of Stars circled about,
 Gild all the spacious firmament,
And, smiling on the panting Rout
 That labour in the steep ascent,
With your resistless influence guide
Of human change th' uncertain tide.

EUSEBEIA, ALETHEIA, SOPHIA.

But oh, you Royal Turtles, shed,
 When you from Earth remove,
On the ripe fruit of your chaste bed
 Those sacred seeds of Love.

CHORUS.

Which no Power can but yours dispense,
Since you the pattern bear from hence.

HOMONOIA, DICÆARCHE, EUPHEMIA.

Stuart race.]

Then from your fruitful race shall flow
 Endless Succession :
Sceptres shall bud, and laurels blow
 About their immortal Throne.

CHORUS.

Propitious Stars shall crown each birth,
Whilst you rule them, and they the Earth.

The Song ended, the two Clouds, with the persons
sitting on them, ascend ; the great Cloud closeth
again, and so passeth away overthwart the Scene,
leaving behind it nothing but a serene Sky. After
which, the Masquers danced their last dance, and
the Curtain was let fall.

The Names of the Masquers.

The King's Majesty.

Duke of LENNOX,	Lord FEILDING,
Earl of DEVONSHIRE,	Lord DIGBY,
Earl of HOLLAND,	Lord DUNGARVAN,
Earl of NEWPORT,	Lord DUNLUCE,
Earl of ELGIN,	Lord WHARTON,
Viscount GRANDISON,	Lord PAGET,
Lord RICH,	Lord SALTON.

The Names of the young Lords and Noble-men's Sons.

Lord WALDEN,	Mr. THOMAS HOWARD,
Lord CRANBORNE,	Mr. THOMAS EGERTON,
Lord BRACKLEY,	Mr. CHARLES CAVENDISH,
Lord CHANDOS,	Mr. ROBERT HOWARD,
Mr. WILLIAM HERBERT,	Mr. HENRY SPENCER.

The Songs and Dialogues in this Book [*Cœlum Britannicum*] were set with apt Tunes to them, by Mr. HENRY LAWES, one of His Majesty's Musicians.

[*This notice, of the Composer, was omitted from the* Masque, *editio princeps,* 1634; *and first added in the* 1640 *edition of Carew's Poems.*]

FINIS.

EXTRA POEMS FROM MANUSCRIPTS:

MORE OR LESS AUTHENTICATED.

EXTRA POEMS, FROM MANUSCRIPTS.

(More or less doubtful, or authenticated.)

To his Mistress retiring in Affection.

[*In* British Museum Addit. MS., 11811, fol. 6.]

FLY not from him whose silent misery
    Breathes many an unwitness'd sigh to thee,
Who having felt thy scorn, yet constant is,
And whom thou hast thy self called only his.
    When first mine eyes threw flames, whose spirit
        moved thee,
    Had'st thou not look'd again I had not loved thee.

Nature did ne'er two different things unite
With peace, which are by Nature opposite.
If thou force Nature, and be backward gone,
O, blame not me, that strive to draw thee on :
    But if my constant love shall fail to move thee,
    Then know my reason hates thee, though I love thee.

On his Mistress looking in a Glass.

[*This version*, Harleian MS. 6057, fol. 8, 9, *agrees with*
  'A Looking Glass ' *of* p. 16, *in first and second stanzas :
  but differs in the remainder, adding a seventh. Also in*
  Cosens' MS., A. 4to, *to which the marginalia refer.*]

THIS flattering Glass, whose smooth face wears
    Your shadow, where a sun appears,
Was once a River of my tears,

a. l. 'they.']   About your cold heart that did make
A circle, where the briny lake
Congeal'd into a Crystal cake

This Glass and shadow seem to say,
'Like us, the beauties you survey
a. l. 'or fly.']   Will quickly break, and fly away.'

Since then my tears can only show
You your own face, you cannot know
How fair you are, but by my woe.

Nor had the world else known your name,
But that my sad verse spread the fame
Of thee, most fair and cruel dame !

Forsake but your disdainful mind,
And in my songs the world shall find
That you are not more fair than kind.

Change but your scorn : my verse shall chase
Decay far from you, and your face
Shall shine with an immortal grace.

                                        TH. C.

EXCUSE OF ABSENCE.

[*In* Cosens' MS. ; *not elsewhere.   Probably genuine.*]

YOU'LL ask, perhaps, wherefore I stay,
    Loving so much, so long away ?
O do not think 'twas I did part,
It was my body, not my heart ;
For, like a Compass, on your love
One foot is fixed, and cannot move :
Th' other may follow the blind guide
Of giddy Fortune, but not slide
'Venter.']   Beyond your service, nor dare venture
To wander far from you, the centre.   T. C.

A Lady's Prayer to Cupid.

[*From* J. Cotgrave's 'Wit's Interpreter,' p. 116, 1655 ;
p. 223, 1671 : *and, like the preceding poem, signed with*
Carew's *initials*, 'T. C.,' *in the late* F. W. Cosens' MS.]

SINCE I must needs into thy School return,
Be pitiful, O Love, and do not burn
Me with desire of cold and frozen Age,
Nor let me follow a fond boy or page.
But, gentle *Cupid*, give me, if you can,
One to my love whom I may call a man ;
Of person comely, and of face as sweet,
Let him be sober, secret, and discreet,
Well practis'd in Love's school : let him within
Wear all his beard, and none upon his chin.

T. C.

Another Version of the Ribbon.

[*Compare* p. 26, *for the* 1640 *ed. printed text.*—Cosens' MS.
B. obl. 80, *an early inaccurate version, differs thus :*]

THIS silken wreath, which circles in mine arm,
Is but an Emblem of that mystic charm, ⌈'that mis-
Wherewith the magic of your beauty binds ⌊take:' C.
My captive heart, and round about it winds
Fetters of lasting love ; that doth entwine
My flesh alone : this makes my soul your shrine.
Consuming age may those weak bonds divide,
But this strong charm no eye shall see untied.
To that, as to a relic, I may give
An outward worship ; but by this I live.
My daily sacrifice and pray'rs to this :
There I but pray a superstitious kiss.
That is the Idol, this the deity :
Religion here is due, there, Ceremony :

I am to this, that's given to my trust,
There I may tribute pay, [but] there I must.
 That order as a layman I may bear ;
 But I become Love's priest when this I wear.
I over this, that over me commands :
This knot your Virtue ties ; but that, your hands.
 This Nature made, but that was made by Art :
 This makes my arm your prisoner, that, my heart

WHEN THE SNOW FELL.

[*This poem is from* Ashmole MS. 38, art. 11, *unsigned, and
following* 'The Amorous Fly'—'While this fly lived,'
etc., our p. 34. *It is printed in* 'Wit's Recreations,'
1645 ; *and* 'Wit's Interpreter,' 1655, 1671 ; *but there,
and elsewhere, the reading is,* 'I saw fair *Chloris* walk
alone,' *which suggests* Robert Herrick *as the author,
whose style it resembles.* It was not included among the
'Hesperides' *of* Herrick ; *it was possibly written by*
William Munsey (*who wrote* 'In the non-age of a
winter's day,' *for* Lawes' *Ayres*). *The title was,* '*Chloris
walking in the Snow.*' *To it music was composed by*
Henry Purcell ; *also by* Christopher Simpson, *in* John
Playford's 'Musical Companion,' p. 49, 1673 ; *but*
Purcell's *was in* Henry Playford's 'Theater of Musick,'
Part iii. p. 20, 1686.]

I SAW fair *Celia* walk alone ;
 When feather'd rain came softly down,

al. lect. 'And J.'] As *Jove* descending from his Tower
 To court her in a silver shower :
The wanton snow flew to-her breast,
Like pretty birds into their nest,
But overcome with whiteness there,

' g. dissolv'd.'] For grief it thaw'd into a tear :
 Thence falling on her garments' hem,

' freez'd.'] To deck her, froze into a Gem.

ODE.

[*This is from* Ashmole MS. 36, art. 198 : *where it follows* 'The Rapture,' *now reprinted on our* p. 45.]

*P*HILLIS, though thy powerful charms
  Have forced me from my *Celia's* arms —
A sure defence against all powers
But those resistless eyes of yours—
Think not your conquest to maintain
By rigour or unjust disdain ;
   In vain, fair Nymph, in vain you strive,
   For love doth seldom hope survive.

THE MOURNFUL PARTING OF TWO LOVERS,
CAUSED BY THE DISPROPORTION OF THEIR ESTATES.

[*Subscribed* 'T. Car.' *by a copyist, not original autograph, this poem is preserved in* Harleian MS. 6057, fol. 6 verso, *and* 7 recto. *There can be no reasonable doubt here : the internal evidence marks it to be by* Carew.]

MY once dear love, hapless that I no more
  Must call thee so, the rich affection's store
That fed our hopes lies now exhaust and spent,
Like sums of treasure unto bankrupts lent.

We, that did nothing study, but the way
To love each other : with which thoughts the day
Rose with delights to us, and with them set :
Must learn the hateful art—how to forget.

We, that did nothing wish, that heaven might give
Beyond ourselves, nor did desire to live
Beyond that night : all this now cancel must,
As is not writ in faith, but words and dust.

But witness those clear vows which lovers make :
Witness the chaste desires that never break
Into unruly heats : witness that breast
Which in thy bosom anchor'd his whole rest,

'Tis no default in us : I dare acquit
Thy maiden faith, thy purpose fair and white
As thy pure self.   Close planets did conspire
Our sweet felicity and hearts' desire,
Faster than vows could bind, so that the star
(When lovers meet) should stand opposed in war.

Since then some higher destinies command,
Let us not stir or labour to withstand
What is past help : the longest date of grief
Can never yield a hope of our relief.
And though we waste our selves in moist laments,
Tears may drown us, but not our discontents.

Fold back our arms ; take Honour's fruitless loves,
That must new fortunes try, like turtle-doves
Dislodged from their haunt : we must in tears
Unwind our loves, knit up in many years.

In this last kiss I here surrender thee
Back to thy self.   Lo ! thou again art free.
a.l. anoth. sad.] Thou in another kiss, as sad, resign'd
The truest heart that Lover e'er did bind.
        Now turn from each, so far, our sever'd hearts,
        As the divorced soul from the body parts.
                                T. CAR.

A HEALTH TO MY MISTRESS.

[*This, with title as above, is from* Harleian MS. 6057, fol.
7 verso, *with the signature* 'Th. Car.'   *It is printed
anonymously in* J. Cotgrave's 'Wit's Interpreter,' p. 42,
1655 ; p. 148, 1671, *as* 'A Health to *his* Mistress.']

'stories,' MS.]

TO her whose beauty doth excel
        Story, we toss these cups, and sell
Sobriety, a Sacrifice,
To the bright lustre of her eyes.
'sips this,' *Ibid.*]   Each soul that sips here is divine :
        Her beauty deifies the wine.   TH. CAR.

To his Unconstant Mistress.

[*Not included in any printed editions of* Carew *before* 1870.
From Harl. MS. 6057, fol. 11 vo, *and* 12, *signed* Th. Car.]

BUT say, you very woman ! why to me
 The fit of weakness and inconstancy ?
What forfeit have I made of word or vow,
That I am rack'd with thy displeasure now ?
If I have done a fault I do not shame
To cite it from thy lips : Give it a name.
I ask the Banns : stand forth and tell me, why ?
Did thy cloy'd appetite urge thee to try
If any other man could do 't as I ?—
I see friends are as clothes, laid up whilst new,
But after wearing cast, though ne'er so true.
Or did thy fierce ambition long to make
Some lover turn a martyr for thy sake ?—
Thinking thy beauty had deserved no name,
Unless some one had perish'd in the flame ;
  Upon whose loving dust this sentence lies :
  ' *Here one was murder'd by his Mistress' eyes ?*'

Or was't because my love to thee was such
I could not choose but blab it—swear how much
I was thy slave, and, doting, let thee know
I better could my self than thee forego ?
  Hearken, ye men ! that so shall love like me :
I'll give you counsel gratis ! if you be
Possess'd of what you like, let your fair friend
Lodge in your bosom, but no secrets send
To seek their lodging in a female breast,
For so much is abated of your rest.
  The steed that comes to understand his strength
Grows wild, and casts his manager at length ;
And the tame lover that unlocks his heart
Unto his Mistress, teaches her an art
To plague himself : shows her the secret way   ['plunge him s.
How she may tyrannise another day.

     M

And now, my fair Unkindness thus to thee !
Mark how wise passion and I agree :
Hear, and be sorry for 't : I will not die
To expiate thy crime of levity.

I walk (not cross-arm'd, neither), eat, and live ;
Yea, for to pity thy neglect—not grieve,
Nor envy him that by my loss hath won,
That thou art from thy faith and promise gone.
Thou shalt believe thy changing moon-like fits
Have not infected me, nor turn'd my wits
To Lunacy : I do not mean to weep,
When I should eat ; or sigh, when I should sleep.
I will not fall upon my pointed quill,
Bleed ink, and Poems or Invention spill,
To contrive ballads, or weave elegies,
For nurses' wearings when the infant cries ;
T. & Iseult.] Nor, like th' enamour'd *Tristrams* of the time,
Despair in prose, or hang myself in rhyme ;
Nor thither run upon my verses' feet,
Where I shall none but fools and madmen meet :
    Who 'midst the silent shades and myrtle walks,
    Pule and do penance for their Mistress' faults.

I'm none of those Poetic malcontents,
Born to make paper dear with my laments,
Orl. Furioso.] Or vile *Orlando*, that will rail and vex,
And for thy sake fall out with all thy sex.
No : I will love again, and seek a prize
That shall redeem me from thy poor despise ;
I'll court my fortune now in such a shape
That will not feign die, nor stern choler take.
Thus launch I off with triumph from thy shore,
To which my last Farewell ! for never more
Will I touch there ; or put to sea again,
Blown with the churlish wind of thy disdain.
    Nor will I stop the course till I have found
    A coast that yields safe harbour and firm ground.

Smile ye, Love's stars ! wing'd with desires, fly
To make my wished-for discovery :
   Nor doubt I but for one that proves like you,
   I shall find ten as fair, and yet more true.

TH. CAR.

['The Enquiry'—'Amongst the myrtles as I walked,' [*Cf.* p. 228.
was given among Carew's, *on our* p. 65; *and also* 'The
Primrose'—'Ask me why I send you here,' *on* p. 73;
although both of them were included among Robert Herrick's
'Hesperides,' 1648, *and strongly resemble his style. Both
belong to the posthumous* 1640 *edition of* Carew, pp. 170, 188,
where 'The Primrose' *is a superior version. Did* Carew
and Herrick *write it, conjointly, in friendly emulation? We
distrust* Herrick's *variations, which are later and weaker.*]

VERSES.

[*From Mr.* Wyburd's MS., *where they immediately precede the
Song of* p. 69, 'Ask me no more where *Jove* bestows :'
a poem indisputably Carew's ; *one often parodied in Civil-
War time, e.g.* 'Ask me no more why there appears'
(*see* pp. 232, 183). *Imitated, without acknowledgment,
by* Alfred Tennyson, *in second edition of his* 'Princess.'
*These Verses are fragmentary. The authorship seems to
be worse than doubtful; without true claim on* Carew.
Included in the Roxburghe Library *edition,* 1870, *they
are retained, under protest, and not accepted as* Carew's.]

HE gave her Jewels in a Cup of Gold,
   Wherein were graven stories done of old ;
And in his hand he held a book, which show'd
The birth-stars of the City, where *Brute* plough'd
The furrows for the wall : on every page
A King was drawn, his fortune and his age ;
But she liked best, and loved to see again
The *British Princes* that had marched with *Spain,*
   Thus enter'd she the Court, where every one
   To entertain her made provision.

[Thus far we might believe the fragment held some Courtly reference to the Queen Henrietta Maria, in sympathy with her antecedent rival, the Infanta of Spain. What follows is mere rambling incoherence: in no way resembling Carew. To print the lines is virtually to condemn them.]

'Naïs,' MS.] *Naïs* had angled all the night, and took
The Trout, the Gudgeon with her silver hook :
The Graces all were busy in the Downs,
In gathering sallets and in wreathing crowns :
The wood-nymphs ran about, and, while 'twas dark,
Cf. Nares, s. v.] With light and lowe-bell caught the amazed Lark :
One with some hairs, pluck'd from a Centaur's tail,
Made springes for the woodcock in the dale :
One spread her net the Coney to ensnare :
Another with her hounds pursued the hare.
Diana, early, with her bugle clear,
Armed with a quiver, shot the fallow deer.
The stately Stag, hit with her fatal shaft,
Shed tears in falling, while the Huntress laugh'd.
All sent their gains to *Hymen* for a present,
The Buck, the Partridge, and the painted Pheasant ;
And *Jove*, to grace the feast of *Hymen's* joy,
Sent thither Nectar by his *Trojan* Boy.
Cætera desunt.] The Graces and the Dryades were there, etc.

THE HUE AND CRY.

[This version, which is the earlier-printed by seven years, differs so greatly from the one similarly-named on our p. 71, reprinted from p. 184 of 'Carew's Poems,' 1640, editio princeps, that the reproduction of both is necessary. There need be no hesitation in assigning solely to Carew their authorship, although the present version appeared in James Shirley's 'Wittie Fair One,' 1633, a comedy acted so early as 1628. 'Would you know what's soft?' p. 70, and 'To his Mistress Confined,' on p. 72, both of them by Carew, no less confusingly adorn Shirley's play, mixed with his own work, and not disclaimed. Perhaps the friends joined in writing the Hue and Cry.]

IN Love's name you are charged hereby
To make a speedy Hue and Cry
After a face, which t'other day
Came and stole my heart away.
For your directions, in brief,
These are best marks to know the thief :
Her hair a net of beams would prove,
Strong enough to captive *Jove*,
Playing the Eagle : her clear brow
Is a comely field of snow.
A sparkling eye, so pure a grey,
As when it shines it needs no day.
Ivory dwelleth on her nose ;
Lilies married to the Rose
Have made her cheek the nuptial bed ;
Lips betray their virgins' weed :
As they only blush'd for this,
That they one another kiss.
But observe, beside the rest,
You shall know this felon best
By her tongue ; for if your ear
Shall once a heavenly music hear,
Such as neither gods nor men
But from that voice shall hear again,
 That, that is she : oh, take her t' ye ;
 None can rock heaven asleep but she.

[*Variations of this song, in* Shirley's Poems, 1646 :—
Dress'd in his Eagle's shape : Her brow
Is a spacious field of snow :
Her eyes so rich, so pure a grey,
Every look creates a day.
And if they close themselves (not when
The Sun doth set) 'tis night again.
In her cheeks are to be seen
Of flowers both the King and Queen,
Thither by all the Graces led,
And smiling in their nuptial bed.
On whom, like pretty nymphs, do wait,
Her twin-born lips, whose virgin state
They do deplore themselves, nor miss
To blush, so often as they kiss,
Without a man.   Beside the rest, *etc.*]

ANOTHER HUE AND CRY.

[*We utterly disbelieve that this can possibly be by* Thomas
Carew. *It has no authentication whatever, beyond the
fact of its presence in Mr.* Wyburd's MS., *along with
several indisputable works by* Carew ; *all more or less
inaccurately transcribed, the variations being generally
corruptions of text. It somewhat resembles* 'Beauties,
have you seen a toy, called Love, a winged Boy?'
which is in 'Prince D'Amour,' 1660. *The song was
written by* Ben Jonson, *and printed in his* 'Hue and
Cry after Cupid :' *a Masque, with Nuptial-Songs, on
the Lord Viscount Haddington's marriage,* 1608 : Henry
Lawes *composed fresh music to it. Earlier, in* 1605,
came 'The Cryer,' *beginning* 'Good folk, for gold or
hire, but help me to a cryer :' *printed by* Anderson
as Michael Drayton's, *in Brit. Poets, iii.* 585, 1793.]

G OOD folk, for gold or hire, One help me to a Crier ;
⠀⠀For my poor heart is gone astray,
⠀⠀⠀⠀After two eyes that pass'd this way.
If there be any man, in town or country can
Bring me my heart again, I'll pay him for his pain.
⠀⠀⠀⠀And by these marks I will you show
⠀⠀⠀⠀That only I this heart do owe,

=own.]⠀⠀⠀It is a wounded Hart, wherein yet sticks the dart ;
⠀⠀⠀⠀Maim'd in every part throughout it,
⠀⠀⠀⠀'Faith and Troth' writ about it :

=heart.]⠀It was a tame Hart and a Dear, and never used to roam ;
But having got this haunt, I fear, 'twill never bide at
⠀⠀⠀⠀home.
⠀⠀⠀⠀For God's sake, passing by the way,
⠀⠀⠀⠀⠀⠀If you my heart do see,
⠀⠀⠀⠀Either impound it for a stray,
⠀⠀⠀⠀⠀⠀Or send it home to me.

[' *The Hue and Cry' of the* Carew-Shirley *lines is transferred into a search for the Lady, instead of after Cupid. All these versions had been suggested by one original,* viz. *this of* Eρως Δραπετης = *Cupid, by* Moschus, *his first Idyll.* Tasso *drew his* Amor Fugitivo *from the same source :—*

Δραπετίδας εμός ἐστιν· ὁ μανυτὰς γέρας ἐξεῖ
Μισθός τοι τὸ φίλαμα τὸ Κύπριδος· ἢν δ' ἀγάγης νιν,
Οὐ γυμνὸν τὸ φίλαμα, τὺ δ', ὦ ξένε, καὶ πλέον ἐξεῖς.]

To Cœlia.

[*A short version of the* Carew *Song on p.* 77, *beginning similarly, but here reprinted as in* J. Cotgrave's ' Wit's Interpreter,' *p.* 28, 1655 ; *p.* 133, 1671.]

R ISE, lovely *Cœlia,* and be kind,
　　Let my desires freedom find ;
　　And we'll make the Gods confess,
　　Mortals enjoy some happiness :
　　　　　Sit thee down.
Cupid hath but one bow, yet can I spy
A thousand *Cupids* in thy eye ;
　　Nor may the Gods behold our bliss,
　　For sure thine eyes do darken his.
　　　　　If thou fearest,
That he'll betray thee with his light,
Let me eclipse thee [from] his sight ;　　　　　[*Misp.* 'with.'
　　And whilst I shade thee from his eye,
　　Oh ! let me hear thee gently cry,
　　　　　'I yield !'

[*Compare the* ' Princess' *song, suggested by* Carew, *ending—*
' Ask me no more : *thy fate and mine are seal'd :*
　I strove against the stream and all in vain :
　Let the great river take me to the main :
　No more, dear love, for at a touch I yield :
　　　　　Ask me no more !'　　　　　*Cf.* pp. 69, 179.]

[*This* Prologue *and this* Epilogue *to an Entertainment at* Whitehall—*probably the same which had included the* 'Four Songs' *given on* pp. 56-61—*form the most important addition to* Carew's *poems furnished by Mr.* Wyburd's MS., *wherein alone they were preserved.* Thomas Killigrew *recorded that* 'The Masque' *was acted (like* 'Cœlum Britannicum') *in* 1633.]

The Prologue to a Play presented before the King and Queen, at an Entertainment of them by the Lord Chamberlain, at Whitehall. [1633.]

SONG.

SIR,

SINCE you have pleased this night t' unbend
   Your serious thoughts, and with your Person lend
Your Palace out, and so are hither brought
A stranger : in your own house not at home ;
Divesting State, as if you meant alone
To make your Servants' loyal heart your throne :
Oh, see how wide these valves themselves display
To entertain his Royal guests ! survey
What Arcs triumphal, Statues, altars, shrines,
Inscribed to your great names, he these assigns :
So from that stock of zeal, his coarse cates may
Borrow some relish, though but thinly they
Cover'd his narrow table : so may these
Succeeding trifles by that title please.
Else, gracious Madam, must the influence
Of your fair eyes' propitious beams dispense,
To crown such pastimes as he could provide
To oil the lazy minutes as they slide.
For well he knows upon your smile depends
This night's success ; since that alone commends
   All his endeavours, gives the music praise,
   Painters and us, and gilds the Poet's bays.

The Epilogue to the same Play.

HUNGER is sharp, the sated stomach dull :
 Feeding delights 'twixt emptiness and full :
The pleasure lies not in the end, but streams
That flow betwixt two opposite extremes.
 So doth the flux from hot to cold combine
An equal temper ; such is noble wine,
'Twixt fulsome must and vinegar too tart.
Pleasure 's the scratching betwixt itch and smart : ['Measures.'
 It is a shifting *Tartar*, that still flies
 From place to place : if it stand still, it dies.
After much rest, labour delights ; when pain
Succeeds long travail, rest grows sweet again. .
  Pain is the base, on which his nimble feet
  Move in continual change from sour to sweet.

 This the Contriver of your sports to-night
Hath well observed, and so, to fix delight
In a perpetual circle, hath applied
The choicest objects that care could provide
To every sense. Only himself hath felt
The load of this great honour, and doth melt
All into humble thanks, and at your feet—
Of both your Majesties—prostrates the sweet
Perfume of grateful service, which he swears
He will extend to such a length of years
  As fits not us to tell, but doth belong
  To a far abler pen and nobler tongue.

 Our task ends here : if we have hit the laws
Of true delight, his glad heart joys : yet, 'cause
You cannot to succeeding pleasures climb,
Till you grow weary of the instant time,
He was content this last piece should grow sour
Only to sweeten the ensuing hour.
But if the Cook, Musician, Player, Poet,
Painter, and all, have fail'd, he'll make them know it,
  That have abused him : yet must grieve at this,
  He should do penance, when the sin was his.

To Mistress *Katherine Neville,*

on her Green Sickness.

[*Compare* p. 101. *Printed anonymously in* Musarum Deliciæ,
1655 ; *but bearing the signature* ' Tho. Carew ' *in* Addit.
MSS. 11811, fol. 11, *and* 23118, fol. 43. *It is also in
the* Wyburd MS., *which alone has not been collated : but
this probably reads in 6th line,* 'That he may never
backward flow,' *and in 12th line,* 'Least to thy heart
he take his course.' *We follow the other MSS. The
evidence, internal and external, amply substantiates the
claim of* Carew *to this poem. He appears to have been
on terms of close intimacy with the* Nevilles, Katherine
and Mary, *and their brother,* Gilbert, *to whom he wrote
from their residence at* Wrest *House and Park, six miles
south of* Bedford, *and not far from* Woburn : *see* p. 125.]

WHITE Innocence, that now liest spread,
　　Forsaken on thy widow'd bed,
Cold and alone, if fear, love, hate,
Or shame recall thy Crimson Mate,
From his dark mazes to reside
With thee his chaste and maiden Bride :—
Least that he backward thence should flow,
Congeal him with thy virgin snow.
　　But if his own heat, with thy pair

Cf. p. 234.]　Of neighbouring Suns and flaming hair,
Thaw him into a new divorce ;
Least that from thee he take his course—
Oh, lodge me there, where I'll defeat
All future hopes of his retreat,
And force the fugitive to seek
A constant station in thy cheek.
　　　So each shall keep his proper place,
　　　I in your heart, he in your face.
　　　　　　　　　　　　Tho. Carew.

ANOTHER OF THE SAME TITLE.

SONG.

[*ot in the early printed editions, or known in* MS. *except*
Wyburd's. *No reader who appreciates the tender beauty
and elegance of* Carew, *when at his best, can willingly
accept for his, this weak and displeasing allegory of a
pale sickly lady, represented as a ' beautous Island,' sur-
rounded like* Albion *and* Venus *by ' her white frothy bed
and native foam,' on such utterly inadequate evidence as
the fact of it being contained in the* Wyburd MS., *the
errors in which are both numerous and glaring. This is
shown by collation with other* MSS. *whenever they are
attainable, or still better, by comparison with the early-
printed text, when any are included in the* 1640 *edition.*]

B RIGHT *Albion,* where the Queen of Love
    Pressing the pinion of her snow-white dove,
  With silver harness o'er thy fair
  Region in triumph drives her ivory chair ;
Where now retired she rests at home
In her white frothy bed and native foam ;
  Where the grey morn, through mists of lawn
  Snowing soft pearls, shoots an eternal dawn
On thy *Elizian* shade : Thou blest
Empire of love and beauty, unpossess'd,   [*Contrast,* p. 33.
  Chaste virgin kingdom ! but create
  Me Monarch of thy free Elective State :
Let me surround with circling arms
My beauteous Island, and with amorous charms
    Mixt with this flood of frozen snow,
    In crimson streams I'll force the red sea flow.

MR. *CAREW* TO HIS FRIEND.

[*In* Ashmole MS. 38, art. 81, *and from it printed by* Bliss *in
his edition of* Anthony à Wood's 'Athenæ Oxonienses,'
ii. 659, 1813–20. *It cannot be considered doubtful. It
bears internally his sign manual, as certainly as the
poem on p.* 187 *lacks it. Moreover,* Wood *and his
excellent annotator, Dr.* Philip Bliss, *erred seldom in
their ascriptions of authorship.*]

LIKE to the hand, that hath been used to play
   One lesson long, still runs the self-same way,
And waits not what the heavens bid it strike,
But doth presume by Custom 'this will like :'
So run my thoughts, which are so perfect grown,
So well acquainted with my passion,
That now they dare prevent me with their haste,
And ere I think to sigh, my sigh is past :
It's past and flown to you, for you alone
Are all the object that I think upon :
   And did you not supply my soul with thought,
   For want of action it to none were brought.

   What though, our absent arms may not enfold
Real embraces, yet we firmly hold
Each other in possession ; thus we see
The lord enjoys his land, where e'er he be.
If kings possess'd no more than where they sate,
What would they, greater than a mean estate ?
   This makes me firmly yours, you firmly mine,
   That something more than bodies us combine.
                FINIS : THO. CAREW.

! were rash to attribute the following saucy and audacious
poem to Thomas Carew, *because it bears* Celia's *name.*
Truly, it has his elegance and light touch. It appears to
have been first printed in Cotgrave's 'Wit's Interpreter,'
p. 106, 1655; *p.* 212, *edit.* 1671; *and there anonymously.*
To it is held resemblance by a daring pre-Restoration
ditty, 'When I my Mistress do intend to flatter.']

LOVE'S FLATTERY.

[Music by Dr.
Colman.

W HEN, *Celia*, I intend to flatter you,
    And tell you lies to make you true,
        I swear
        There's none so fair :
    And you believe it too.

Oft have I match'd you with the Rose, and said
No Twins so like hath Nature made ;
        But 'tis
        Only in this :—
    You prick my hand, and fade.

Oft have I said there is no precious stone,
But may be found in you alone ;
        Though I
        No stone espy—
    Unless your heart be one.

When I praise your skin, I quote the wool
That silk-worms from their entrails pull ;
        And show
        That new-fall'n snow,
    Is not more beautiful.

Yet grow not proud, by such Hyperboles !
Were you as excellent as these,
        While I
        Before you lie,
    They might be had with ease.

Four unauthenticated Epigrams.

[Robert Herrick, *true poet and divine though he was, indulged
himself occasionally, and amused his boon companions,
by writing several* Epigrams : *which we might have lost
without serious bereavement. Vulgar personalities, or*
Nugæ Venales, *such as the following meritless four,
rashly attributed to* Carew, *in* Harl. MS. 6917, *are far
more akin to some trifles by* Herrick. *After all, it counts
well for* Carew *that we know the very worst follies that
had ever been attributed to his pen, and yet that these
held so little evil. They are included here unwillingly.*]

On *Munday* of *Oxford*.

GOD bless the Sabbath, fie on worldly pelf !
  The week begins on *Tuesday: Munday* has
    hanged himself.

Epigram.

CALL *Philip* 'flat-nose,' and he frets at that :
  And yet this *Philip* hath a nose that's flat.

On one that died of the Wind-Colic.

HERE lies *John Dumbelow*, who died because he
    was so :
If his tail could have spoke, his heart had not broke.

On a Child's Death.

A CHILD, and dead ! alas, how could it come ?
  Surely the Thread of Life was but a thrum.

A PARAPHRASE OF CERTAIN PSALMS.

These are nearly all transcribed from Ashmole MS. 38, art. 15. Psalm civ. *is also in* Brit. Museum Addit. MS. 22, 118, fol. 36. *But for* Psalm cxix., *imperfect, possibly mutilated, and not collated anew, the sole authority is the* Wyburd MS. *They have no higher literary merit than* Milton's *attempts. The atmosphere of* Sternhold *and* Hopkins *surrounds them, like miasma. But it should be remembered that they were copies, of rough drafts, not corrected by the author. This has been ungenerously forgotten by one so notable as the Rev. Dr. Augustus* Jessopp, *who—in the Dict. Nat. Biog., ix. 63, 1887— tells of* Carew *having been 'stricken down by mortal sickness,' so that 'it looks as if his life had been shortened by his irregular habits;' also that* Hales *of* Eton *'seems to have thought very meanly of him, and made no secret of his low opinion;' which 'low opinion' casts discredit solely on the said* Hales *himself, and any Biographer who endorses the Etonian's slanders and betrayal of Confessional-secrets, thus infamously revealed after* Carew's *death: but see note, p. 248. He is careful to add that 'Carew has left some wretched attempts at versifying a few of the Psalms;' winding up with 'the illness that led him to a maudlin kind of repentance seems to have come upon him when he was in the country.' From an ecclesiastic who writes thus, no penitent could gather any comfort or direction: nor from* John Hales.]

PSALM I.

I.

HAPPY the man that doth not walk
　　In wicked counsels, nor hath lent
His glad ear to the railing talk
　　Of scorners, nor his prompt steps bent
　　To wicked paths, where sinners went.

2. But to those safer tracts confined,
    Which God's Law-giving finger made :
Never withdraws his wearied mind
    From practice of that holy trade,
    By noon-day's sun or midnight's shade.

3. Like the fair plant whom neighbouring floods
    Refresh, whose leaf feels no decays ;
That not alone with flattering buds,
    But early fruits, his Lord's hope pays :
    So shall he thrive in all his ways.

4. But the loose Sinner shall not share
    So fix'd a state ; like the light dust
That up and down the empty air
    The wild wind drives with various gust,
    So shall cross-fortunes toss th' Unjust.

5. Therefore, at the last Judgment-day,
    The trembling sinful soul shall hide
His confused face, nor shall he stay
    Where the elected troops abide,
    But shall be chased far from their side.

6. For the clear paths of Righteous men
    To the all-seeing Lord are known ;
But the dark maze and dismal den,
    Where Sinners wander up and down,
    Shall by his hand be overthrown.

PSALM 2.

1, 2, 3.

WHY rage the Heathen ? wherefore swell
    The People with vain thoughts ? why meet
Their Kings in counsel to rebel
    'Gainst God and Christ, trampling His sweet
    But broken bonds under their feet ?

4, 5, 6.

Alas ! the glorious God that hath
  His throne in heaven, derides th' unsound
Plots of weak Mortals : in His wrath
  Thus shall He speak : 'My self have crown'd
  The Monarch of My holy ground.'

7, 8.

I will declare what God hath told ;
  'Thou art My Son ; this happy day
Did Thy incarnate birth unfold :
  Ask, and the Heathen shall obey,
  With the remotest earth, Thy sway.'

9, 10, 11.

Thy Rod of Iron shall, if Kings rise
  Against Thee, bruise them into dust,
Like pots of clay : therefore be wise,
  Ye Princes, and learn judgments just :
  Serve God with fear : tremble, yet trust.

12.

Kiss, and do homage to the Son,
  Lest His displeasure ruin bring :
For if the fire be but begun,
  Then happy those that themselves fling
  Under the shelter of His wing.

PSALM 51.

1.

GOOD God, unlock thy magazines
  Of Mercy, and forgive my sins.

2. Oh, wash and purify the foul
  Pollution of my sin-stain'd soul.

3. For I confess my faults, that lie
  In horrid shapes before mine eye.

N

4. Against Thee only and alone,
In Thy sight, was this evil done,
That all men might Thy Justice see
When Thou art judged for judging me.

5. Even from my birth I did begin
With mother's milk to suck in sin.

6. But Thou lovest truth, and shalt impart
Thy secret wisdom to my heart.

7. Thou shalt with 'ysop purge me, so
Shall I seem white as mountain snow.

8. Thou shalt send joyful news, and then
My broken bones grow strong again.

9. Let not Thine eyes my sins survey ;
But cast those cancell'd debts away.

10. Oh, make my cleans'd heart a pure cell,
Where a renewed spirit may dwell.

11. Cast me not from Thy sight, nor chase
Away from me Thy spirit of grace.

12. Send me Thy saving health again,
And with Thy Spirit those joys maintain.

13. Then will I preach Thy ways, and draw
Converted sinners to Thy law.

14, 15. Oh God, my God of health, unseal
My blood-shut lips, and I'll reveal
What mercies in Thy justice dwell,
And with loud voice Thy praises tell.

16, 17. Could sacrifice have purged my vice,
Lord, I had brought Thee sacrifice ;
But though Burnt Offerings are refused,
Thou shalt accept the heart that's bruised :
The humbled soul, the spirit oppress'd,
Lord, such oblations please Thee best.

18. Bless *Sion*, Lord ! repair with pity
The ruins of Thy Holy City.

19. Then will we holy dower present Thee,
And peace offerings that content Thee ;
And then Thine Altars shall be press'd
With many a sacrificed beast.

PSALM 91.

1, 2, 3.

MAKE the great God thy Fort, and dwell
In Him by faith and do not care
(So shaded) for the Power of hell,
   Or for the cunning Fowler's snare,
   Or poison of th' infected air.

4, 5. His plumes shall make a downy bed,
   Where thou shalt rest : He shall display
His wings of truth over thy head,
   Which, like a shield, shall drive away
   The fears of Night, the darts of Day.

6, 7. The winged Plague that flies by night,
   The murdering Sword that kills by day,
Shall not thy peaceful sleeps affright,
   Though on thy right and left hand they
   A thousand and ten thousand slay.

8, 9, 10. Yet shall thine eyes behold the fall
   Of sinners ; but, because thy heart
Dwells with the Lord, not one of all
   Those ills, nor yet the plaguy dart,
   Shall dare approach near where thou art.

11–13. His Angels shall direct thy legs,
   And guard them in the stony streets :
On lion's whelps and adder's eggs
   Thy steps shall march ; and if thou meet
   With Dragons, they shall kiss thy feet.

14, 15, 16.

When thou art troubled, He shall hear,
　And help thee, for thy love embraced
And knew His name ; therefore He'll rear
　Thy honours high, and, when thou hast
　Enjoy'd them long, save thee at last.

PSALM 104.

1.

a. l. ' glorious.']

M Y Soul the great God's praises sings
　　Encircled round with Glory's wings ;

2.

Clothed with light, o'er Whom the sky
Hangs like a starry canopy ;

3.

Who dwells upon the gliding streams,
Enamel'd with His golden beams :
Enthroned in clouds, as in a chair,
He rides in triumph through the air.

4.

The winds and flaming Element
Are on His great Ambassage sent.

5.

The fabric of the Earth shall stand
For aye, built by His powerful hand.

6, 7, 8, 9.

The floods, that with their wat'ry robe
Once cover'd all this earthly Globe,
Soon as Thy thundering voice was heard,
Fled fast, and straight the hills appear'd :
The humble valleys saw the Sun,
Whilst the affrighted waters run
Into their channels, and no more
Shall drown the Earth, or pass the shore.

10.

Amongst those Vales the cold springs flow,
And wash the mountains' feet below.

11.

Hither for drink the whole herd strays :
There the wild Ass his thirst allays :

12.

And on the boughs that shade the spring
The feather'd Choir shall sit and sing.

13, 14, 15.

When on her womb Thy dew is shed
The pregnant Earth is brought to bed,
And, with a fruitful birth increased,
Yields herbs and grass for man and beast :
Heart-strengthening bread, care-drowning wine,
And oil that makes the face to shine.

16.

On *Lebanon* His cedars stand :
Trees full of sap, works of His hand.

17.

In them the Birds their cabins dight :
The fir-tree is the Stork's delight.

18.

The wild Goat on the hills, in cells
Of rocks the hermit Coney, dwells.

19.

The Moon observes her course ; the Sun
Knows when his weary race is done.

20.

And when the Night her dark veil spreads,
The wilder beasts forsake their sheds :

21.

The hungry Lions hunt for blood,
And roaring beg from God their food.

22, 23.

The Sun returns : these beasts of prey
Fly to their dens, and from the day ;
And whilst they in dark caverns lurk,
Man till the evening goes to work.

24.

How full of creatures is the Earth
To which Thy wisdom gave their birth !

25.

And those that in the wide Sea breed,
The bounds of number far exceed.

26.

There the huge Whales with finny feet
Dance underneath the sailing fleet.

27, 28, 29, 30.

All these expect their nourishment
From Thee, and gather what is sent.
Be Thy hand open, they are fed,
Be Thy face hid, astonished :
'withhold,'⎤ If Thou withdraw their Soul, they must
Add. MS. ⎦ Return unto their former Dust :
If Thou send back Thy breath, the face
Of th' Earth is spread with a new race.

31.

God's glory shall for ever stay ;
He shall with joy His works survey.

32, 33.

The steadfast Earth shall shake, if He
Look down, and if the mountains be
Touch'd, they shall smoke ; yet still my verse
Shall, whilst I live, His praise rehearse.

34.

In Him with joy my thoughts shall meet ;
He makes my meditations sweet.

35.

The Sinner shall appear no more :
Then, O my Soul, the Lord adore !

THO. CAREW.   [Add. MS.

PSALM 113.

1, 2, 3.

YE children of the Lord, that wait
  Upon His will, sing Hymns divine,
From henceforth to time's endless date,
  To His name : praised from the first shine
  Of th' Earth's Sun, till it decline.

4, 5, 6.

The hosts of Heaven or Earth have none
  May to His height of glory rise ;
For who like Him hath fix'd His throne
  So high, yet bends down to the skies,
  And lower-Earth, His humble eyes ?

7, 8, 9.

The Poor from loathed dust He draws,
  And makes them regal state invest
'Mongst kings ; He gives His people laws :
  He makes the barren mother rest
  Under her roof, with Children blest.

PSALM 114.

1, 2. WHEN the seed of *Jacob* fled
   From the cruel *Pharaoh's* land,
 Judah was in safety led
  By the Lord, whose powerful hand
  Guided all the *Hebrew* band.

3, 4. This the Sea saw, and dismay'd
t. 'flies.']   Fled : swift *Jordan* backward makes :
  Mountains skip, like rams afraid ;
  And the lower hillocks shake,
Ash. MS.,]
' afraid.'] Like the tender lambs [that quake].

5, 6. What, O Sea, hath thee dismay'd ?
  Why did *Jordan* backwards make ?
  Mountains why, like rams afraid,
  Skipt ye ? wherefore did ye shake,
  Hillocks, like the lambs that quake.

7, 8. Tremble, O thou steadfast Earth,
  At the presence of the Lord !
  That makes rocks give rivers birth,
  And by virtue of Whose word
  Flints shall flowing springs afford.

PSALM 119.

[*From Mr.* Wyburd's MS., *no other copy known.*]

ALEPH. *Beati Immaculati.*

1. BLEST is he that spotless stands
  In the way of God's commands.

2. Blessed he that keeps His word :
  Whose entire heart seeks the Lord ;

3. For the man, that walketh in
  His just paths, commits no sin.

4. By Thy strict commands we are
Bound to keep Thy laws with care.

['thine,' *Wyb.*

5. O that my steps might not slide
From Thy statutes' perfect guide.

6. So shall I decline Thy wrath,
Treading Thy commanded path ;

7. Having learn'd Thy righteous ways,
With true heart I'll sing Thy praise.

8. In Thy statutes I'll persever :
Then forsake me not for ever !

[' perséver.'

BETH. *In quo corriget?*

9. How shall Youth, but by the level
Of Thy word, be kept from evil ?

10. Let my soul, that seeks the way
Of Thy truth, not go astray.

11. Where, lest my frail feet might slide,
In my heart Thy words I hide.

12. Blest be Thou, O Lord ! O show
How I may Thy statutes know.

13. I have publish'd the divine
Judgments of Thy mouth with mine ;

14. Which have fill'd my soul with pleasure
More than all the heaps of treasure.

15. They shall all the subject prove
Of my talk and of my love.

16. Those, my darlings, no time shall
From my memory let fall.

GIMEL.   *Retribue servo tuo.*

17. Let Thy grace, O Lord, preserve me,
That I may but live to serve Thee.

18. Open my dark eyes, that I
May Thy wondrous laws descry.

19. Let Thy glorious light appear :
I am but a pilgrim here.

20. Yet the zeal of their desire
Hath even set my heart on fire.

21. Thy fierce rod and curse o'ertaketh
Him that proudly Thee forsaketh.

22. I have kept Thy laws, O God :
Turn from me Thy curse and rod !

23. Though combined Princes rail'd,
Yet thy Servant hath not fail'd

24. In their study to abide ;
For they are my joy, my guide.

DALETH.   *Adhæsit pavimento.*

25. For Thy word's sake, give new birth
To my soul that cleaves to earth.

26. Thou hast heard my tongue untwine
All my ways : Lord, teach me Thine !

27. Make me know them, that I may
All Thy wondrous works display.

28. Thou hast said the word : then bring
Ease to my soul, languishing.

29. Plant in me Thy laws' true love,
And the Veil of lies remove.

30. I have chosen Truth to lie
    The fix'd object of mine eye.

31. On Thy word my faith I grounded,
    Let me not then be confounded.

32. When my soul from bonds is freed,
    I shall run Thy ways with speed.

HE. *Legem pone.*

33. Teach me, Lord, Thy ways, and I
    From that road will never fly.

34. Give me knowledge, that I may
    With my heart Thy laws obey.

35. Unto that path my steps move,
    For I there have fix'd my love.

36. Fill my heart with those pure fires,
    Not with covetous desires.

37. Blind to vain sights, let me be ;   [Transposed.
    But Thy ways let me see.   'To . . be B.'

38. Make Thy promise firm to me,
    That with fear have served Thee.

39. 'Cause Thy judgments ever were
    Sweet, divert the shame I fear.

40. Let not him, for justice, perish,   [*t.* 'in justice.']
    That desires Thy laws to cherish.

VAU. *Et venias super me.*

41. Let Thy loving mercies cure me,
    As Thy promises assure me ;

42. So shall the blasphemers see
    I not vainly trust in Thee ;

43. Take not quite the words away
   Of Thy truth, that are my stay :

MS. 'even till.']

44. Then I'll keep Thy laws, until
   Winged time it self stand still.

45. And, whilst I pursue Thy search,
   With secure steps will I march.

46. Unashamed I'll record,
   Even before great kings, Thy word.

47. That shall be my joy, for there
   My thoughts ever fixed were ;

48. With bent mind and stretch'd-out hands
   I will seek Thy loved commands.

ZAINE.   *Memor esto Verbi tui.*

49. Think upon Thy promise made,
   For in that my trust is laid ;

50. That, my comfort in distress :
   That hath brought my life redress.

51. Though the proud hath scorn'd me, they
   Make me not forsake Thy way ;

52. Thy eternal judgments brought
   Joy to my rememb'ring thought ;

53. With great sorrow I am taken,
   When I see Thy laws forsaken :

54. Which have made me songs of mirth,
   In this pilgrimage of Earth.

55. Which I mindful was to keep,
   When I had forgot to sleep :

56. Thy commands I did embrace,
   Therefore I obtain'd Thy grace.

HETH. *Portio mea, Domine.*

57. Thou, O Lord, art my reward :
To Thy laws my thoughts are squared ;

58. With an humble heart I crave,
Thou wilt promised mercy have.

59. I have mark'd my ways, and now
To Thy ways my feet I bow.

60. Nor have I the time delay'd,
But with haste this journey made,

61. Where, though bands of sinners lay
Snaring nets, I keep my way.

62. I my self at midnight raise,
Singing Thy just judgments' praise.

63. I converse with those that bear
To Thy laws obedient fear.

64. Teach me them, Lord, by that grace
Which hath fill'd the world's wide space.

.   .   .   .   .   .
.   .   .   .   .   .

[*Cætera desunt.*]

PSALM 137.

1. SITTING by the streams that glide
Down by *Babel's* towering wall,
With our tears we fill'd the tide,
Whilst our mindful thoughts recall
Thee, O *Sion*, and thy fall.

2. Our neglected harps unstrung,
 Not acquainted with the hand
Of the skilful tuner, hung
 On the willow trees that stand
 Planted in the Neighbour Land.

3. Yet the spiteful foe commands
 Songs of mirth, and bids us lay
To dumb harps our Captive hands,
 And, to scoff our sorrows, say,
 'Sing us some sweet *Hebrew* lay !'

4. But, say we, 'Our holy strain
 Is too pure for heathen land ;
Nor may we God's Hymns profane,
 Or move either voice or hand
 To delight a savage band.'

5. Holy *Salem*, if thy love
 Fall from my forgetful heart,
May the skill, by which I move
 Strings of Music tuned with art,
 From my wither'd hand depart.

6. May my speechless tongue give sound
 To no accents, but remain
To my prison-roof fast bound,
 If my sad soul entertain
 Mirth, till thou rejoice again.

7. In that day remember, Lord !
 Edom's breed, that in our groans
They triumph ; and with fire and sword
 Burn their City, hearse their bones,
 And make all one heap of stones.

8. Cruel *Babel !* thou shalt feel
 The Revenger of our groans,
When the happy Victor's steel,
 As thine [had] our's, shall hew thy bones,
 And make all one heap of stones.

9. Men shall bless the hand that tears
   From the Mothers' soft embraces
Sucking Infants, and besmears
   With their brains the rugged faces
   Of the rocks and stony places.

[*Dr.* Philip Bliss *printed this* Psalm 137, *from the* Ashmolean MS. 38, art. 115 ; *where alone it was preserved : see* Athenæ Oxonienses, ii. col. 659–666. *It was therefrom cited inaccurately in* Notes and Queries, Second Series, vol. x. p. 223, *by* J. M. Gutch. *Also it was reprinted in* 'Gathered Riches from the Older Poets,' p. 134, 1865. *It is uncertain whether* Carew *continued these paraphrases, with* 'TETH,' *the ninth portion of the* Psalm 119 *of* p. 205, *or versified any other of the Psalms additionally.*]

Here end the Unauthenticated Poems from
manuscripts.

FINIS.

NOTES

POEMS OF THOMAS CAREW.

.

o

Appendix Notes.

Note 1.—On the annotations by T. Davies and John Fry.—
The detection of Similarities, or so-called 'parallel passages,'
has been the harmless hobby of many an amateur editor, for
whose busy-idleness it furnished laborious trifling. But in
regard to Thomas Carew, it was needless. He borrowed
little from other writers, and seems to have been free
from the restless ambition that drives men to desert their
own choice, and attempt to rival other masters of distinctly
varied taste and power. Few of the pretended discoveries
claimed by T. Davies, in 1772, and by John Fry of Bristol,
1810, deserve fresh record. Their explanatory notes were
devoted to the mere commonplaces of mythology (such as
Semele, p. 44; *Danæ*, 147; *Amalthea's* Horn of Plenty, 127;
Janus, 97, 99; *Bethesda*, 79; *Daphne*, 119; *Plutus*, 115;
the Ordeal by Fire, 57, etc.). These might now be deemed
impertinent or redundant, unless their use were sanctioned
by a belief in popular ignorance. Of T. Davies's critical
estimates five samples suffice: 1st, 'We shall observe,
once for all, that elegance characterizes all our Poet's Love
Pieces. This song [viz., "Gaze not on thy beauty's pride,"
p. 11], with the *Persuasions to Love* [meaning, *to Joy*, p. 14],
etc., and several other Poems, which the judicious reader
will easily distinguish, are incontestible proofs of it.'—D.
This 'truism' is innocent; but another note is offensive,
alike false and calumnious. 2nd, On the 'Elegy' (p. 17),
Davies wrote thus :—'The time is too distant to trace out
this Lady's name with any certainty; probably she belonged
to the Pennington family, who were then well known. Our
Poet is not so successful in grave elegy as in love sonnets.
Perhaps he was not so sincere in his grief as in his love.
When the fancy wanders after frivolous pointedness and
epigrammatic conceit, it shows too well that the heart is at
ease.'—D. Unable to discern the thicket mentioned in the
final stanza of 'A Pastoral Dialogue' ('As *Celia* rested in the
shade,' our pp. 38–40), Davies 'wrote himself down' under

the proper initial, to this effect, 3rd, 'That the reader may
not be surprised at our author's having entitled this piece *A
Pastoral Dialogue,* in which *we do not find even the most dis-
tant allusion drawn from pastoral life,* it may be necessary
to inform him, that it was a prevailing custom in our author's
time to style almost every poetical dialogue, of which Love
was the subject, pastoral. Most of the wits of Charles's
court left propriety to be studied by the following age.'—D.
Another specimen of this sapient critic. On the final stanza
of the other 'Pastoral Dialogue'—'This mossy bank they
press'd' (pp. 41, 42), here, 4th, is the comment :—'It is im-
possible to pass over these three lines with inattention. The
delicacy of the thought is equalled only by the simplicity of
the description. Those soft sensations, which arise in lovers,
when their joys and sorrows meet, *as a man of genius only can
describe them, so a man of taste only can conceive them.*'—D.

Criticism was at a low ebb in 1772, but Davies's comment
suited other 'men of taste.' 5th, He patronisingly estimates
the 'Inscription on the Tomb of the Duke of Buckingham'
(p. 54) :—'This little poem is not destitute of some pathetic
touches, expressive of the illustrious lady's grief, who is
supposed to utter them ; but the eight concluding lines,
instead of being the mournful monody of a widow, degrade
it into the wretched conceit of a poetaster. *But this was the
fustian of the times.*'—D.

John Fry considered that 'candies the grass' (p. 1) was
closely imitated from Michael Drayton's 'Quest of *Cinthia,*'

> ' Since when those frosts that Winter brings,
>   Which *candy* every green.'—*Poems,* 1627.

Also, ' When *Hyems* bound the floods in silver chains,
          And hoary frosts had *candied* all the plains.'

This is from William Browne's *Britannia's Pastorals,*
Book I. song 4, printed in 161¾. In the same Song, the
words 'pretty whispering gale,' Fry supposed, suggested
Carew's 'Go, thou gentle whispering wind' (p. 9). If
this system of private detection be well pursued, it seems
difficult for any one to employ language at all ; since every
word had been previously used by somebody. In the case of
' those streaks of doubtful light' (p. 41), there is undeniable
resemblance to the parting of the lovers in *Romeo and Juliet,*
act iii. scene 7. Thus, when we read the glowingly indignant
rebuke, given by Carew to the ungrateful public which
had rejected D'Avenant's play of *The Just Italian* (p. 120),
as a dramatic faction in London often indulges its spiteful-
fickleness against any of its spoilt favourites, we are reminded

of Coriolanus, with his scathing denunciation of the rabble,
'You common cry of Curs, whose breath I hate, as reek of
the rotten fens,' etc. : we read Carew's just denunciation of
the many-headed mob, inapt for rising to 'all that exceeds
Red-Bull and *Cock-pit* flight,' as were the groundlings whom
Hamlet scorned, because they 'for the most part are capable
of nothing but inexplicable dumb shows and noise.' Even so,

> ' Now noise prevails, and he is taxed for drouth
> Of wit, that with *the cry* spends not his mouth.
> Yet ask him reason why he did not like ?
> Him, why he did ? their ignorance will strike
> Thy soul with scorn and pity.'

Carew knew well his Shakespeare, Jonson, and Fletcher; and
remembered the '*common cry*,' but he was no plagiarist.

Note 2.—On the varying titles of the Poems.—Transcribers
of selected verse in commonplace books, MS. miscellanies
(to which we owe the preservation of many early poems that
would otherwise have perished, unprinted, amid the civil-war
disturbances and havoc), took liberties alike with the titles
and the text. Few among them can be accepted trustfully.
Inaccuracies are great and numerous, lines omitted, words
changed in ignorance or perversity in the best, while grosser
blunders meet us in the worst. It is seldom or never that
any one manuscript can be depended on throughout; the
originals by Carew are totally lost, whereby we might have
ascertained the genuine reading to be followed.

In general, as might have been expected, although not
published until certainly a year after his death, *the earliest
printed text of the Poems*, 1640 (but of the 'Masque,' *Cœlum
Britannicum*, the editio princeps, 1634), is by far the purest.
Two of Robert Herrick's short pieces may have crept in,
unawares (pp. 65 and 73), the *Hesperides* not having been
printed, with them in it, until 1648 ; and also an address
written by Edmund Waller to the Duke of Buckingham,
on his recovery from sickness (p. 100), for Waller indulged
in more fulsome flattery than Carew could ever do; and
there sounds in it the false ring of Waller, a turncoat and
sycophant throughout his long life : moreover the poem is
printed among his own. It has the excess of mythological
allusion (Lethæan lake, Orpheus and Euridice, Adonis and
Venus, Phœbus, 'Neptune and his sea-born niece'), by
Waller employed *ad nauseam*. Carew's own sentiments
were expressed strongly in 1634, in the Masque (p. 133),
and earlier in the Elegy on John Donne, 1631 (p. 112) :—

> ' They will recall the goodly exiled train
> Of Gods and Goddesses, which in thy just reign
> Was banish'd nobler poems ; now with these,
> The silenced tales i' th' *Metamorphoses,*
> Shall stuff their lines and swell the windy page ;
> Till verse, refined by thee in this last age,
> Turn Ballad-rhyme, or those old idols be
> Adored again with new apostacy.'

These are the only 'doubtful' poems given, outside of the group 'chiefly from MSS.' (beginning with p. 169, and extending to p. 208) ; unless we also count hesitatingly the ascription to Carew of two songs, 'Farewell, fair Saint,' and the 'Methodus Amandi,' of pp. 92, 103–105, which may have belonged to another T. C., Thomas Carey. Several of the MS. Poems share the same doubt. Where they are really good they are probably Carew's, for Carey was inferior as a versifier.

It is not necessary to record the innumerable variations, between print and manuscript versions, the best reading being taken after careful balancing of evidence. Every MS. has been collated and transcribed, while this edition was being prepared, personally (for hired transcribers are not trustworthy), except the unavailable Wyburd and Cosens MSS. *No pains have been spared to either restore or preserve the true text throughout,* as completely as possible.

3. *Miscellaneous Notes.*—On p. 2, in the words additional to the original title, ' His Counsel to his Mistress,' ' Mistress' merely implies the object of his affectionate attention ; and not the modern corrupt insinuation. These words are won from the British Museum Harleian MS. 6931, fol. 25 ; also from Additional MSS. 11811, fol. 4, and 22118, fol. 39 ; where the reading is, ' You are fayre as *Helen,* fresh as *May;*' moreover, in the Bodleian Library Ashmole MS. 47, art. 101, is a similar reading ; there it is entitled, ' An Admonition to coy Acquaintance.' It is remarkable and suggestive, that the lines are addressed, in the 1640 edition, ' To A——— L——.' Similarly initialed are two other poems, written about the same date, by Richard Lovelace, the author of '*Lucasta,*' to his cousin. She was the Honourable Lady Anne Lovelace. Probably the same Lady Anne Lovelace, born a Wentworth, who was so near being married by Sir John Finch, after 1635 (p. 82), and who really was married, not much later, to John, Lord Lovelace, second Baron (p. 83). She was a younger sister of Lady Mary Wentworth (p. 53), who died in 1632, aged eighteen, eldest daughter of Sir Thomas

Wentworth, afterwards Earl of Cleaveland, 162⅘; Anne Crofts, their mother, being the daughter of Sir John Crofts of Saxham, County Suffolk (see pp. 24, 27, and Addit. MS. 24189, iii. 255 of Hunter's *Chorus Vatum*). Lovelace's poems begin respectively, 'With what delight the royal captive's brought,' and 'This Queen of Prey, now prey to you' (*Library of Old Authors*' edition of *Lovelace*, 1864, pp. 104, 108). Also Sir John Suckling addresses one whose initials are the same, A. L. (but she is styled 'Mistress A. L.,' not 'Lady,' though this may be an error in copying), unless the initials are an intentional transposition of L. A. for '*Lutea Allanson*,' so named in ed. 1659, *alias* Allison of pp. 62, 66, in *Library of Old Authors : Suckling*, 1892, beginning 'Though you *Diana*-like have liv'd still chaste, Yet must you not, fair, die a maid at last.' The other, ' Upon Mrs. A—— L——,' begins, with unstinted laudation of the lady :—

> ' Thou think'st I flatter, when thy praise I tell,
> But thou do'st all hyperboles excel ;
> For I am sure thou art no mortal creature,
> But a divine one, throned in human feature :
> Thy piety is such, that heaven by merit
> If ever any did, thou should'st inherit,' etc.

Page 5.—'If when the Sun at noon displays.' This is one of the songs by Carew to which Henry Lawes, Milton's friend, composed the music, and printed them in his *Ayres and Dialogues*, Book I. 1653 ; Book II. 1655. A list of these songs is given in a note on p. 104, *ante*. Compare p. 167.

Page 6.—*The Assyrian King*=Nebuchadnezzar ; *Dan*. iii.

Page 10.—'Give me more love, or more disdain.' Comparisons have been made with Richard Lovelace's translation of 'Done moy plus de Pitie, ou plus de Creaulte, car sans ci je ne puis pas vivre, ne morir :' title, A La Bourbon : 'Divine destroyer, pity me no more !' 1649. Also to William Stanley's 'So much of absence and delay,' etc., 1656.

Pages 11, 29.—A Calenture is 'a distemper peculiar to sailors in hot climates, wherein they imagine the sea to be green fields, and will throw themselves into it.' (J.'s *Dict*.)

Page 13.—The second stanza, 'Young men fly,' etc., is found, without the opening, in *Festum Voluptatis*, 1639, by S. P., supposed initials of the compiler, Sam Pick. Other

songs by Carew, not needing to be specified individua
were habitually reprinted, more or less mutilated s
marred in text from doubtful transcripts, in various poeti
miscellanies: *Wit's Recreations*, 1640; John Cotgrave's *W
Interpreter*, 1655, 1671; *Academy of Complements*, 16
New Academy of Complements, 1671; *Westminster Drolle
1671*; *Holborn, London, Choice* and *Windsor Drolleries*, c
In fact, few of them lacked his popular songs.

Page 15.—'Know, *Celia*, since thou art so proud.' Hei
Jacob, of Merton College, Oxon., 'the greatest prodigy
criticism in his time,' according to Anthony à Wo
translated into Latin this poem by Carew, entitling
'Αντιτεχνος, *ad ingrate pulchram*. It appears to be l
One variation of Carew is in *Holborn Drollery*, p. 22, 16
beginning, 'Know, Lady, since you are so proud.'

Ibid.—'And with it ympt the wings of Fame.' Althou
it was frequently used of old, and occurs in Shakespeai
King Richard II., act ii. scene 1, the Hawking-word *i*
or *ymp* is now virtually obsolete, and unknown except
commentators or linguists.

It signifies the graffing part of a new feather into one tl
is worn and broken, in the wing or tail.

Davies noted, 'This phrase is borrowed from Falconry.
imp is to add a new piece to a broken stump.' Examples
'*Imp* out our drooping country's broken wing.'—*K*
Richard II., act ii. scene 1, line 292.

George Chapman's *Conspiracy of Byron*, 1608:—'I
plumes only *imp* the Muses' *wings.*'

Spenser's *Hymn of Heavenly Beauty*, 1596, lines 137, 1

'Thence gathering plumes of perfect speculation,
To *impe the wings* of thy high-flying mynd.'

Also, in his *Faërie Queene*, Book IV. canto ix., line 39,

'And having *ympt* the head to it agayne.'

In Phineas Fletcher's *Purple Island*, 1633, canto i. 24,

. . . '*imping* their flaggy *wing*,
With thy stol'n plumes.'

In Milton's *Sonnet* XV., on Fairfax,

. . . 'though new rebellions raise
Their Hydra heads, and the false North displays
Her broken league to *imp* their serpent *wings.*'

In John Cleaveland's satire, *The Rebel Scot*, line 30,

> 'Help, ye tart Satirists, to *imp* my rage,
> With all the scorpions that should whip this age.'

In Browne's *Britannia's Pastorals*, 161¾, Book I. song ii.,

> 'She'll tell you what you call virginity
> Is fitly liken'd to a barren tree,
> Which, when the gard'ner on it pains bestows,
> To graft an *imp* thereon, in time it grows
> To such perfection,' etc.—Lines 571–575.

Ibid., Book II. song ii. (Christopher Brooke), lines 309, 310,

> 'And when thy temples' well-deserving bays
> Might *imp* a pride in thee to reach thy praise.'

In Massinger's *Roman Actor*, 1629 (lic. 1626), act v. scene 2,

> 'Could I *imp* feathers to the *wings* of Time.'

Also, 'with a white feather *imp'd* in her tail,' Richard Brome's *Jovial Crew*, 1641.

Elsewhere cited, from Charles Colman, D. Mus., in Lines prefixed to Lawes' *Ayres*, Book II., concerning Music,

> 'She droop'd and flagg'd before, as Hawks complain
> Of the sick feathers of their wing and train ;
> But thou hast *imp'd the wings* she had before.'

The phrase had become a mere poetic commonplace.

Page 16.—'He that loves a rosy cheek.' Written before 1632, when it appeared in Walter Porter's *Madrigals and Ayres*, with music, lacking the third stanza of the poem.

Page 22.—Additional 'Good Counsel to a Young Maid' (the other so entitled being on p. 11), second stanza, Trowbesh MS. reads 'heated face :' the 1640 text has '*sweaty*,' a word not then deemed offensive. From the same Trowbesh MS. are adopted a few other changes, such as in 'A Rapture,' on p. 47, '*pinnace*' for 'pine,' and the final rhymes on p. 50, '*enshrined*' with '*kind*' instead of 'adores' with 'whores.' Also in 'The Second Rapture,' here advanced to follow close on the other Rapture, the MS. correction gives '*aboue* thirteen,' which early printers had mis-read '*about;*' and '*love*' for '*lust,*' twice. Similarly, the Trowbesh MS. is again followed, clearing the meaning by simple transposition, in the fourth stanza of p. 90, 'You that will a wonder know.' The earliest printed text, 1651 edition, read unintelligibly, ' As fair Pillars understand | Statues Two, | Whiter than the Silver Swan,' etc., and, in next stanza, ' as the miss.' But compare, "So was her heavenly body comely rais'd | On *two fair columns,*" etc.—*Britannia's Pastorals,* I. iv. 254.

Three poems, 'Grieve not,' 'You that will,' and ' As one that strives' (reprinted here on pp. 88, 90, 91, respectively), are not known to have appeared in print before the third edition, 1651, '*Some Additional Poems by the Same Author.*'

Pages 24, 27.—'*To Saxham.*' Harl. MS. 6931, fol. 24, gives the title wrongly as 'A Gent. on his Entertainment *at Saxham, in Kent;*' but the locality is in Suffolk; where dwelt Carew's friend, John Crofts, Cup-bearer to King Charles I. ; Cecila Crofts became Mrs. Killigrew (p. 81). The first wife of Sir Thomas Wentworth had been Anne Crofts, mother of the Ladies Maria and Anne Wentworth (pp. 82, 83, 237). About 1632 Charles I. visited Saxham.

On p. 25, it is unnecessary to relinquish the appropriate word ' *Votary*' (Harl. MS.), although Addit. MS. 11811 reads ' *Volary,*' and Davies explains it as ' A great bird-cage, in which the birds have room to fly up and down :' an *Aviary.* We need not disturb the 1640 text, ' *Votary.*'

Pages 29, 71, 99.—*Lucinda,* in these two poems, is the Lady Lucy Hay, Countess of Carlisle, the second wife, and widow, of John Hay, first Earl of Carlisle. She was born a Percy, daughter of Henry, eighth Earl of Northumberland, and has been rightly styled, by Bishop Warburton, the 'Erinnys of England ;' since her wanton fascination and heartless treachery wrought evil widely. In her day she had been accounted successively the mistress of John Wentworth Earl of Strafford and afterwards of his bitter enemy and destroyer, John Pym (whom she had saved from arrest at the abortive attempt against the Five Members in 1642, by betraying Charles's secret, learnt from Queen Henrietta). She was held in more rapturous admiration than reverential respect by friends, as is shown in the copy of verses written by Sir John Suckling, 'Upon my Lady Carlisle's walking in Hampton-Court-Gardens,' being a 'Dialogue between *T. C.* and *J. S.,*' printed posthumously in the *Fragmenta Aurea,* 1646, reprinted in the *Poems,* 1648, p. 32, and beginning happily thus, in imitation of Carew's love of nature :—

DID'ST thou not find the place inspired?
    And flowers, as if they had desired
No other Sun, start from their beds,
And for a sight steal out their heads?
Heard'st thou not music, when she talk'd,
And did'st not find that, as she walk'd,
She threw rare perfumes all about,
Such as Bean-blossoms newly out
      Or chafed spices give?

Whereto Suckling's reply is of the *nil admirari* sort :—

J. S.

I must confess, those perfumes, *Tom*,
I did not smell; nor found that from
Her passing by aught sprang up new;
The flowers had all their birth from you:
For I passed o'er the self-same walk,
And did not find one single stalk,
    Or anything that was to bring
    This unknown after after-spring.   ⌈As in an
                                                             ⌊after-math.

Thom[*as Carew*].

Dull and insensible ! could'st see
A thing so near a Deity
Move up and down, and feel no change?

J[*ohn*] *S*[*uckling*].

None, and so great, were alike strange !
I had my thoughts, but not your way;
All are not born, Sir, to the Bay;
Alas ! *Tom*, I am flesh and blood,
And was consulting how I could
In spite of Masks and Hoods descry
The parts denied unto the eye :
I was undoing all she wore,
And had she walk'd but one turn more,
    Eve in her first state had not been
    More naked, or more plainly seen.

Let it be remembered that, whatever sensuality is here
shown, in Suckling's rejoinder, it is his own confession, of
his own evil thoughts and imaginings, and given in his own
words. His evidence is tainted, and it recoils against

himself.   His friend '*Thom*' merely catches the ball on the rebound, and sings prolongedly Lucinda's praise :—

Thom[*as Carew*].

> ' 'Twas well for thee she left the place ;
> There is great danger in that face :
> But had'st thou view'd her, [yet more nigh],
> And upon that discovery
> Searched after parts that are more dear,
> As fancy seldom stops so near,
>   No time nor age had ever seen
>   So lost a thing as thou had'st been.'

That the Lady Lucy would neither blush nor feel angry, at anything said or sung out of the mouths of such babes and sucklings, we can readily believe.   No one felt aggrieved at warmth of expression in the Masques or Lyrics ; it was frigidity or formality that provoked disgust, and, in reaction against Puritanic hypocrisy, excused errors of the poets.

Page 32.—Upon the King's Sickness. Date, 1633. William Cartwright wrote a contemporary poem, 'On his Majesty's Recovery from the Small Pox ' (*Poems*, p. 192, 1651),

> ' I do confess the over-forward tongue
> Of public duty turned into a wrong,
> And after-ages, which could ne'er conceive
> Our happy *CHARLES* so frail as to receive
> Such a disease, will know it by the noise
> Which we have made in showing forth our joys,' etc.

Page 34.—Cleaveland has an inferior poem on this theme.

Page 35.—In some MSS. (Ashm. 36 and Cosens) the locality is erroneously stated to have been the vault or gallery at York House.   Arundel Gardens, in the time of Carew, occupied the ground now known as Norfolk Street, Strand, with Arundel Street, Howard, and Surrey.   The entire space covered by the gardens, the terraces, and the town house of the Earls of Arundel and Dukes of Norfolk, is shown in Hollar's prints.   The statues here mentioned, the celebrated Arundelian marbles, described by John Selden in *Marmora Arundeliana*, were given later to the University of Oxford.

Page 36.—There may have been some faint remembrance of this 'Seek not to know my Love ' when the author of ' A Rhodomontade on his Cruel Mistress ' wrote the following epigram.   It well describes Lucy, the Countess of Carlisle. In Ashmole MS. 38, art. 237, it begins, ' Ask not to know : '—

SEEK not to know this Woman ; for she's worse
    Than all ingredients cramm'd into a Curse.
Were she but ugly, peevish, proud, a whore,
Perjured or painted—so she were no more—
I could forgive her, and connive at this,
Alleging 'Still, she but a Woman is !'
        But she is worse, and may in time forestall
        The Devil, and be the damning of us all.

Page 39.—The Marigold.   A later version than Carew's
poem formed the foundation of a popular street-ditty and
broadside, 'printed for the assigns of Tho. Symcocke,' and
entitled 'The Maid's Comfort.' Beginning similarly, 'Down
in a garden sits my dearest love,' it is preserved by one
unique exemplar, in the Roxburghe Collection, I. 242.   (See
Roxburghe Ballads, vol. ii., end of part iv., 1872.)

LOVE'S RIDDLE RESOLVED.

DOWN in a garden sate my dearest Love,
    Her skin more soft than down of swan,
More tender-hearted than the Turtle-dove,
    And far more kind than bleeding Pelican.
    I courted her, she rose, and blushing said,
    'Why was I born to live and die a maid ?'
With that I pluck'd a pretty Marygold,
Whose dewy leaves shut up, when day is done ;
'Sweeting,' I said, 'arise ! look, and behold,
A pretty riddle I'll to thee unfold :
    These leaves shut in as close as cloistered Nun,
    Yet will they open when they see the Sun.'
'What mean you by this riddle, Sir ?' she said ;
'I pray expound it.'   Then I thus began,
'Are not Men made for Maids, and maids for men ?'
With that she changed her colour, and grew wan.
    'Since that this Riddle you so well unfold,
    Be you the Sun, I'll be the Marygold.'
                          Wit's Interpreter, 1655, p. 27.

The ballad-maker spun it out to fifteen stanzas, ending,

Comfort she found, and straight was made a Wife ;
It was the only thing she did desire :
And she enjoys a Man loves her as life,
And will do ever, till his date expire.
    And this, for truth, report hath to me told,
    He is her Sun, and she his Marygold.   (1620–42).

'An Answer' meets us in *Acad. of Comp.*, 1650, 1671 :—

ANSWER TO 'THE MARIGOLD.'

SHOW me no more the Marigold,
   Whose leaves like grieved arms do fold !
My longings nothing can explain
But Soul and Body rent in twain.
Did I not moan, and sigh and groan,
    And talk alone,
I should believe my Soul were gone from home.

She's gone, she's gone away ! she's fled,
Within thy breast to make her bed ;
In me there dwells her tenant, Woe,
And sighs are all the breath I blow.
Then come to me ! One touch of thee
    Will make me see
Whether, living thus, alive or dead I be.

In Clement Robinson's *Handefull of Pleasant Delites,* 1584
(a book which Shakespeare knew), is *A Nosegay always sweet :*

'*Marigold* is for Marriage, that would our minds suffice,
Lest that suspicion of us twain by any means should rise.'

John Lyly says in his panegyric on Queen Elizabeth
(*Euphues and his England,* 1580 : 1868, p. 462), 'This is she that
resembling the noble Queen of *Navarre,* useth the *Marigold*
for her flower, which at the rising of the Sun openeth her
leaves, and at the setting shutteth them ; referring all her
actions and endeavours to Him that ruleth the Sun.'

Page 48.—'*The Rapture.*' Pietro Aretino had grown to
be proverbially supreme for licentiousness, in consequence of
his comment on the ' Postures ' of Julio Romano and Marc
Antonio, as the younger Crébillon became afterwards with
'The Sofa.' William Browne, in *Britannia's Pastorals,*
Book I. song ii., line 766, alluded to Aretine as a corrupter
of youth, and his own self-expostulates against such writing
is not without force :—

' Whose well-tuned ears, chaste object-loving eyne,
Ne'er heard nor saw the works of *Aretine.*'

It would have utterly destroyed the scholarly value of this
edition of Carew, to have omitted 'The Rapture,' or even
'The Second Rapture' which is brought into sequence with
it. They are indiscreetly warm and outspoken, it is true
but not a tenth part so vicious as are the sickly sentimenta
pruriencies and pruderies of our *Fin de Siècle* poets. Afte

all, let it be remembered, Thomas Carew was a man, with a man's failings, but also with a man's courage and gentleness. We disbelieve the jesting slander unwarrantably brought against him by Sir John Suckling, and consider that Hales of Eton had no less calumniously exaggerated any charges of immorality, whilst pluming himself in the conceit that he was not as other men—even as this Publican. No proof exists that Carew ever descended to be a seducer or an adulterer. 'If he loved rashly, his life paid for wrong,' in his failure to attain a higher social rank than 'sewer to His Majesty, and gentleman of the Privy Chamber.'

Unwilling to disturb the text (beyond a rectification of 'aboue' for the misprint '*about*'—an unusual looseness of phrase at such early date), we hesitate as to the girl's age : Carew could have had no tainted passion for unripe fruit. Juliet, of the Capulets, was not fourteen years old, by 'a fortnight and odd days—come Lammas-eve'—when her mother wished her to marry (and married she became, speedily), saying,

'Well, think of marriage now! Younger than you
Here in Verona, ladies of esteem,
Are made already mothers. By my count,
I was your mother much upon these years
That you are now a maid.'

This was in Italy, indeed, but Shakespeare seldom wanders far from home, for local colour or chronological exactness. It was not unusual to 'contract' and to solemnise such early weddings in England, especially among the gentry and nobility. Thirteen is the misprinted text of Carew, 1640 :— 'Give me a wench about thirteen !'

We must read 'above' if we retain 'thirteen ;' but 'above fifteen' is the Trowbesh MS. correction. Listen to a song by Carew's contemporary William Cartwright (Ben Jonson said, 'My son Cartwright writes like a man') : the song, *circâ* 1640, belongs to his play *The Ordinary*, act iii. scene 3. It is sung by one unseen, the lover thinking meanwhile, 'My Fair is hallowing her lute with her blest touch.'

LOVE ADMITS NO DELAY.

(*Music by HENRY LAWES.*)

COME, O come! I brook no stay :
He doth not love that can delay :
See how the stealing Night
Hath blotted out the light,
And tapers do supply the Day.

To be chaste is to be old,
And that foolish Girl that's cold
   Is fourscore *at fifteen :*
   Desires do write us green,
And looser flames our youth unfold.

The Lover (*Meanwell*) now rightly guesses that, not his mistress, but her waiting-maid, *Priscilla*, has been singing :—

  'It cannot be her ! her voice was ne'er profaned
  With such immodest numbers.'

He scarcely awaits the final stanzas, but they follow thus :

See, the first taper's almost gone !
Thy flame, like that, will straight be none,
   And I, as it, expire,
   Not able to hold fire ;
She loseth time that lies alone.

O let us cherish then these powers,
Whiles' we yet can call them ours :
   Then we best spend our time,
   When no dull zealous Chime
But sprightful kisses strike the hours.

Abraham Cowley sings thus, in 'The Inconstant,' 1647,

' I never yet could see that face which had no dart for me ;
From *fifteen years* to fifty's space, they all victorious be.'

The judicious epicure in love would rather accept two sweethearts, each of fifteen years old ; than one, of thirty.

Tom D'Urfey illustrates the same precocity of virginal charms, with commendable discretion, in his quaint ditty,

KINGSTON CHURCH :

A SONG.

SWEET, use your time ; abuse your time
  No longer, but be wise !
Young lovers now discover you
  Have beauty they can prize.
But if you're coy, you'll lose the joy,
  So curst will be the fate :
The flower will fade, you'll die a maid,
  And mourn your chance too late.

At *thirteen years* and *fourteen years*
The virgin's heart may range ;
'Twixt fifteen years and fifty years
You'll find a wondrous change :
Then, whilst in tune, in May and June,
Let love and youth agree,
For if you stay till Christmas day
The devil shall woo for me.

Pages 54, 55.—Few students of history in these later days are able or willing to concede any praise, howsoever justly due, to George Villiers, first Duke of Buckingham. The wave of democracy is bursting on us, and all courtiers or royalists are overwhelmed. Yet we see no room to doubt the perfect sincerity of Carew's tributary lines, and their virtual truth, towards the generous patron and friend who was slain by the gloomy fanatic, John Felton, at Portsmouth, in 1628.

As to the 'conceit,' about the monument having been wept by the mourning and widowed Duchess (who had loved her husband devotedly, in spite of his infidelities, which she did not see), critics should remember that it was the fashion of the day, and that nearly every public writer sought to indulge in such popular tricks of style. The phrases 'hatch'd a cherubin' (p. 53), 'unkneaded dough-baked prose' (p. 111), 'surfeit on grief . . . upon what *cates* you sit, glutting your sorrows' (p. 109), 'grew a Bird of Paradise' (p. 34), 'nest of spice' (p. 43), or the strained fancies about the King's sickness of small-pox in 1633 (p. 32), are not in conformity with our modern canons. Prudery and super-subtle fastidiousness may disparage such poems for an occasional flaw ; but much worse can often be found in the writings of Donne, of Cowley, and of Waller : such faults as are amply exemplified, and criticised with unmitigated severity by Sam. Johnson, in his *Lives B. P.*, article *Cowley*. Suckling was preserved from such errors by his finer sense of humour, which detected the burlesque side of all emotion. But no one thought the less of Carew for any strained hyperbole. All can admire his 'Eddy' (p. 12), or 'Lips and Eyes,' p. 4 ; yet each is based on what is termed a conceit. Why rail at a fleeting fashion, seeing that we ourselves of later time are slaves to similar, or worse ?

Page 61.—This address to Ben Jonson, although a rebuke or his intemperate outburst of scorn against the witless public, is full of noble friendship and admiration. The man had been accounted foremost of his day, dictator, tyrant, and benefactor, whose applause gave fame, and whose censure

P

was condemnation. We love well his rugged honesty and independence, also his indisputable genius. It was no idle boast of his, that he was descended from the Johnsons of Annandale, for all the finer qualities of the true Scot met in him. 'O rare Ben Jonson!'

With his warm appreciation of Jonson, we may feel sure that if Carew had survived the dramatist long enough he would have written a later contribution to 'Johnsonius Verbius.' The absence therefrom of any such poem clearly marks the date of Carew's own death as 1638.

Ben Jonson's comedy, the 'New Inn; or, The Light Heart:' This inauspiciously-named comedy was produced on the stage, 19th January 16$\frac{29}{30}$; but so badly acted that the fickle and irresponsive public condemned it unheard, not suffering it to continue to the end, even at a single performance. In Jonson's own words, it was 'most negligently played by some, the "King's Servants;" and more squeamishly beheld and censured by others, the King's Subjects, 1629.' He printed it in 1631, and the bitterness of his indignation, aroused by such treatment as he had received, found expression in the celebrated 'Ode' (To Himself), beginning,

> ' Come, leave the loathed Stage,
>   And the more loathsome Age!
> Where pride and impudence, in faction knit,
>   Usurp the chair of Wit;
> Indicting and arraigning every day
> Something they call a play.
>   Let their fastidious, vain
>   Commission of the brain
> Run on and rage, sweat, censure, and condemn,
> They were not made for thee: less thou for them.'

Five stanzas follow. Jonson was then in his fifty-seventh year, and his had been a stormy life, in many ways, so that he had become aged before his time. No wonder is it that he felt the sting of ingratitude and insult keenly. His autocratic rule had not been borne so long without a suppressed rebellion, and the vicious tribe of obscure satirists took advantage of their opportunity to poison the wound. Owen Feltham, author of 'Resolves,' 1626, became the foremost assailant, beginning his mocking 'Answer' thus:—

> ' Come, leave this saucy way
>   Of baiting those that pay
> Dear for the sight of your declining wit:
>   'Tis known it is not fit
> That a stale poet, just contempt once thrown,
>   Should cry up thus his own,' etc.   (60 lines.)

Jonson's friends came forward in his defence, Thomas Randolph and honest John Cleaveland repeating the same form of Ode ; Randolph beginning, 'Ben ! do not leave the stage, 'Cause 'tis a loathsome age, For pride and impudence will grow too bold ;' and Cleaveland starting thus, 'Proceed in thy brave rage, Which hath raised up our stage, Unto that height as Rome in all her state, or Greece might emulate.' But Thomas Carew wrote, as he would have spoken, temperately, firmly and affectionately, in mild remonstrance. His exhortation of 'Trust thou to after days !' was the wiser policy. Well sang our noble Walter Savage Landor, in 1859, echoing his own loved Milton's 'Veniet cordatior ætas ; Siquid meremur sana posteritas sciet' (*Poemata*) :—

> ' A few will cull my fruit, and like the taste,
> And find not overmuch to pare away.
> The soundest apples are not soonest ripe,
> In some dark room laid up when others rot.'

And surely this is also true of Thomas Carew himself, whose unhasting care was censured by the trifler Suckling, coarsely reproaching his Muse as 'hard-bound.' The elegance and accurate polish of poems is not won without *labor limœ.*

Page 64.—In the eighth line '*compare*' is used as a noun, equivalent to 'comparison,' sometimes misprinted 'compard.' Of the variations here, we follow the 1640 edition, and Harl. MS. 6057, '*tresses*,' not the affectedly 'twin'd haires' of other MSS. ; and 'Fair Goddess ! *since* thy feature,' not '*for*.'

> ' But, as you are divine in outward view,
> So be within as fair, as good, as true.'

Of date probably earlier than 1640, and contained in that year's edition of *Wit's Interpreter* (there entitled, 'What is most to be liked in a Mistress '), reprinted into *Choice Drollery*, 1656, is a song embodying Carew's prayer :—

UPON KIND AND TRUE LOVE.

'TIS not how witty, nor how free,
    Nor yet how beautiful she be,
But how much kind and true to me :
Freedom and Wit none can confine,
And Beauty like the sun doth shine,
But Kind and True are only mine.

Let others with attention sit
To listen, and admire her wit :
On that same rock I'll never split.

Let others dote upon her eyes,
And burn their hearts for sacrifice :
Beauty's a calm where danger lies.

But Kind and True have long been tried,
A Harbour where we may confide,
And safely there at anchor ride.
From change of winds we there are free,
And need not fear Storms' tyranny,
Nor Pirate, though a Prince he be.

Like another song, that accompanied it in *Choice Drollery,*
1656, probably by the same author, 'Upon his Constant
Mistress,' beginning, 'She's not the fairest of her name'
(*i.e.* Freeman), it is anonymous ; but both are said to have
been written by Aurelian Townsend, Carew's friend, who is
mentioned affectionately on pp. 113–115. (See p. 243.)

Cf. p. 179.] *Pages* 65, 73.—It seemed better to include these two
doubtful poems, 'The Enquiry' and 'The Primrose,' both
of them belonging to the 1640 edition of Carew, although
it is possible they may be Robert Herrick's, they being
printed in 1648, as Nos. 263 and 582 of the *Hesperides.* But
in 'The Enquiry,' the allusion to the tulip bears affinity to
'leaves of crimson tulips,' of p. 90, which is Carew's.

Whether we give to Herrick or to Carew 'The Enquiry'
(celebrating Elizabeth Wheeler), with its fourth line that
explains the title—'Where may I find my Shepherdess?' we
recall the Reply, written by Aurelian Townsend (p. 243) :—

HIS MISTRESS FOUND.

THOU Shepherd, whose intentive eye
O'er every lamb is such a spy,
No wily fox can make them less,—
Where may I find my Shepherdess?

A little pausing, then said he,
'How can that jewel stray from thee?
In Summer heat, in Winter cold,
I thought thy breast had been her fold.'

That is indeed the constant place
Wherein my thoughts still see her face,
And print her image in my heart ;
But yet my fond eyes crave a part.

With that, he smiling said, 'I might
Of *Chloris* partly have a sight ;
And some of her perfections meet
In every flower was fresh and sweet.

' The growing Lilies bear her skin,
The Violet her blue veins within ;
The blushing Rose new blown and spread,
Her sweeter cheek, her lip the red.

' The winds that wanton with the Spring
Such odours as her breathing bring.
But the resemblance of her eyes
Was never found beneath the skies.

' Her charming voice, who strives to hit,
His object, must be higher yet ;
For heaven and earth, and all we see
Dispersed, collected is but She ! '

Amazed at this discourse, me thought,
Love with ambition in me wrought,
And made me covet to engross
A wealth, would prove a public loss.

With that I sigh'd : ashamed to see
Such worth in her, such want in me :
And, closing both mine eyes, forbid
The world my sight, since she was hid.

Page 66.—'O my dearest, I shall grieve thee.' For
this we have decided to retain the old spelling in the
title, ' *Love's Complement ;* ' meaning the total fulfilment of
Beauty, for Love's entire satisfaction : not merely a modern
' Compliment,' as a flattering phrase. Of old the word held
both meanings, as is shown in the title of ' *The Academy of
Complements,*' 1640, etc., though even there also it suggests
' *of Completion.*'

Sometimes called ' Celia Altogether.' Half a century
earlier, before 1593 (we need not here enquire how the idea
had been expressed in more remote antiquity), Christopher
Marlowe had written to the same effect, in a poem seldom
remembered. It was printed *circá* 1597, at end of the ' At
Middleborugh ' earliest known edition of ' *Epigrammes and
Elegies,*' but disguisedly marked ' Ignoto.' (Although it was
speedily forgotten, the poem which followed next to it, in
1597, was revived in popularity by *Wit's Interpreter,* 1655,
and *Westminster Drollery,* 1671, the lines beginning ' Fair
wench, I cannot court thy sprightly eyes,' altered into
' Madam, I cannot,' etc.) Marlowe's so-called ' SONNET,' is
of the loosely-constructed *Quatorzain* sort that Shakespeare
used later for his own ' Sonnets.' Marlowe's may fairly be
deemed the original suggestion for Carew's song.

I LOVE thee not for sacred Chastity :
    Who loves for that ? nor for thy sprightly wit.
I love thee not for thy sweet modesty,
Which makes thee in Perfection's throne to sit.

I love thee not for thy enchanting eye,
Thy beauty's ravishing perfection :
I love thee not for unchaste luxury,
Nor for thy body's fair proportion.

I love thee not for that my soul doth dance
And leap with pleasure, when those lips of thine
Give musical and graceful utterance,
To some (by thee made happy) poet's line.

text, 'slender.']   I love thee not for voice or [fingers] small,
But wilt thou know, wherefore ? fair sweet ! for all.

Here is another SONG (found of no earlier date than 1669) :-

I LOVE thee, not because thou'rt fair,
    Or 'cause thou art virtuous too ;
Though in them both is power enough
    To make a Prince to woo.

Nor love I thee for those sweet lips,
    Nor for thy dimpled chin ;
Though in them both is power enough
    To tempt a Saint to sin.

Nor love I thee for those bright eyes,
    Which shine like Lamps of Love :
'Twas not these lovely curled locks
    Did my affection move.

Nor love I thee for those fair cheeks,
    Where damask roses grow,
Nor for that lovely neck of thine,
    And breasts like hills of Snow.

Nor love I thee, because thou once
    Disdain'dst my love to see.
Was there e'er such amorous flames
    As may be found in me ?

Since Love and Virtue now are lodged
    Within thy breast to grow ;
I'll love thee still in spite of Fate ;
    And let the world this know.

Whosoever wrote the 21 lines, 'From a Gentleman to his Mistress,' printed in 1655 (*Wit's Interpreter*, p. 69), beginning, 'Temptation breeds those love-attracting flowers, That grow upon thy cheeks, Love's bowers,' indulged himself boldly in plagiarism from Carew's 'O my dearest, I shall grieve thee,' stealing without change the red coral lips, and other couplets. In 'Disdain Return'd,' beginning, 'Wert thou much fairer than thou art, which lies not in the power of art,' the final (third) stanza runs thus:—

> 'I love thee not because thou'rt fair,
> Softer than down, smoother than air;
> Nor for the *Cupids* that do lie
> In every corner of thine eye:
>> Would you then know what it may be?
>> 'Tis I love you 'cause you love me!'

Page 69.—In 1658, when the scattered Cavaliers began to look forward confidently to the approach of more settled times, and even of a Restoration to the monarchy, some of them gathered the fugitive verses; as E. Phillips, Sir John Menzies, and Dr. James Smith had done in 1656 with at least three collections (*Sportive Wit, Parnassus Biceps*, and *The Muses Recreation*). By a well-understood hint, they entitled one *Wit Restored*. They therein gave Carew's 'Ask me no more whither do stray,' as 'The Reply,' after this commencement:—

A QUESTION.

'I ASK thee whence those ashes were
 Which shrine themselves in plaits of hair?'
Unknown to me: sure each morn dies
A Phœnix for a sacrifice.

'I ask whence are those airs that fly
From birds in sweetest harmony?'
Unknown to me; but sure the choice
Of accents echo'd from her voice.

'I ask thee whence those active fires
Take light, which glide through burnish'd air?'
Unknown to me: unless there flies
A flash of lightning from her eyes.

'I ask thee whence those ruddy blooms
Perch on her cheeks, [as] scarlet gowns?'   [*t.* 'Pierce.
Unknown to me: sure that which flies
From fading Roses, her cheek dyes.

' I'll ask thee of the Lily, whence
It gain'd that type of Innocence ? '
Unknown to me : sure Nature's deck
Was ravish'd from her snowy neck.

Then follows (unacknowledged as being his) ' The Reply '
by Carew, ' Ask me no more, whither do stray, the golden
atoms of the day ? ' (our p. 69 ; but, transposing the stanzas
into different order, as in *Lawes' Ayres,* thus, 2nd, 3rd, 4th,
1st, and 5th).   Next comes, from *Wit's Interpreter,* 1656 :—

THE LOVER'S MISTAKE.

TELL me no more, Her eyes are like
    To rising Suns, that wonder strike ;
For if 'twere so, how could it be
They could be thus eclipsed to me ?

Tell me no more, Her breasts do grow
Like melting Hills of rising Snow :
For if 'twere so, how could they lie
So near the Sunshine of her eye.

Tell me no more, the restless spheres
Compared to her voice fright our ears ;
For if 'twere so, how then could death
Dwell with such discord in her breath ?

No, say, Her eyes portenters are
Of ruin, or some blazing Star :
Else would I feel from that fair fire
Some heat to cherish my desire.

Say that her breasts, though cold as snow,
Are hard as marble when I woo ;
Else they would soften and relent,
With sighs inflamed from me sent.

Say that, although She, like the Moon,
Is heavenly fair, yet change as soon ;
Else she would constant once remain,
Either to Pity or Disdain :

That so, by one of them, I might
Be kept alive or murder'd quite ;
t. ' For 'tis."]   'Tis no less cruel than to kill,
Where life doth but increase the ill.

The Mock-Song.

[*Cf.* p. 235.

I TELL you true, whereon doth light
 The dusky shade of banish'd Night;
For in just vengeance heavens allow
It still should shine upon your brow.

I tell you true where men may seek
The sound which once the Owl did shriek;
For in your false dividing throat
It lies, and death is in its note.

I tell you true, whither doth pass
The smiling look out of a glass;
It leaps into your face, for there
A falser shadow doth appear.

I'll tell you true, whither are blown
The airy wheels of Thistle-down;
They fly into your mind, whose care
Is to be light as Thistles are.

I tell you true, within what nest
The stranger Cuckoo's eggs do rest;
It is your bosom, which can keep
Nor him, nor them, where one should sleep.

The Moderatrix.

[*Lady's Answer.*

I'LL tell you where's another Sun,
 That sets, as rising it begun:
It is my self, who keeps one sphere;
And were the same, if men so were.

What need I tell, that life and death
May pass in sentence from one breath?
So issue, from my equal heart,
Both love and scorn for men's desert.

I'll tell you in what heavenly hell
An Angel and a Fiend may dwell:
It is mine eye, whose glassy brook
Sends back the gazer's diverse look.

I'll tell you in a diverse scale
One weight can up and downwards hale;
You call me Thistle; *you,* a Rose;
I neither am, yet both of those.

I'll tell you where both frost and fire
In peace of common seat conspire ;
My frozen breast, that flint is like,
Yet yields a fire if you will strike.

Then you that love, and you that loathe,
With one aspect I answer both :
For round about me glows a fire,
Can melt and harden gross desire.

Man Replies.]　　　　　THE AFFIRMATIVE ANSWER.

OH no ! Heaven saw men's fancies stray
　　To idolize both dust and clay ;
That emblem gave that they might see
Your Beauty's date but dust must be.

No *Philomel* when Summer's gone
Hastes to the wood, her rape to moan :
(Unwilling her's,) ashamed to see
Your (unlike her's) unchastity.

Oh no, those Stars fly but the sight
Of what you act in dead of night :
Ashamed themselves should Pandars prove
In your unsatiate beastly love.

Oh no, that Rose, when *June* is past
Looks pale as with a poisonous blast ;
And such your beauty, when-as Time
Like Winter shall o'ertake your prime.

Oh no, the *Phœnix* shuns the place,
And fears the lustful fires t' embrace
Of your hot breast and barren womb,
As Death, or some perpetual Tomb.

This is a ' most lame and ' impudent ' conclusion.'
might have avoided Carew's song if they could no
' rush in, where angels fear to tread.' But irrevere
parody or caricature what it affects to admire.]
Carew's original ' Ask me no more ! ' was reprinte
other purloined poems, and actually *mis*-attrib
William Herbert, Earl of Pembroke. Of the ' E
' Mock ' (on p. 233), a version appeared in the *Wes
Drollery,* 1671 ; it cannot be called an improvement

I 'LL tell you true, whither do stray
   The darkness which succeeds the day ;
For Heaven's vengeance did allow
It still should frown upon your Brow.

I'll tell you true, where may be found
A voice that's like the Screech-Owl's sound ;
For in your false deriding throat
It lies, and death is in its note.

I'll tell you true, whither doth pass
The smiling look seen in the glass ;
For in your face reflect' it there
False as your shadow doth appear.

I'll tell you true, whither are blown
The angry whirls of Thistle-down ;
It flies into your mind, whose care
Is to be light, as Thistles are.

I'll tell you true, within what nest
The Cuckoo lays her eggs to rest :
It is your bosom, which can keep
Nor him nor them : Farewell, I'll sleep.

But of all idle and unprofitable labours the writing
lampoons on false maidens or cast mistresses is the worst.
Poets cannot thereby amend them, and if it could be done,
it would lead to no happiness ; they being damaged articles,
and not wanted back again. Carew himself knew this well,
and kept constant to a single love, in whom he found ample
variety, owing to her changeful humours.

Another imitation is the 'Dialogue concerning Hair
between a Man and a Woman,' which begins with the man's
self-answered enquiry, 'Ask me no more, why I do wear my
hair so far below my ear.' Patherike Jenkyns has a song,
beginning 'Ask me not why the Rose doth fade.' It is
entitled 'On the Death of his Mistress,' and is in his
Amorea, 1661. There is another memorable parody, or
Mock-Song, as it was called, of Carew's original. It was
written by Thomas Jordan, author of *Poetical Varieties*,
numerous civil-war ballads, and a few Civic Entertainments
for Lord Mayor Shows, after the Restoration. This parody
was circulated in 1642, when it was alike popular and
persecuted. Also known as 'Pym's Anarchy.' It is in '*Royal
Arbor of Loyal Poesie, consisting of Poems and Songs,*' 1664.
It powerfully describes the early days of mob tyranny,
which Carew fortunately survived not long enough to see.

The Resolution. 1642.

A SK me no more, why there appears
Daily such troops of Dragoneers?
Since it is requisite, you know ;
They rob *cum privilegio.*

Ask me not why the gaol confines
Our Hierarchy of best Divines?
Since 'tis allow'd, by full consent,
'The Privilege of Parliament.'

Ask me no more, why from *Black-wall*
Such tumults come unto *White-hall?*
Since some in Parliament agree
''Tis for the Subjects' Liberty !'

Ask me not, why to *London* comes
So many muskets, pikes, and drums,
So that we fear they'll never cease ?
a. l. 'protect.] 'Tis to procure the Kingdom's peace !

John, Lord
Finch of *Ford-* Ask me no more, why little *Finch*
wych : fled From Parliament began to flinch?
1641, p. 82. Since such as dare to hawk at kings
May easily clip a *Finch's* wings.

Ob. 11 *May* 1640.] Ask me no more, why *Strafford's* dead,
Or why they aim'd so at his head ?
Faith, all the reason I can give,
'Tis thought he was too wise to live.

Ask me no more, where's all the plate
Brought in at such an easy rate ?
It to the Owners back they'll bring,
In case it fall not to the King.

Edw. Dering. Ask me not, why the House delights
Sir Roger Not in our two wise *Kentish* Knights ?
Twysden. Their counsel never was thought good,
Because they were not understood.

Alex. Lesley. Ask me no more, why *Lesley* goes
a. l. Livesley. To seize all rich men as his foes ?
Whilst country farmers sigh and sob :
Yeomen may beg, when Knights do rob.

Ask me no more, by what strange slight
London's Lord Mayor was made a knight ?   ⸢Sir *Isaac*
Since there's a strength sprung out of war,   ⸤*Pennington.*
That can at once both make and mar.

Ask me no more, why in this age
I sing so free without a cage ?   [*i.e.* outside.
My answer is, I need not fear :
All *England* doth the burden bear.

Ask me no more (for I grow dull),
Why *Hotham* keeps the town of *Hull ?*
This answer I in brief do sing :
All things were thus when *Pym* was K[ing].

Tom Jordan altered these words, after 1648, into ' I'll answer ye one word for all : All things are thus when kings do fall.' The last stanza, unless it were a post-script, serves to date the ballad as immediately following after Sir John Hotham's treasonable refusal to admit King Charles into Hull, at the end of April 1642. Hotham met his fate, nevertheless, at the hands of the Parliament, along with his son : ' Treason doth never prosper,' Harrington said.

Page 73.—See note on p. 65. There are variations in the other version, which is No. 582 in the *Hesperides,* 1648 ; where it reads, ' This *sweet Infanta* of the Year? . . . *thus* bepearl'd . . . *I will* whisper . . . are *mix'd* with tears.' Second stanza, ' *I will answer* : These discover What *fainting hopes* are in a lover.' Carew's own rendering is the earlier and better : we need not doubt that he wrote it.

Page 78.—1640 text is, ' Rose, sticking upon,' not ' worn.'

Page 81.—See note p. 248, on Cecilia Crofts and Thomas Killigrew. The Bride's strewing of nuts at wedding feasts preceded throwing the stocking, and struggling for points.

Page 82.—Sir John Finch (*cf.* p. 233) failed to confirm his ' election ' of the lady, and she remained Anne Wentworth until she was married by John, 2nd Lord Lovelace. Whether she had been fickle, or some difficulty about dower flutter'd the Finch and made it take wing, is not apparent. But criminals on trial found out ' how the stern Law breathes ' harsh sentences after personal disappointment had invaded the Bench. When ' cruelty is sunk to hell ' it finds a way back again. It had not far to travel, upward, at that time.

Page 88.—'Grieve not, my *Celia*,' was added in 1651 (with pp. 90, 91): *Some Additional Poems by the Same Author.*

Page 89.—There is no external evidence to confirm the attribution of this song to Carew. Given anonymously in *Wit's Interpreter.* It were well to see it established as his, even on manuscript authority, although such is frequently valueless. 'Come, my *Celia!*' is worthy of him.

Page 90.—We have to transpose words, not innovate fresh, to make the fourth stanza intelligible. It reads, ' As two fair Pillars understand Statues two.' These ' two suns in a heaven of snow ' meet us on p. 186. They shone before, on p. 64. They reappear at beginning of 'The Lover's Mistake ' (our p. 232), in answer to Carew's 'Ask me no more.'
Also, in the song beginning " Swift as the feet of *Leda* I, will to *Olympus'* flower'd bosom fly," we read, ' Her neck's a tower of snow,' and of her eyes 'You'd swear two Suns at once broke through the skies.' With the 'Lover's Mistake,' it was printed in *New Academy of Complements*, 1669.

Page 92.—'Farewell, fair Saint !' The external evidence is wholly in favour of the other T. C., Thomas Cary, or Carey, of the Bedchamber, whom Henry Lawes, or his publisher, John Playford, distinctly names in 1655 as the author. Anthony à Wood, in his *Fasti*, i. 352, mentions Henry Carey, 'the frequent translator of books,' afterwards Earl of Monmouth, having been admitted B.A. of Exeter College, Oxon., Feb. 17, 164¾, and then adds :—' Thomas Carey of the same Coll. was admitted on the same day. This Thomas (who was younger brother to the said Henry Carey) was born in Northumberland (while his father, Sir Robert Carey, was Warden of the Marches towards Scotland), proved afterwards *a most ingenious poet*, and was author of several poems printed scatteredly in divers books ; one of which, beginning, "*Farewell, fair Saint*," etc., had a vocal composition of two parts set to it, by the sometime famed musician, Henry Lawes. Upon the breaking out of the rebellion in 1642, he adhered to his Majesty, *being then of the bedchamber* to, and much esteemed by, him. But after that good king had lost his head, he [*T. C.*] took it so much to heart, that he fell suddenly sick, and died before the expiration of the year 1648 [*i.e.* which extended to 25 March 164⅝, Old Style], aged 58, or thereabouts. Soon after, his body was buried in a vault (the burying-place of his family) under St. John Bapt. chappel, within the precincts of St. Peter's Church in Westminster.'

H. Lawes' *Ayres*, 1653, has both names in full :—1st. Mr.
Tho. Cary, son to the Earl of Monmouth, and of the Bed-
chamber to his late Majesty. 2nd. Mr. *Thomas Carew*, Gen-
tleman of the Privy Chamber, and Sewer to his late Majesty.

' *Carew* of ancient *Caru* is, and *Carru* is a plough ;
  Romans the trade, *Frenchmen* the word, I do the name avow,'
          —Tho. Westcote's *View of Devonshire*, p. 106.

On the other hand, it is to be remembered that (except two
songs in Lawes' *Ayres*, these in dispute) the available materials
extant by which to judge of Thomas Carey's holding the
requisite poetical powers, to contest even these few leaves
of the wreath worn by Thomas Carew, are wofully inadequate.
We take a favourable specimen, an extract, *verbatim et
literatim*, from Thomas Carey's descriptions in Jean Puget
de la Serre's *The Mirrour which flatters not*, translated in
163⅝, the very time of Carew's last sickness.

Relating to the First Emblem.

WHEN haughtie thoughts impuffe thee, then   [*text*, 'than.'
      Dictate thy selfe, *Thou art but Man*,
A fabrick of commixed Dust,
That's all the prop of humane trust.
How dares a Clod of mould'ring Clay
Be proud, decaying every day ?
And yet there is a way beside,
Wherein may be a lawful Pride.
When sly *temptations* stirre thee, then
Againe the word, *Thou art a Man !*
Rouze up thy Spirits, doe not yeeld,
A brave resistance wins the Field.
Shall a soul of *Heavenly* breath
Grovell so farre, its worth beneath :
Foully to be pollute with slime,
Of any base and shameful crime ?
Thou art a *Man*, for Heaven borne,
Reflect on *Earth* disdainefull scorne,
Bee not abus'd, since Life is *short*,
Squander it not away in sport :
Nor hazard heaven's eternal Joyes
For a small spurt of worldly Toyes.
Doe *Something* ere thou doe bequeath
To *wormes* thy flesh, to Aire thy breath ;
Something that may, when thou art dead,
With *honour* of thy name be *read* ;

Something that may, when thou art cold,
Thaw frozen Spirits, when 'tis told ;
Something that may the grave controule,
And show thou hast a *noble* Soule.
   Doe SOMETHING, to *advance* thy bliss
Both in the other World and This.

TOWER-HILL,   By THOMAS CARY.
Antepenultimâ Augusti, 1638.

Page 97.—The Roman temple of 'Bifrons' Janus was closed during times of peace. Carew wrote this Ode before 1637, 'When first the *Scottish* wars began.'

Page 99.—*Lucy Countess of Carlisle* has been already mentioned on page 218 ; but seeing how Carew gave poetic expression to sympathy for the widowed Countess of Anglesea (p. 108), in 1630, we remember that Davenant's address to the Countess of Carlisle, in her similar bereavement, touches on her grief, so far as she chose to give any outward indication of mourning, in 1636. The lines deserve notice. They are entitled, 'To the Countess of *Carlisle*, on the Death of the Earl her Husband,' and begin thus :—

' This cypress folded here, instead of lawn ;
   These tapers winking, and these curtains drawn,
   What may they mean ? unless to qualify
   And check the lustre of your eye, you'll try
   To honour darkness and adorn the night,
   So strive, thus with your Lord to bury light.
   Call back your absent beauties to your care !
   Though clouded and conceal'd, we know you are
      The Morning's earliest beam, life of the day,
      The Even's last comfort, and her parting ray.

But why these tears ? that give him no relief,
   For whom you waste the virtue of your grief :
   Such as might be prescribed the earth to drink
   For cure of her old curse ; tears, you would think
   Too rich to water (if you knew their price)
   The chiefest plant derived from Paradise.
   But O ! where is a Poet's faith ? how far
   We are misled : how false our numbers are !
   Our Love is passion ; our Religion, rage ;
   Since to secure that mighty heritage . . .' etc.

At the same date, on the same occasion, Edmund Waller apostrophized ' The Countess of *Carlisle* in Mourning ' :—

' When from black clouds no part of sky is clear,
But just so much as lets the sun appear,
Heaven then would seem thy image, and reflect
Those sable vestments, and that bright aspect.
A spark of virtue by the deepest shade
Of sad adversity is fairer made ;
   Nor less advantage doth thy beauty get :
   A *Venus* rising from a Sea of Jet !' . . . .

What follows does not make pretension to seriousness,
but is insincere laudation only, unworthy of being called
poetry. Thomas Carew in his more sustained elegiac verse
always writes with tenderness and feeling. His friendship
like his love was a reality. Whatever were his faults or
follies, they in no degree exceeded the average failings of
young men in his time, of good family but restricted means,
alternately courted and repelled by the heartless women of
beauty and gallantry who lured so many to destruction.

The adulation paid by Waller to the Countess of Carlisle
was so entirely restricted to praise of her sensual charms,
her beauty and amatory yielding, that he betrays himself in
the lines to this Circe, celebrative ' Of Her Chamber : '—

THEY taste of death that do at Heaven arrive ;
   But we this paradise approach alive.
Instead of DEATH, the dart of LOVE does strike
And renders all within these walls alike.
The high in titles, and the shepherd, here
Forgets his greatness, and forgets his fear :
All stand amazed, and gazing on the Fair,
Lose thought of what themselves or others are :
Ambition lose ; and have no other scope,
Save CARLISLE'S favour to employ their hope.
The *Thracian* could (tho' all those tales were true   *[Orpheus.*
The bold Greeks tell) no greater wonders do ;
Before his feet so sheep and lions lay,
Fearless and wrathless, while they heard him play.
The gay, the wise, the gallant, and the grave,
Subdued alike, all but one passion have :
No worthy mind, but finds in hers there is
Something proportioned to the rule of his :
While she with cheerful but impartial grace,
(Born for no one, but to delight the race
   Of men) like *Phœbus,* so divides her light,
   And warms us, that she stoops not from her height.

                                  Q

Page 108.—*Elizabeth, Countess of Anglesea.* She was a daughter of Thomas Sheldon, Esq., of Houby, in Leicestershire, and her two children were named respectively Charles (who succeeded to the title of his father, Christopher, in 1630, as the second and final Earl of Anglesea, dying *sine proles* in 1659, when his titles became extinct), and Anne, married, first, to Thomas, Viscount Savile, afterwards Earl of Sussex, who died in 1646 ; her second husband was Barde, of Weston. Elizabeth married again, the Hon. Benj. Weston.

The Countess had been 'led captive by the rebels, at the disforesting of *Pewsam,*' Wilts., 1630 (granted by James I. to *Chr. Villiers*) ; the rioters had held common-rights of pasturage, attested by this current rhyme :—

' When *Chipp'nam* stood in *Pewsham's*-Wood,
    Before it was destroyed,
A Cow might have gonne for a groat a yeare :
    But now it is denoyed.'

Davenant has a fantastic 'Song' on that rioting. It is unsympathetic, and mere flattery of her beauty :—

O WHITHER will you lead the fair
    And spicy Daughter of the Morn ?
Those manacles of her soft hair
    Princes, though free, would fain have worn.

What is her crime ?--what has she done ?
    Did she, by breaking Beauty, stay
Or from his course mislead the sun ;
    So robb'd your harvest of a day ?

Or did her voice, divinely clear,
    (Since lately in your Forest bred,)
Make all the trees dance after her,
    And so your woods disforested ?

Run, run ! pursue this *Gothic* rout,
    Who rudely Love in bondage keep ;
Sure all old lovers have the gout :
    The young are over-watch'd, and sleep.

Amid the anguish could such banter console her ? Wa the 'toothache,' of p. 79, really 'cured by a kiss ?' 'Owei Meredith' asked in '59, 'Is it worth while to guess at all this ?

Page 114.—*Aurelian Townsend.* This poet has bee unjustly neglected, seldom mentioned in modern day and his poems are still uncollected, they being scattere throughout MS. miscellanies, and very seldom bearing hi

name as author. He is not characterised, only alluded to, by
Suckling in his 'Session of the Poets,' in fact disparagingly,
after George Sandys (see p. 117), as though unbefittingly
coupled with one greater than himself — '*Sandys* with
Townsend, for they kept no order.' Carew addressed him
affectionately, but either mistakenly imagined him to have
been the writer of 'The Shepherd's Paradise,' instead of
the Hon. Walter Montague, or else left such an ascription
to be conceived, by the indefiniteness of his own phraseology.
The two friends evidently loved better to toy with themes of
love and pastoral pleasures, than such grim realities as the
career and death of Major Dugald Dalgetty's hero and
leader, Gustavus Adolphus, 'The Lion of the North, and
Bulwark of the Protestant Faith,' of whom praise enough
was forthcoming elsewhere. By Aurelian Townsend were
written the Dialogue betwixt Time and a Pilgrim, beginning,
'"Aged man that mows these fields."—"Pilgrim, speak,
what is thy will?"'—the poem reprinted on our p. 228,
"Thou Shepherd, whose intentive eye ;" and 'A Bacchanal,'
commencing with "Bacchus, *Iacchus*, fill our brains !"
His truly charming verses 'To the Lady May,' begin
"Your smiles are not, as other women's be, only the drawing
of the mouth awry" (*Speculum Amantis*, 1889, p. 126).
They were recovered from one of the Malone MSS. in the
Bodleian Library, and printed by Arthur Henry Bullen,
best of all poets' editors, whose taste and discrimination
far outweigh the criticism of men who 'murder to dissect.'
Townsend's masques are, 1.—*Albion's Triumph*. Personated
in a Masque at Court, by the King's Majesty and his
Lords, the Sunday after Twelfth Night, 1631. In 4to,
12 leaves. 2.—*Tempe Restored*, a Masque, presented before
King Charles I. at Whitehall, on Shrove Tuesday, 1631, by
the Queen and fourteen of her ladies. 4to, 1631. The
scenery was by Inigo Jones, as in our *Cœlum Britannicum.*

There must assuredly have been a singular frankness
and affectionate simplicity in the disposition of Carew. Of
his friendship for others, and their feelings towards him,
convincing proofs remain. We have no signs of petty
jealousy and spite, no warfare waged against rivals for fame
or wealth and courtly favour, or the smiles of beauty. This
was an honest swordsman who disdained to soil his weapon
with a foul blow. His praise of Jonson, at the moment
when that rugged dramatist was feeling bitterly the slights
and 'spurns which patient merit from the unworthy takes'
—not that Ben was ever specially patient—is characterised
by a manly truthfulness, which neither degenerates into

servile adulation nor poisons the wound already made by
such an enemy as Owen Feltham.

Sir John Suckling was incapable of understanding Carew,
in his final days of sickness and depression, as he had been
(and this is conceding much) in their earlier days of reckless
gallantry.   His vile address 'To T—— C——' etc., 'Troth,
Tom, I must confess I much admire,' and ending, ' For
evermore the water runs away,' is nothing more than
coarse badinage, without foundation : in any case not
necessarily addressed to Carew, although they were of close
acquaintance ; but many other Toms were open to a similar
aspersion, since 'T. C.' might apply to Thomas Carey, to
Thomas Crosse, and other T. C. poets.   Of higher interest
is the mention made of Carew by Suckling in his ' Session
of the Poets,' although here again there is more paltry and
mischievous malignity of tone than can be justified.

> ' A Session was held the other day,
> And *Apollo* himself was at it (they say) ;
> The Laurel, that had been so long reserved,
> Was now to be given, to him best deserved.
>
> Therefore the wits of the Town came thither,
> 'Twas strange to see how they flock'd together,
> Each strongly confident of his own way,
> That day thought to carry the Laurel away.
>
> .   .   .   .
>
> *Tom Carew* was next, but he had a fault,
> That would not well stand with a Laureat ;
> His Muse was hard-bound, and th' issue of 's brain
> Was seldom brought forth but with trouble and pain ;
>
> All that were there present did agree
> A Laureat Muse should be easy and free :
> Yet sure, 'was not that, but 'twas thought that his Grace
> Consider'd he was well, he had a Cup-bearer's place.'

p. 246.]

p. 253.]

Suckling has a letter to Carew, concerning 'Countesses'
and ' The Lady of Highgate ' (vol. ii. p. 221, *Lib. of Old
Authors*' edit., 1892).   With more hearty good-will than this
professed satirist and witling, William Davenant wrote, in
badinage, a poem addressed to Carew, printed in 1638
playfully anticipating the death of his friend, but little
thinking the grim reality was near.   The *King-Street* here
mentioned, where Carew resided when in town, absent from

his Windsor 'Sunninghill,' was *King-Street, Westminster* (not the later-built King-Street, St. James's: *Introduction,* p. xxiii.). Davenant's lines follow here :—

To *THOMAS CAREW.*

UPON my conscience, whensoe'er thou diest—
  Though in the black, the mourning time of Lent,
There will be seen, in *King's-street* (where thou liest)
  More triumphs than in days of Parliament.

How glad, and gaudy then will Lovers be !
  For every Lover that can verses read
Hath been so injured by thy Muse and thee,
  Ten thousand thousand times he wish'd thee dead.

Not but thy Verses are as smooth and high
  As glory, love, or wine from wit can raise ;
But now (the devil take such destiny !)
  What should commend them, turns to their dispraise.

Thy wit's chief virtue is become its vice,
  For every Beauty thou hast raised so high,
That now coarse faces carry such a price
  As must undo a Lover that should buy.

Scarce any of the Sex admits commerce ;
  It shames me much to urge this to a friend :
But more that they should so mistake thy verse,
  Which meant to conquer, whom it did commend.

WILL D'AVENANT.

Page 117.—*Verses to George Sandys.* His *Paraphrase upon the Psalmes of David,* and upon the Hymnes dispersed throughout the Old and New Testaments, was published in 1636 ; *A Paraphrase upon the Divine Poems* with his name in full, 1638. His *Ovid's Metamorphoses Englished* was of 1626 ; Dryden praised him as the best versifier of his time. To the first Paraphrase, Carew prefixed lines :—

OUR graver Muse from her long dream awakes,
  Peneian Groves and *Cirrha's* caves forsakes ;
Inspired with zeal she climbs th' ethereal Hills
Of *Solyma,* where bleeding balm distills ;
Where Trees of Life unfading youth assure,
And Living Waters all diseases cure.

Few critics have written of Carew with more sweetness and discrimination than Dr Trench, the late Archbishop of Dublin, to hear whom when he lectured at St. Mary's in our undergraduate days at Cambridge the students crowded every available seat. A man of noble presence, in all ways distinguished and admirable. He wrote, 'Carew is commonly grouped with Waller, and subordinated to him. He is immensely his superior. Waller never wrote a love-song like this ['Ask me no more where Jove bestows,' our p. 69] ; while in many of Carew's lighter pieces there is an underlying vein of earnestness, which is wholly wanting in the other.'—*Houschold Book of English Poetry*, p. 403.

Again, of the lines addressed to George Sandys (p. 117), R. C. Trench wrote, 'This poem will acquire a profound interest, for those at least who count there is something better in the world than Art ["for Art's sake," as the later phrase runs], when we read it in the light of the fact mentioned by Lord Clarendon in his *History of the Rebellion* [*Life of Clarendon*, Pt. I., par. 33] about the author, namely, that "after fifty years [a mistake: *read, forty years from birth*], spent with less severity and exactness than it ought to have been, he died with the greatest remorse for that license, and the greatest manifestations of Christianity that his best friends could desire ;" so that in the end the hope which he ventures here timidly to utter was fulfilled, and one thorn "from the dry leafless trunk on Golgotha" did prove to him more precious "than all the flourishing wreaths by laureates worn."'—*Ibid.*, p. 405. After such an estimate one can but smile at Augustus Jessop 'damning with faint praise' Carew's work, as being 'chiefly songs and "society verses," *composed it is said with great difficulty* [this drives Suckling's expression of "hard-bound" most ungenerously], but melodious and highly polished, though characterised by the usual conceits and affectation of his time.' The criticism of Headley is that, 'Carew has the ease without the pedantry of Waller, and perhaps less conceit.' (See p. 254.)

Cf. p. 244.]

Page 118.—*Henry Carey*, second Earl of Monmouth and Baron Carey of Lippington, Yorkshire, son of Robert; married Lady Martha Cranfield, lived in retirement during the rebellion, 'a generous scholar ;' and died 13th June, 1687.

Sir John Suckling also addressed lines 'To his muchhonoured, the Lord *Lepinton* (*sic*) upon his Translation of *Malvezzi*, his *Romulus* and *Tarquin*,' beginning, 'It is so rare and new a thing to see Ought that belongs to young nobility, In print,' etc. (*Suckling*, i. 17, *Lib. O. Authors*).

Page 119.—Of Thomas May, translator of Lucan's *Pharsalia*, 1627, and later ensnared by the Parliament, when piqued at some refusal of a pension from the king, but like Enobarbus, repenting of treachery and desertion, who died in misery and humiliation, the summary by Clarendon is conclusive : 'He fell from his duty and all his former friends, and prostituted himself to the vile office of celebrating the infamous acts of those who were in rebellion against the king ; which he did so meanly, that he seemed to all men to have lost his wits when he left his honesty ; and so, shortly after, died miserable and neglected, and deserves to be forgotten.'—*Life of Clarendon*, 1857. The early use of *Letter-Lock safes* is shown in lines 24, 25.

Page 122.—'To My Friend, Will D'Avenant :' this was the heading of a poem beginning, 'I crowded 'mongst the first to see the Stage,' printed on p. 166 of the 1640 edition of *Poems by Thomas Carew, Esquire*, and it has reappeared in subsequent editions, including that of 1870, without any one observing that the lines in question are imperfect, and were written by neither Carew nor Cary, *alias* Carey, but by another friend of Will D'Avenant, William Habington, the author of *Castara*. Hence the lines are removed from position in our p. 122 ; they do not find place among the 'Doubtful Poems,' seeing that they are not by any means doubtful : they are reprinted here instead. When wrongly inserted among Carew's Poems, in 1640, instead of stopping at end of the fourteenth line ('Master or Bachelor, in Comedie'), there were added unnecessarily six lines, *genuinely by Carew*, which had formed the termination of his own poem addressed to Davenant, as *he* called him—not 'D'Avenant' —which had been printed, prefixed, in the first edition of '*Madagascar, with Other Poems*. By W. Davenant, London, 1638.' The duplicated lines—when rightly placed—marked the union of romance and history, the finale of Carew's Madagascar poem, 'When I behold,' etc., now on p. 122. Signed *Thomas Carew*, in the original version, 1638.

> ' We of th' adulterate mixture not complain,
>   But thence more Characters of Virtue gain ;
> More pregnant Patterns of transcendent worth,
> Than barren and insipid Truth brings forth :
>   So oft the Bastard nobler fortune meets,
>   Than the dull issue of the lawful sheets.'

(These are the source of Wycherley's couplet, that won for him the patronage of Barbara, Duchess of Cleaveland :—

'When parents are slaves, their brats cannot be any other :
Great wits and great braves, have alway a Punk to their
mother.'—*Love in a Wood,* 1672.)

To my Friend, *Will Davenant.*

I CROWDED 'mongst the first to see the Stage
  (Inspired by thee) strike wonder in our age,
By thy bright fancy dazzled ; where each scene
Wrought like a charm, and forced the audience lean
To th' passion of thy pen. Thence Ladies went,
Whose absence Lovers sigh'd for, to repent
Their unkind scorn ; and Courtiers, who by art
Made love before, with a converted heart,
    To wed those virgins whom they'd woo'd t' abuse ;
    Both render'd *Hymen's* proselytes by thy Muse.

But others, who were proof 'gainst Love, did sit
To learn the subtle dictates of thy Wit ;
And as each profited, took his degree,
Master or Bachelor in Comedy.

[Instead of stopping here—where 1640 edit. wrongly adds
the Carew six lines—*Habington's* address continued thus,—
we print now in *italic* type to distinguish *the omitted lines*] :—

Who on the Stage, though since, they ventur'd not
Yet on some Lord or Lady had their plot
Of gain or favour ; every nimble jest
They speak of thine, b'ing the entrance to a feast,
  Or nearer whisper : most thought fit to be
  So far concluded wits, as they know thee.

                 But here the Stage thy limit was, kings may
Canute.] *Find proud ambition humbled at the sea,*
          Which bounds dominion : but the nobler flight
          Of Poesy hath a supremer right
            To empire, and extends her large command
            Where'er th' invading sea assaults the land.

Ev'n Madagascar *(which so oft hath been*
Like a proud virgin tempted, yet still seen
Th' enemy court the wind for flight) doth lie
A trophy now of thy wit's victory :
  Nor yet disdains destruction to her state,
  Encompass'd with thy laurel in her fate.

1638.   William Habington.

Page 123.—The Hon. Walter Montague was author of the *Shepherd's Paradise*, a Pastoral Comedy mentioned on p. 114; a play privately acted before the King in 1633 (and possibly in 1629), of which Queen Henrietta bore a part. Prynne's libellous attack on the stage and dancing, being published at the time, was supposed to specially refer to her: Prynne's language deservedly encountered rebuke and punishment. The Inns of Court prepared a Masque, James Shirley's *Triumph of Peace*, played at Whitehall on Feb. 2, 163¾, before their majesties. This was within a week before Prynne's appearance at the Star Chamber. He received a heavy sentence for this *Histriomastix*. Montague's Pastoral is ridiculed by Suckling, in his 'Session of the Poets,' stanzas xx. and xxii., describing a contest for the Laureateship:— [*Cf.* p. 244.

> ' *Wat Montague* now stood forth to his trial,
> And did not so much as suspect a denial;
> But witty *Apollo* asked him first of all,
> If he understood his own Pastoral?
>
> For if he could do it, 'twould plainly appear
> He understood more than any man there,
> And did merit the Bays above all the rest:
> But the Monsieur was modest, and silence confess'd.'

He is styled 'the Monsieur' because of his recent travels in France, from which he had returned to Carew's satisfaction. We find a note in the 1836 *Selections* from Suckling, by his unsatisfactory namesake and mutilator the Rev. Alfred S., 'Wat Montague wrote the *Shepherd's Paradise*, published in 1629 [according to one Brit. Mus. copy, perhaps true date: same sheets, 1659], 8vo. He was a papist, and suspected of having been concerned in the conversion of Lady *Newburgh*. On that occasion, it is said in a letter of Lord Conway's, "The King did use such words of *Wat Montague* and Sir *Tobie Matthew*, that the fright made *Wat* keep his chamber longer than his sickness would have detained him."' W. M. published, in 1648, *Miscellanea Spiritualia; or Devout Essays*, 4to; and a *Second Part* to it in 1654; also, in 1656, *The Accomplished Woman*, 8vo.

Page 130.—No reasonable doubt hinders the acceptance of this Masque as Carew's. (Bolton Corney denied it, in *Notes and Q.*, with no authority as a critic.) The only other claim advanced, on insufficient evidence, is in favour of Sir William D'Avenant, who might possibly have assisted, if aid had been required. D'Avenant has scarcely received justice, for he is somewhat ponderous in his poetry and rhetorical in his dramas. But Carew loved him, and even Suckling (who, *more suo*, girded at him about the 'mischance' in France, with as little truth as in his lampoon on 'T. C.') mentioned him with a sort of kindness, by acknowledging 'the handsomeness of his Muse,' in *A Session of the Poets.*

Page 175.—Ode to Phillis. This poem might have the less claim to be held the work of Carew, insomuch as it was given imperfectly by the Ashmol. MS. 36, wherein it follows '*A Rapture.*' So late as December, 1680, a popular song of 'Fair *Phillis*, your prevailing charms' was known and named as a tune, at Viscount Stafford's execution ; perhaps a ballad-adaptation of our '*Phillis*, though thy powerful charms' (see *Roxburghe Ballads*, iv. 227, 1881) ; to which music may have been composed by Henry Lawes. A second MS. gives the entire song. It is in the collection made by Catherine Gage of Sussex, the Right Hon. Lady Aston (known as '*Tixall Poetry*,' Staffordshire, p. 125, and half-edited by Sir Walter Scott, who knew not the other MSS., in 1813). This charming Ode was worth our tracing, even though it were not by Carew ; we may find the music. We give it here complete (1st stanza alone was on p. 175) :—

*P*HILLIS, though thy powerful charms
    Have forced me from my *Celia's* arms—
A sure defence against all powers
But those resistless eyes of yours ;
Think not your conquest to maintain
By rigour or unjust disdain :
    In vain, fair Nymph, in vain you strive,
    For Love doth seldom Hope survive.

Although I languish for a time,
Whilst all your glories in their prime
Do justify your cruelty,
By that same force that conquer'd me ;
Yet Age will come, at whose command
Those troops of Beauties must disband :
    A Tyrant's strength, once took away,
    What Slave so dull as to obey ?

Those threatening dangers to remove,
Make me believe at least you love ;
Dissemble well, and by that art
Preserve and govern well my heart.
But if you'll learn a nobler way
To keep your Empire from decay,
    And so for ever fix your Throne,
    Be kind, but kind to me alone.

This is so thoroughly in accordance with Carew's own style of pleading and sentiment that we need no longer hesitate before accepting it as his. The '*Tixall Poetry*' was nearly all made as a commonplace book of gathered favourites : it is thus similar to most MSS. miscellanies. We have identified the authors of the chief songs.

Page 176.—The allusion to 'Honour's fruitless loves' is in harmony with Carew's playful banter, on p. 45, against the monstrous conventionalism, 'Giant Honour,' as an enemy of Love. This was afterwards glanced at, in the anonymous poem called *Stipendiarae Lachrymae*, 1654, which tells of Carew being seen among the spectral forms in Hades :—

> 'There, purged of the folly of disdaining
>   *Laura* walk'd hand in hand with *Petrarch* join'd,   [*Cf.* p. 49.
> No more of "Tyrant Giant Honour" 'plaining ;
>   There *Sidney* in rich *Stella's* arms lay 'twined :
> *Carew* and *Suckling* there mine eye did find.'

The better half of George Wither was a true poet, amatory and idyllic, as shown in his lovely *Mistress of Phil' Arete ;* before he degenerated into dreary pietism, the worse half being a prosaic Puritan. To him is attributed the authorship of a polemical tract entitled *The Great Assizes Holden in* Parnassus *by* Apollo *and his Assessors,* 1645. It is a halting half-hearted apology (the censure of a much too 'candid friend,') for Carew's warmth, as expressed in 'A Rapture' (p. 45), admitting or pleading 'Yet may some chaster Songs him render free,' from the having been challenged on nomination as a Parnassian juryman or assessor. Apollo rebukes the advocatus diaboli, the accuser, by a furious glance, and Carew is weakly described, after death, as regretting his having written anything which the 'unco guid and rigidly righteous' Puritans counted as licentiousness. He is made to concede, apologetically, regarding 'A Rapture,'

> '"This Song of mine
> Was not infused by the Virgins Nine,   [= The Muses.
> Nor through my dreams divine upon this Hill,
> Did this vain *Rapture* issue from my quill,
> No *Thespian* waters, but a *Paphian* fire
> Did me with this foul ecstacy inspire :
> I oft have wished that I (like *Saturn*) might
> This infant of my folly smother quite,
>   Or that I could retract what I had done
>   Into the bosom of Oblivion." '

The collectors of anecdotes are always rummaging dust-heaps in search of whatever may injure the reputation of men who were beloved and famous. No dirt is too foul for their busy fingers, and they find unveracious gossips to help them liberally. Isaak Walton, seeking materials for a projected memoir of John Hales of Eton (Sir Edward Hales married Carew's widowed sister, Lady Cromer), revealed unsuspiciously the baseness of Hales, in setting afloat by one 'Mr. Anthony Farrindon,' and 'by others'

f. p. 284.] [one Lady Salter is named], that 'Mr. Thomas Cary, a poet of note, and a great libertine in his life and talk, and one that had in his youth been acquainted with Mr. Ha., sent for Mr. Hales to come to him in a dangerous fit of sickness, and desired his advice and absolution, which Mr. Hales, on a promise of amendment, gave him : this, I think, was in the country [perhaps at Sunninghill]. But Mr. *Cary* came to London, fell to his old company, and into a more visible scandalous life, and especially in his discourse, and being taken very sick, that which proved his last, and being much troubled in mind, procured Mr. Hales to come to him *in this his sickness and agony of mind, desiring earnestly, after a confession of many of his sins,* to have his prayers and his absolution. Mr. Hales told him he should have his prayers [Hales's prayers ! ! ! from whom small mercy would have been found by the "woman who had been a sinner" or the penitent on the Cross, or by Mary Magdalen out of whom the Lord had cast seven devils], but *would by no means give him either the sacrament or absolution.'* Then to exalt himself, sacrilegiously, Hales told a woman,

R. K.] and 'that bad Delilah told !' Samson's Delilah had some excuse ; she betrayed the secret of one who had been, and still was, the irreconcilable enemy of her own allies, the Philistines. Treacherous and wanton though she might be, doubly a hireling, bribed for evil, she was nevertheless their avenger. But where could be found any justification of Hales, or of his gossips ? Probably he lied, unblushingly, when he told the chattering women who repeated the tale to Walton. If Hales had spoken truly, it was a culpable desecration of the Confessional ; but, if falsely, what language stigmatizes him too severely ?

Page 180.—' *Nays,*' in the MS., is probably for *Naïs* (the name occurs in a novel by Emile Zola, 'Naïs Micoulin ').

' *With light and low bell* caught the amazed lark' alludes to a fowling practice, where the hand-bell was used by night to frighten the birds and make them 'lie close,' till by more violent noise and dazzling with a lantern, they were alarmed

and flew into the net. (Strutt's *Sports*.) They drew a lark
down to earth by glitter of a mirror in sunshine, a daze or
dare. The falconer's term, '*Imp*,' is on p. 216.

Page 182.—*The Song of Jealousy*. As already indicated
on p. 182, the 'Prologue' and 'Epilogue' reprinted thereon
and on p. 183, were probably connected with the same
entertainment at Whitehall to which belong the songs of
'Jealousy,' of 'Feminine Honour,' 'Separation of Lovers,'
and 'Incommunicability of Love,' and also the two songs
that follow them, 'From a Lover' and 'From a Lady,' on
our pp. 56 to 61. As to the date, it was decidedly 1633,
shown in a note written by Tom Killigrew to Cecilia Crofts,
whose marriage at Oatlands, 29th June, 1636, is celebrated
in Carew's song, p. 81, 'The morning stormy.' Killigrew
introduced the 'Song of Jealousy' into his tragi-comedy
'*Cicilia and Clorinda*,' Part Second, act v., scene 2, and
printed it, with this declaration :—'This song was written
by Mr. *Thomas Carew*, cup-bearer to *Charles I*., and sung
in a Masque at *Whitehall*, anno 1633. And I presume to
make use of it here, because in the first design 'twas writ at
my request, upon a dispute held betwixt Mistress *Cecilia
Crofts* and myself, where he was present ; she being then
Maid of Honour. This I have set down, lest any man
should believe me so foolish as to steal such a poem from so
famous an author ; or, so vain as to pretend to the making
of it myself : and those that are not satisfied with this
apology, and this song in this place, I am always ready to
give them a verse of my own. *Written by* Thomas Killigrew,
resident for Charles II. in Venice, 1651.' (She died, 163⅜.)

Robert Baron, in his *Pocula Castalia*, 1650, p. 102, has
a poem, 'Truth and Tears,' containing an affectionate
reference to Carew, printed twelve years after his death :—

> 'Sweet *Suckling* then, the glory of the Bower,
> Wherein I've wanton'd many a genial hour,
> Fair Plant ! whom I have seen *Minerva* wear,
> An ornament to her well-plaited hair,
> On highest days ; remove a little from
> Thy excellent *CAREW* ! and thou, dearest *TOM*,
> *Love's Oracle !* lay thee a little off
> Thy flourishing *Suckling*, that between you both
> I may find room : then (strike when will my fate),
> I'll proudly part to such a princely seat.
>   But you have Crowns : our god's chaste darling tree [Laurel.
> Adorns your brows with her fresh gallantry.'

In verses 'To his Honoured Friend, *Thomas Stanley*, Esquire, upon his Elegant Poems,' James Shirley mentions Carew (whom he had known; see pp. 180, 181):—

Cf. Baron, *supra.*]

> '*CAREW*, whose numerous language did before
> Steer every genial soul, must be no more
> The Oracle of Love; and might he come
> But from his own to thy *Elysium*,
> He would repent his immortality
> Given by loose idolaters, and die
> A tenant to these Shades; and by thy ray
> He need not blush to court his *Celia*.'

As was mentioned in the *Introductory Memoir*, p. xxiii., Clement Barksdale sent a book to Thomas Carew, early in March, 163⅘, with the following lines inscribed (afterwards printed in *Nympha Libethris*, 1651):—

> '*AD THOMAM CAREW*, APUD *J*[OH.] *C*[ROFTS]
>   CUM *DAVENANTII* POEMATIS.
>
> '*T*EQUE meum, cùm triste fuit mihi tempus, amorem,
>   Officiis dico demeruisse tuis:
> Meque tuum, si forte occasio detur, amorem,
>   Officiis dices demeruisse meis.
> Si placet, interea, hoc grandis non grande Poetæ
>   Ingenii dignum munus habeto tui.'

'Mr. [Henry] Headley, in his *Biographic Sketches*, p. 39, has justly observed that "*Carew* has the ease, without the pedantry of *Waller*, and perhaps less conceit. He reminds us of the best manner of Lord *Lyttelton*. *Waller* is too exclusively considered as the first man who brought versification to anything like its present standard. *Carew's* pretensions to the same merit are seldom sufficiently either considered or allowed." Lord *Clarendon*, however, has remarked of his poems that "for the sharpness of the fancy, and for the elegance of the language in which that fancy was spread, they were at least equal, if not superior, to any of that time."'—*Spec. Early Eng. Poets*, George Ellis, 1801.

Cf. p. 246.]

Ellis gives no less than thirteen specimens of Carew, including unhesitatingly 'The Primrose' and 'The Inquiry,' beside the 'Dialogue,' beginning "Tell me, *Utrechia*" (here reprinted on pp. 65, 73, 103). Ellis' taste was sound, though inclined to be fastidious, and his choice of Carew's Poems was excellent, viz., 'Sweetly breathing vernal air' (p. 125); 'Think not, 'cause men flattering say'—'If the quick spirits in your eye '—'When you the sunburnt pilgrim see '—'Gaze not on thy beauty's pride '—'Mark how the bashful morn in vain ' —'Know, *Celia*, since thou art so proud '—'Wonder not though I am blind '—and the exquisite poem which seems to concentrate in itself the best qualities of Carew's love-songs, 'Ask me no more where *Jove* bestows, when June is past, the fading rose' (see pp. 2, 11, 14, 15, 22, 30, 39, and 69).

Henry Hallam wrote, on '*The Primrose*,' [our Carew, p. 73], 'Herrick gives the second line strangely, "This sweet Infanta of the year," *which is little else than nonsense;* and all the other variations are for the worse. I must leave it in doubt whether he [Herrick] borrowed and disfigured a little, or was himself improved upon.' [What! ten years before he published his version?] Hallam adds: 'I must own that he [*Herrick*] *has a trick of spoiling what he takes.*' He gives as an example, Herrick's perversion of Suckling's '*little mice*' into '*snails*.'—*Lit. of Europe*, iii. 267, 1872.

John Fry's inability for the task of critical selection was denounced by Barron Field, who styled the volume printed at Bristol in 1810, 'The most drivelling piece of pedantry that we have ever witnessed' (*Quarterly Review*, iv. 173); for Fry had copied the 1642 misprint '*Faleme*,' carefully reproduced, instead of '*Falerne*' (p. 128), and had totally omitted the 'Deposition from Love,' 'New Year's Sacrifice,' 'Willing Prisoner,' the 'Epistle to Ben Jonson,' 'Elegy on Donne,' the 'Hue and Cry,' and the lines 'To My Mistress in Absence' (our pp. 14, 19, 29, 34, 61, 71, 111). Barron Field marked the advantage gained in reprints by giving to true poetry the modern spelling, '*save where the orthography of a poet influences his rhyme,* as Chaucer's and Spenser's does every moment, and therefore "the whole ought to be sacred."' We adopt the rule of modern spelling.

Ezekiel Sandford gave twenty-six poems by Carew, in vol. iv. pp. 377–406, of his *Works of British Poets,* 1819.

END OF APPENDIX NOTES.

THE following letters from Thomas Carew to Sir Dudley Carleton are mentioned in the *Introductory Memoir* (pp. xvii, xviii). Of Carew there are so few memorials extant, in addition to his poems, that the reproduction of them here, in modernised spelling, may be welcome. First, this, from London, telling of his interview with George, Lord Carew, at Woodstock, dated 2nd September, 1616, and duly addressed to Sir Dudley Carleton at the Hague.

'Right Honourable, my most singular good Lord,—

'I have been thus long in giving your Lordship account of the success of my business, by reason of my Lord *Carew's* absence from this town, where after I was arrived, and had a while consulted with my father and other friends, it was thought fit I should repair unto him to the Queen's Court ; which then, with the King and Princes, was at *Woodstock*, where I delivered your Lordship's letter. His answer to me was, that he had already in that employment a Master of Arts, whose seven years' service had not yet deserved to be so displaced ; and added, that I, being his kinsman, might expect from him all those greatest courtesies whatsoever, whereunto his nearness of blood did oblige him, which I should always find him ready to perform ; but to admit me into his family as a servant, " it were a thing (said he) far beneath your quality, and which my blood could not suffer without much reluctance." I told him that *my coming was not to supplant any man*, but that I thought this late addition of honour might have made those small abilities which I had acquired by my travels and experience in your Lordship's service, of use to his, which I did humbly prostitute [*i.e.*, proffer or prostrate] before his Lordship ; who if he thought not my youth unworthy so great honour, I should esteem my self no ways disparaged by his service. He replied that my languages, and whatever serviceable parts I had, would rust in his service for want of use, and therefore prayed me to propose to my self any other means wherein he might pleasure me ; were it the service of some other who had more employment and better means of preferment for a Secretary, or whatsoever project I could devise ; wherein he promised not only to employ his credit but his purse, if need were : and so referred me to his return to *London* for his answer to your Lordship's letter, at what time he would talk more at large with me and my father about his business. This is the issue of my hopes, with my Lord *Carew, nor am I likely to gain any thing, at his return hither, from him, but fair words and compliment.*

'Your Lordship's letters to my Lord of *Arundel,* because it was necessary for me to wait upon my Lord *Carew,* and could at no time see him but with the King, from whose side he seldom moveth, I left with Mr. *Havers* to be delivered to him ; of whom I learned that he was as yet unfurnished of a Secretary ; wherefore, according to your Lordship's instructions, my father's counsel, and my own inclination, I will labour my admittance into his service ; wherein I have these hopes, the present vacancy of the place, the reference my father had to his Grandfather, and the knowledge which by your Lordship's means he had of me at *Florence,* wherein, if need be, and if Mr. Chamberlain shall so think good, I will engage my Lord *Carew,* and where-unto I humbly beseech your Lordship to add your effectual recommendation ; which I know will be of more power than all my other pretences, which you will be pleased with your most convenient speed to afford me, that I may at his return hither (which will be with the King some twenty days hence), meet him with your Lordship's letters, and that I may in case of refusal return to your service the sooner ; from which, I profess (notwithstanding all these fair shows of preferment), as I did with much unwillingness depart, so do I not without great affliction discontinue ; my thoughts of their proper and regular motion not aspiring higher than the orb of your Lordship's service ; this irregular [motion] being caused by your self, who are my *Primum mobile ;* for I ever accounted it honour enough for me to *Correre la fortuna del mio Signior,* nor did I ever aim at greater happiness than to be held, as I will always rest,

'Your Lordship's | most humble devoted | to your service,

THO. CAREW.'

'*London,* this 2 of *September,* 1616.'

Endorsed :—'To the Right Honble my most singular good L Sr *Dudley Carleton,* Knight, L Ambassad^r for his Maj^ty wth the States of the United Provinces of the Low Countries at the *Hague.*'

'Tom Carew, the 2d of 7^ber 1616.'

Second. We have a letter, nine days later :—

R

'Right Honble. my most singular good Lord,—

'Since my last to your Lordship of the 2nd of this present [month], my Ld *Carew's* repair to town gave me occasion to attend his resolution at his lodging: which he delivered with much passion, protesting that he did not therefore refuse me because he had no intent to take care or charge of me, for I should upon any occasion be assured of the contrary, but merely for that he should have no employment for me, and therefore prayed me, since he tendered herein my own good more than his particular interest, to surcease this suit, and prevail my self of him in another kind ; to the same effect was his excuse to my father, so as that string hath failed ; but as there was ever more appearance, so do I conceive better hope of good success, with my Lord of *Arundel*, and the rather because my Lord *Carew* hath so willingly engaged himself in my behalf, and promiseth to deal very effectually for me, but chiefly when I shall have your Lordship's recommendation, which I daily expect,' etc. (11 Sept., 1616).

Jul. Cæsar,⎤
iv. 2, *l.* 15.⎦

Third. From Tunstall, Kent, 20 Sept., 1616. It tells of one whom Brutus called 'a hot friend, cooling.'

'My Lord of *Arundel's* in definite answer, whereby he holds me in suspense, though not without hope of good success ; for he protesteth that if he can by any means satisfy the pretences of two competitors, who are with daily importunity recommended unto him from his hon^ble and especial good friends, which (he says), he will endeavour, and hopes to effect, he will then with all willingness embrace my service, the tender whereof he takes very kindly : thus much he hath professed unto my Ld *Carew*, who made the first overture to Mr. *Shireborn* [*Sherburn ?*], who in your Lordship's name seconded that recommendation,' etc. . . .
'I have in this interstice had leisure to see my Sister, Grandmother, and other my friends in *Kent*, who remember their most affectionate services to your L^p and my Lady.'

This shows that, whatever were the cause of estrangement of the Carletons, they lacked no outward show of friendliness and courtesy. This was deceptive. Perhaps Thomas Carew, as was natural, lost hope, and soon fell into idler habits. His father was already sinking into comparative poverty, and died before the next two years ended. He had yielded to desponding fears about his family. Nine years earlier he had written his own epitaph :—

'*Heu, quae, quanta et qualia vidi! Satis mihi vixi, si satis Deo. Pertæsus levitatis, vanitatis et inconstantiæ hujus vitæ; æternam appeto, ut Deo fruar et requiescam in pace. Amen.*'

He had lost many of his children early. Martha alone, twice married, survived to reach what is termed a 'good old age.' Her brother, the younger Sir Matthew Carew, became a gallant soldier, who died early in Ireland, fighting for his king.

The future success which Thomas, youngest of the three, was thereafter to win, alike in literary excellence and in court favour with his sovereign (by whom he was esteemed the choicest in wit and poetic grace), his father could not foresee. His own wealth had gone; and he died before the after-math of hope or happiness. If we possessed the later letters of Thomas Carew, written in the heyday of prosperity and friendship, we should find in them nothing of our modern pessimism; our unwholesome self-analysis; our proneness to torture every petty detail into an evil meaning; our unrest and dissatisfaction whatever befalls us: our distrust of ourselves, of human nature, and of Providence. His was a cheerful philosophy, and he has left us much for which we owe gratitude. The confusion of the Civil-War, which followed swiftly after his death, accounts for the disappearance of his manuscripts, and familiar letters. But among the poems, we hold several that rank high as epistles to the men whom he loved: he contrasts (p. 125) his pleasant home at Wrest, near Woburn Park, with the stern grandeur recently beheld in the far North, that Tweedside where Gilbert Neville then abode. By these poems, if we are not distrustful, we can enter into the charmed circle, and see him, as his many friends had seen him: one whom fairest women and bravest men both loved and honoured.

BIBLIOGRAPHY OF THOMAS CAREW.

(*A Hand-List.*)

CŒLUM BRITANNICUM. A Masque at White-hall in the Banquetting-House, on Shrove-Tuesday-Night, the 18 of February, 1633. London : Printed for *Thomas Walkley*, and are to be sold at his Shop neare *White-Hall*. 1634. Quarto. [See p. 129.]

Of the four editions of the 'Poems by Thomas Carew' it is probable that the first and best was seen through the press by one of his surviving friends, not unlikely to be Aurelian Townsend (whom he had addressed affectionately in an 'Elegiacal Letter' (p. 114 ; see also pp. 228, 242), and who had Carew's own manuscripts to guide him. Unfortunately Carew's death was sudden, after weakening attacks of illness ; the loss of his own final corrections and personal supervision is irreparable. *Cœlum Britannicum* was included, with its separate title-page, in the four editions of the *Poems* :—

1.—POEMS. By THOMAS CAREW, Esquire. One of the Gentlemen of the Privie-Chamber, and Sewer in Ordinary to his Majesty. London, Printed by *I. D.* for *Thomas Walkley*, and are to be sold at the sign of the flying Horse between Brittain's Burse and York-House, 1640. Sm. 8vo. A, 2 leaves ; B—S 6, in eights. The Poems end with 'The Mistake' (our p. 80) on its p. 106 ; followed on p. 107 by title of the Masque. The Poems have the 'Imprimatur, Matthew Clay, April 29, 1640 on *verso* of title : reproduced on our pp. xxxi, xxxii.

2.—POEMS. By *Thomas Carew*, Esquire. One . . . Majesty. *The Second Edition revised and enlarged.* London [etc., same printer, publisher, and locality] 1642. [Tho. Walkley makes an addition of eight poems these given on the 1642, pp. 207, 210, 211, 212, 215, 217, 221, and 222. The *first* of these, 'To my Lord Admiral on his late Sickness and Recovery' (our p. 100), was certainly *added wrongly* by Walkley, it being Edmund Waller's. The *second* is entitled 'On Mistress *N.* to the Greene Sicknesse' (our p. 101); *third,* 'Upon a Mole in *Celia's* Bosom' (p. 102); *fourth,* 'An Hymeneal Song' (p. 83); *fifth,* 'A Married Woman' (p. 85); *sixth,* 'A Divine Love' (p. 85); *seventh,* 'Love's Force' (p. 87); and *eighth,* 'A Fancy' (p. 88).]

3.—POEMS, with a Maske : By *Thomas Carew,* Esq. ; One of the Gent. of . . to his late Majestie. The *Songs* were set in *Musick* by Mr. *Henry Lawes,* Gent. of the King's Chappell, and one of his late Majestie's Private Musick. *The Third Edition revised and enlarged.* London, Printed for *H. M.* and are to be sold by *J. Martin* at the signe of the Bell in St. *Pauls*-Church-Yard. 1651. [A group of three extra poems is here first added, on its pp. 217, 218, and 219, as *Some Additional Poems by the same Author.* They are, *first,* 'To his Mistress :' "Grieve not, my *Celia*" (our p. 88); *second,* 'In praise of his Mistress :' "You that will a wonder know" (p. 90); and *third,* 'To Celia on Love's Ubiquity : "As one that strives" (p. 91).]

4.—POEMS, SONGS AND SONNETS. Together with a Masque. By Thomas Carew, Esq. One of . . . Private Musick. *The Fourth Edition revised and enlarged.* London, Printed for *H. Herringman* at the *Blew Anchor* in the *Lower Walk* of the *New Exchange,* and are to be sold by *Hobart Kemp* at the sign of the *Ship* in the *Upper Walk* of the New Exchange, 1671. The separate title to Masque is dated 1670. [The group of three extra poems, previously mentioned, are here again added, on its pp. 226, 227, and 228 ; as *Some Additional Poems by the same Author,* already given in the 1651 *third edition :* and therefore *not* printed for the first time in 1671, as was misleadingly asserted in the 1870 edition.]

No authoritative editions follow. Very little demand was made for them, while public taste was debased, and the earlier poets neglected, until Thomas Warton in 1778, and Thomas Percy in 1765 (ridiculed by Samuel Johnson), set a better fashion of studying 'The Old Singers.' Not until 1772 was a fresh issue made of the '*Poems, Songs, and Sonnets:* Together with a *Masque;* By Thomas Carew, Esq., etc. . . . to King Charles I. *A New Edition.* London: Printed for T. Davies, in Russell Street, Covent Garden, MDCCLXII.' (See pp. 211, 212.)

Next, near the close of the century, *Carew's Poems,* with the *Masque,* were included in Dr. Robert Anderson's useful, tolerably accurate, but not scholarly, edition of the *British Poets,* wherein these poems occupy pp. 671 to 723 of vol. iii., 1793. They are also reprinted in Alexander Chalmers's similar double-column edition of the *English Poets,* vol. v., 1810.

'A Selection from the Poetical Works of Thomas Carew,' London, Printed for Longmans, Hurst, & Co., and sold by Thomas Fry & Co., No. 46 High Street, Bristol, 1810, is chiefly noteworthy for having preceded what had been intended to be a more complete edition (mentioned in *The Gentleman's Magazine* of January 1811 as being 'in preparation,' and in *Bibliographical Memoranda,* 1816, declared to be 'in the Press'), but not known to have been published: it was told, in a prospectus, dated 1814, that 'it will be illustrated with Portraits of the Authour and his Wife, from a rare medal by Warin.' This is a false statement, doubly: 1st, of Carew having had a wife (even though she had been the lady whose pseudonym was '*Celia,*' or some later consoler), for we refuse to accept it as proved, on such totally inadequate evidence: no medallion portrait of the lady being forthcoming or known to be extant. No one else saw it but Fry: (as Paul Dombey said, 'I don't believe that story').

Cf. p. viii.] And, 2nd, *The medal is not of Carew, but of Cary.*

The Works of Thomas Carew were 'reprinted from the original edition of 1640,' issued in 1824 : Edinburgh, Printed for W. and T. Tait :—Edited by Mr. Thomas Maitland, a Lord of Session. 125 copies printed. The appendix poems, additional, from eds. 1642 and 1651, alone are modernised in spelling. [*Not seen.*]

Robert Southey gave a large selection from Carew, including the entire *Masque*, in 1831 ; but it was merely hack-work, and he left any slightest revision to the chances of the printing office, or the untrained energies of what he playfully called his 'Harem' of sisters-in-law (we know what sort of accuracy might be expected from the Irrepressible sex) : as a Moderator of the General Assembly, *circâ* 1856–7, once profanely in his place had declared of *Macphail's Edinburgh Ecclesiastical Journal* (obiit 1863), that it was 'Edited by Divine Providence.' Southey was a noble 'man of letters,' over-burdened in too many ways, so that he was always hurrying his 'copy.' That he had reprinted seventeen of Carew's choice poems and the Masque deserves gratitude. His criticism is unworthy of himself and of his subject, though it sufficed for his female coterie and their proprieties : 'Carew's wit and his accomplishments qualified him for a courtier, and his morals would not have disqualified him, even at the court of Charles the Second' (p. 732) : *Ipse dixit.*

The Poetical Works of Thomas Carew, etc., London : H. G. Clarke and Co., 66 Old Bailey, bears date 1845. It is summarised by W. C. Hazlitt as 'an edition of no value, and chiefly a reprint of that of 1824.'

His own edition of 1870, the Roxburghe Library large quarto, was published by Messrs. Reeves and Turner, of London, handsomely printed and bound, dedicated to (the now, late) Frederick William Cosens, F.S.A., and furnished with an elaborate array of references to transcripts from MSS., etc. It gives *verbatim* several letters written by the poet Carew, with his signature in fac-simile (written at Tunstall,

on 20th September 1616, in an epistle to Sir Dudley
Carleton, whom he had by that time left, after having
joined him as secretary in 1614). These letters
(p. 256) show not the poetic attainments of Carew :
compare the *Calendar of State Papers, Domestic*, James I.,
vol. 88, Nos. 67, 77, 87 ; *Ditto*, of Charles I., 1638,
April 1–17 (certainly after the decease of Carew), vol.
387, No. 31, and May 25–31, vol. 391, No. 99.

Mr. W. C. Hazlitt has done life-long service for
literary students, by innumerable and laborious works,
especially of Bibliography, in which department he
stands eminent. He is personally entitled to respect
and esteem ; moreover as being the grandson of that
true critic, William Hazlitt ; and the worthy son of
a second William Hazlitt, the author and Registrar,
still alive and honoured : who had shown his own
great love for the writings of our Poet, by giving
to his son William the additional baptismal-name of
'CAREW.'

In the present edition, 1893, *The Poems of Thomas
Carew* are for the first time added by Messrs. Reeves
and Turner to the *Library of Old Authors*, now their
sole property. The editor, Joseph Woodfall Ebsworth,
of Molash Priory, Kent, to whom they generously
entrusted the work unrestrictedly, has followed his own
judgment throughout in determining the text, which
had been often obscured and perverted. He alone is
responsible, if aught be blamed. There is no better
'Golden Rule' than Theobald's (p. 270). The former
mis-readings deserved unhesitating rejection. He hopes
speedily to send forth similarly a trustworthy new
edition of 'ROBERT SOUTHWELL'S POEMS,' to follow
these of THOMAS CAREW.

TABLE OF FIRST LINES

TO THE

POEMS OF THOMAS CAREW, 1893.

(*Library of Old Authors' Edition.*)

[*No historical work ought ever to be published without a full Index. Every printed collection of 'Letters and Life' requires similar help for the student, making easier any reperusal of particular passages. Also, each new edition of a Standard Poet should be furnished with a good* 'Index of First Lines,' *in addition to a* 'Table of Contents.' *Without these the book, especially a collection of Songs, or other short poems, is wofully defective; and the omission furnishes perpetual reproach alike against the Editor and the Publisher. It shows that the work has not been a labour of love, but merely a cheap substitute for a better edition. Some future day may give us the greatly-needed* 'Index of First Lines of all Early Poems;' *meanwhile the present Editor has been for years preparing one of* 'All Known Songs and Ballads, in print or manuscript, of date before 1805;' *though intended solely for his private use.*

Here are the First Lines of the Poems and Songs by Thomas Carew; *not neglecting the few of doubtful authenticity, or the collateral poems quoted in the Notes.*]

'I ever labour to make the smallest deviations that I possibly can from the text; never to alter at all where I can by any means explain a passage into sense; nor ever by any emendations to make the author better when it is probable the text came from his own hands.'
    —*Lewis Theobald, to Warburton.*

INDEX.

CELIA.

(ECHO OF 'A LEAVE-TAKING.')

HERE let us close the record.   Will she pause?
*   Vainly we strive against unbending laws.*
Love's slavery ends not with the joyless day:
Worship misplaced is Sin's embitter'd cause.
Woman heeds little in true Poet's lay:
Seeks not his love—seeks but her own applause.
*   She will not pause!*

CAREW.

THEY come back to us in our lonely hours,
*   The friends we loved, the singers of sweet song,*
The unrepining conquerors of wrong,
Who in the Past were crown'd with thorns or flowers,
When Fortune beckon'd them to Love's own bowers—
*   Such, in the saddest life, may chance erelong:*
*   Men loyal, stainless, gentle and yet strong,*
Unhurt by storm, as we by April showers.

Could we repay them for their toils, their cares!
*   They gave us help; and can we nothing give?*
With them we may not tread the hot ploughshares,
*   Who in close-guarded pathways walk and live:*
How then requite these givers of all good?—
Sole guerdon yield we: our heart's gratitude.

                        J. W. E.

19, xi. '89₂

INDEX.

Printed by BALLANTYNE, HANSON & CO.
Edinburgh and London

www.ingramcontent.com/pod-product-compliance
Lightning Source LLC
Chambersburg PA
CBHW020809060726
47498CB00017B/1204